The New
Total War
of the 21st Century

And the Trigger of the Fear Pandemic

The New
Total War
of the 21st Century

And the Trigger of the Fear Pandemic

By Gregory R. Copley

SPECIAL ISSA PREMIER EDITION

THE INTERNATIONAL
STRATEGIC STUDIES
ASSOCIATION

GREGORY R. COPLEY

The New
Total War
of the 21st Century

And the Trigger of the Fear Pandemic

PUBLISHED BY

THE INTERNATIONAL STRATEGIC STUDIES ASSOCIATION

PO Box 320608,
Alexandria, Virginia 22320,
United States of America.
Telephone +1 (703) 548-1070.
Email: Marketing@StrategicStudies.org
www.StrategicStudies.org

Manufactured in the United States of America.

Special ISSA Premier Edition

ISBN-13: 978-1-892998-26-2

US$34.50 plus shipping and handling

Some of the content of this book is based on, or appeared in, reports by the
author in *Defense & Foreign Affairs* **Strategic Policy** journal, produced by the
International Strategic Studies Association.

Bearing in mind that I may not have many more books in me, I would like to pay homage to some who have been of profound importance to me.

THIS BOOK IS DEDICATED TO

Dr Stefan Thomas Possony (1913-1995),
the father of the discipline of Grand Strategy,
and the genius and constant friend
who transformed my life.

To
Dr Assad Homayoun (1932-2020),
the brilliant, considerate, and thoughtful mentor
who always caused me to read more, think more,
and care more.

To
Pamela, Marchioness of Tana, my wife,
and our remarkable families, for the
support, inspiration, and courage they
have shown.

To
His Imperial Highness
Prince Ermias Sahle-Selassie Haile-Selassie,
President of the Crown Council of Ethiopia,
who continues to inspire us that there is
reason to hope for a
better future for mankind.

And To
The great engineer, Dr Harold Clough, my partner
in what we came to call "the freedom movement".
He has contributed vastly to the Australian
economy, but even more extensively to the
opening of minds to rational discourse.

Some Acronyms Used

A2/AD: Anti-Access/Area Denial doctrine/capability to dominate a geopolitical space.

AI: Artificial intelligence.

ANZUS: Australia-New Zealand-US (security alliance); signed in 1951.

BRI: Belt and Road Initiative (People's Republic of China ideological doctrine); known until May 2017 as One Belt, One Road (OBOR).

CIS: Commonwealth of Independent States, comprised of sovereign states which were formerly part of the Soviet and earlier Russian empires.

COVID-19: Shorthand for the 2019 version of coronavirus. CO (corona), VI (virus), and D (disease). Originally referred to as "2019 novel coronavirus" or "2019-nCoV".

CPC: Communist Party of China, aka Chinese Communist Party (CCP).

CPTPP: Comprehensive and Progressive Agreement for Trans-Pacific Partnership, also known as TPP11 or TPP-11.

CPSU: Communist Party of the Soviet Union (now defunct).

ECB: European Central Bank.

EU: European Union.

EW/ECM: Electronic warfare/electronic countermeasures.

FSB: *Federal'naya sluzhba bezopasnosti Rossiyskoy Federatsii*. Federal Security Service (Russia).

FSO: *Federalnaya Sluzhba Okhrany*. Federal Protective Service (Russia).

GDP: Gross Domestic Product.

HMS: Her/His Majesty's Ship.

ID: Information dominance (doctrine and operations).

IP: Intellectual property.

IT: Information technology.

IW: Information Warfare.

MIT: Turkish National Intelligence Organization (*Milli Istihbarat Teskilati*).

MOOTW: Military operations other than war.

NATO: North Atlantic Treaty Organization, North Atlantic Alliance.

NGO: Non-governmental organization.

PLA: People's Liberation Army, the Armed Forces of the People's Republic of China, with a range of subsidiary forces, including Ground Forces, Air Force (PLAAF), Navy (PLAN), Strategic Support Force (SSF), etc.

PRC: People's Republic of China.

ROC: Republic of China, still the formal name for Taiwan.

SCO: Shanghai Cooperation Organization.

SDI: Strategic Defense Initiative (US).

SLBN: Submarine-launched ballistic missile with nuclear payload.

SOE: State-owned enterprise.

SSBN: Nuclear-powered submarine with ballistic missile launch capability.

UKUSA Accords: aka "Five Eyes" signals intelligence-sharing alliance, originated between US and UK in 1943, and now includes the US, UK, Canada (1948), Australia (1956), and New Zealand (1956). Plus third-party "associates".

USSR: Union of Soviet Socialist Republics (now defunct), replaced by the Russian Federation (within reduced boundaries) and the Commonwealth of Independent States (CIS).

Contents

"You may not be interested in war,
but war is interested in you."

— mis-attributed to Soviet Minister of War Leon Trotsky[1]

---

1   Who actually said: "You may not be interested in the dialectic, but the dialectic is interested in you." The mis-attribution was a deliberate literary ploy in Alan Furst's 1988 novel, *Night Soldiers*.

Author's Note

WAR IS COMPLEX, and became exponentially more complex as the 21st Century grew. Then a simmering conflict became a "total war" of a new type, erupting in 2020, openly and irrevocably from a Beijing epicenter.

The opening volleys of this war came to most of the world as a *barrage of fear* "heard 'round the world". It was the most effective opening salvo of any offensive, 1941's Pearl Harbor included.

Fear was the initial weapon and doctrine of the new total war; and coronavirus was the gunpowder which fueled it. Fear can change everything: economics, politics, love and hate, and the balance of power. Life itself.

The world had begun moving toward this amorphous new, global "total war" even as the Cold War ended three decade earlier. I watched it take form. A new world finally crystallized as the war burst into the open in 2020. And all the world's people were drafted into this unique and titanic battle for survival, dominance, and all that prosperity can deliver.

So the "new way of total war" emerged, inevitably, as a combination of historical practice and current expediency, of novel technologies with prosaic doctrine; and the stultifying paralysis of re-learned ignorance. We are prey to instantaneous, seismic electrification of unverified rumors pulsed into the new crowds on the global street. How do we wage this war?

It would be tempting to believe that the new type of

total war of the 21st Century would be all about the People's Republic of China (the PRC). The Communist Party of China (CPC) had, by 2020, become one driver in how this amorphous form of warfare was developing. But the evolution of "total war" to a very new format was a logical evolution of warfare, and, more particularly, of how societies compete for survival.

This book is not just about whether the PRC or US would dominate the aftermath of the 2020 crisis, but about an even bigger, longer-term framework.

It is, though, worth bearing in mind some key markers when reading this book: the November 3, 2020, US Presidential and Congressional elections; the July 23, 2021, centenary of the foundation of the Communist Party of China; the 2049 centenary of the takeover of mainland China by the CPC; and so on.

In my 2018 book, *Sovereignty in the 21st Century*, I noted the "global civil war" as part of this evolving pattern of conflict; it was, by 2020, increasingly evident.

Manmade milestones measure change, define prestige by being anniversaries or deadlines for accomplishment, and define or challenge power structures.

But *underpinning* this framework defined by the will of individuals and groups lies a tsunamic surge of human demographic change which is the motor of socioeconomic waves. This underpinning drives the growth or regression of food supply, scientific and technological capabilities; how people gather, and how they act.

It drives *everything* which affects human societies.

— Gregory R. Copley, June 2020.

Preface

Everybody's War

WAR — THIS GLOBAL WAR; THIS TOTAL WAR for "global domination" — raged all around as I was writing this book in 2020. It was a struggle in which, literally, the fate of human society would be determined for the coming century.

Few people were thinking of that. Most were panicked, gripped with fear, over the reality that an era of certainty, comfort, and wealth was over.

The future seemed to have vanished from the horizon.

It had not.

It merely had become a clouded vista of turbulent conflict of a new type.

The streets were quiet. Too quiet. Much of the world was entering a psychologically pivotal economic depression. The skies clear. Air traffic was eerily absent; at its lowest level for decades.

It was, at that time, a war running silently and deeply in the frightened substrate of societies and uncertain economic structures; in the aching layers deep in us all, in every clan and pocket of humanity.

It was about surviving the worldwide economic, social, and demographic transformation which had reached an iconic tipping point in 2020, after an evolution which had taken more than a century.

Regardless of the intent of politicians and generals, it was a transformation and a war largely being led by demographic and social trends.

We were facing the aftermath of the now-expired pandemic-like growth of wealth, health, and human numbers. That had begun after World War II, and lasted for almost seven decades.

How well we could understand and manage the new contextual trends would determine the wealth or poverty, freedom or subservience, progress or regression of the world.

The new global war's "big push" began in the last months of 2019 with the pervasive fear pandemic which the coronavirus disease — COVID-19 (or SARS-CoV-2), as it came to be called — created as it emerged from Wuhan, in Hubei Province of the People's Republic of China. The coronavirus epidemic was itself, in fact, fairly innocuous in historical terms with its impact on long-term demographics; albeit frightening for many in terms of randomness of contagion.

But the world *after* the fear pandemic which COVID-19 stimulated would be a new world; a true break from the previous hundred years.

The fear pandemic merely marked an inflection point after a significant process of decline had already begun.

Declines in human numbers and wealth; the collapse of linear growth in technology and the evaporation of all the material things which we had taken for granted: these retreats were already well in evidence by 2020 when the coronavirus triggered the fear pandemic. And it all came together as a mass confluence of rivers of decline which dictated who would seize control of the latter 80 percent of the 21st Century, and how.[2]

Just as supply chain evolution (logistics) largely determined Allied success in World War II and the post-war period, a transformed approach to supply chain thinking would dominate the post-2020 crisis. The gradual evolution in the late 20th Century toward the "just in time" approach would, after 2020, be marked by the rise of "just in case" preparations for supply chain alternatives.

So it was already a different world by 2020, even if societies and institutions were slow to realize it.

The wars had only just begun. And they were being determined at a social level — because, among other things, it was at a social level that panic occurred and economies were transformed, particularly in 2020 — which drove economic and military outcomes.

Now we needed to understand how they would evolve and how the games of nations would be fought.

To a greater degree than ever before in history, the

2   See, for example, Copley, Gregory R.: *UnCivilization: Urban Geopolitics in an Age of Chaos*. Alexandria, Virginia, 2012: The International Strategic Studies Association (ISSA). *Sovereignty in the 21st Century and the Crisis for Identity, Cultures, Nation-States, and Civilizations*. Alexandria, Virginia, 2018: ISSA's Zahedi Center. And Bricker, Darrell and Ibbitson, John: *Empty Planet: The Shock of Global Population Decline*. New York, 2019: Crown Publishing.

wars of the 21st Century had become truly total; truly pervasive. Some of the most critical forces on the chessboard were no longer under the direct control of governments. This would be the great challenge to societies, mostly to elected as well as to autocratic governments.

*   *   *

WARFARE IS SOLELY ABOUT the imposition of will.

Human will enables all things, from the control of lands to the supply of food and the possibility of survival. At its heart, all warfare — all life — is a psychologically- and emotionally-driven exercise.

How we influence and dominate minds — including our own — is the ultimate skill of the warrior. It is the skill of survival and prosperity.

It was during the Vietnam War in the 1960s that the "anti-war movement" became weaponized in and against the West as a proxy form of psycho-political warfare. We have to understand that, just as we have to understand the general history of our strategic context over the past century and more. Without that comprehension we cannot understand what was happening in 2020, and what would happen in the balance of the 21st Century.

So we will get to that in this book.

What happened to the strategic environment of the 20th Century was largely built around the rise to dominance of the crowd, and the assault on hierarchy.

With the fall of crowns across Eurasia and Africa

came the rise of republics and a new era of globalism. We might come to regret some aspects of how we made the transition through that fateful 20th Century, but regrets require memory. And that, too, we had lost. The fall of crowns — of constitutional monarchies — marked the end of multi-generational identity thinking and the start of short-term, materialistic republicanism or "crowned republicanism", in which the lure of immediate gratification of the crowd replaced the dignity and ethics of the past.

Crowds and mobs have always existed, of course, and have always had a receptivity to being captured and used; that is their nature.[3]

But the International Section (IS) of the Communist Party of the Soviet Union (CPSU) had, particularly under Boris Ponomarev (1905-95), made the capture and use of crowds a science to build and control social groundswells. And how Russian-born, anti-communist Evgeny Messner (1891-1974) had helped conceptualize the "hybrid war" theory, which helped shape "war by all means".[4]

The way in which the "anti-war" and "anti-nuclear" movements were shaped was to prove an indication of the massive change in the way wars would be fought in the coming century. Psycho-political actions morphed with other forms of proxy warfare.

3   See, particularly, Canetti, Elias: *Crowds & Power*. New York, 1981: Continuum. Originally published by Claassen Verlag, Hamburg, in 1960 as *Masse und Macht*. And LeBon, Gustave: *The Crowd: A Study of the Popular Mind*. Viking, 1960. Our edition: New York, 1896: The Macmillan Co.
4   Messner was not in the same camp as Ponomarev. He was an ardent anti-communist, an officer in the Russian Imperial Army, forced into exile in Yugoslavia, then fighting against the USSR through World War II. He died in Buenos Aires in 1974.

Proxy war, so difficult to control (but seeming tanta-
lizingly less risky and less expensive than direct, formal
war), became the preferred form of conflict, particularly after the end of the Cold War in 1990. Attempts
to formalize it and control it as "hybrid warfare"
merely saw conflict enter a grey zone which soon embraced all of society.

Those broad, so-called "anti-war" and "anti-nuclear" efforts of the 1960s and '70s were primarily intended to stop or limit the US and its allies from militarily challenging communist attempts to dominate
South-East Asia. Grassroots social activism in North
America, Europe, and Australasia, heavily supported
by clandestine front groups of the communist leadership in Moscow, mostly unknown to its targets, began
to influence the political and media thoughts and actions of Western governments.

It is now no secret that the Soviet attempt at that
time was aimed at minimizing and neutralizing resistance to its own proxy military adventurism in Asia. It
is easy, in the 21st Century, to forget that the Soviets
were as concerned about competition from their com-
rades in the People's Republic of China (PRC) as they
were about competition with the West.

Proxy warfare, including psycho-political operations, had been considered the warfare of choice of
weaker powers or of nuclear powers, which had to be
careful not to trigger direct confrontation among
themselves. But, in fact, indirect warfare had *always*
been the *first* choice of grand strategists (if not always

of military strategists) since the time of Sun-tzu, two-and-a-half millennia ago, and probably earlier.

The Soviet proxy and hybrid information dominance campaigns after World War II were partially successful, as they were from 1917 to 1945[5]. They created a warfare style and momentum which outlasted the Soviet Union itself, heralding the start of a new, grassroots form of strategic political engagement which was to be supercharged by the advent of mass interactive communications such as the Internet and social media.

An article by "anti-war" activist Charlotte Keys in the US *McCall's Magazine* in 1966 hypothesized "Suppose They Gave a War and Nobody Came". The title became a slogan for the Soviet front groups and the proxy US co-opted movements.

Little did Mrs Keys — or *McCalls*, or perhaps even the Soviets — realize that the broad use by the Soviets of psychological warfare (information dominance) techniques of triggering mass actions in target societies such as the US would presage an ongoing activism which would profoundly escalate in the 21st Century.

That escalation would be fired by wealth, the Internet, and urbanization.

Now we are faced with the realization of a new hy-

5 Even the rationale for the "Russian Revolution" (in fact only a *putsch* followed by massive suppression of the population of Russia and its Empire) was based on extensive psychological manipulation. Essentially, the Soviets built all their global offensive operations around psychological warfare and their defensive operations — out of necessity — around kinetic or conventional warfare. That balance or mix was to change after World War II gave the Soviets significant military capability, although the extent to which that was hampered by poor economic capabilities meant that psychological strategies were consistently at the forefront of Soviet capabilities.

pothesis: Suppose They Gave a War and *Everybody Came.*

It is this state of affairs which affects how conflict is conducted in the 21st Century. In some ways, it signals a substantial shift to information dominance warfare, including proxy and hybrid operations, and indirect operations designed to pre-determine strategic outcomes.

It is a state of affairs which has re-defined the meaning and conduct of democracy. It is fair to say that some modern *concepts* of democracy had, by 2020, become so weaponized that they sometimes began to represent the antithesis of freedom at individual and societal levels.

But it was not merely "the state" which was driving a suppression of freedoms in the name of democracy. Mass movements in urban areas were themselves becoming driving forces in *co-opting* and transforming concepts of "democracy", effectively ending freedoms.

The question was whether this process would, or could, prevail, or whether it would merely just reinforce global and national divisions.

The 21st Century began the great polarization between urban-dominated globalist ideologies on the one hand, and regionally-dominated nationalists on the other. But this also began to see an overlay in which rigid, mass-oriented ideology — in this case globalism in its several forms[6] — adopted a *cloak* of democracy

6   ie: *globalism* is an ideology; *globalization* is the phenomenon of actual trade infrastructure and mechanics.

against the reviving nationalists who often emphasized individual freedom.

But just as "globalism" and "democracy" were nowhere clearly understood, neither was the meaning and philosophical depth of the concept of "freedom". And at their cores, "globalism" and "democracy" (in the 21st Century iteration) often came to represent the *surrender* of responsibility to others, rather than the *assignment* of certain tasks within free societies. "Freedom" implies the acceptance of responsibility by the individual.

And if, as this study suggests, the world was now in a war to which everybody had come, then the ideological underpinnings would be important to both propagandist groups in the contest: nationalists and globalists. It was a titanic struggle on which we had embarked, whether or not we were aware of the fact.

The global economy had become brittle by the end of 2019, and the coronavirus-inspired fear pandemic of early 2020 drove almost every economy in the world into either recession or structural transformation.

One of the pillars of the post-Cold War architecture — the People's Republic of China — had suffered severe setbacks well before 2020: setbacks which could see it enter a path of decline and possible instability.

So it was possible, even probable, that the "inevitable" rise of the PRC could well be still-born, or at least constrained or distorted in its infancy. And that the European Union might itself founder if it did not transform. That the US, and most of the states of the

West, of Africa, Asia, and Latin America would continue to face their own forms of dysfunction.

That is not to say that we saw the PRC reduced to impotence. Quite the contrary: in many ways the new phase of the war had just begun in 2020, and the Communist Party of China (CPC) grasped the chaos of the 2020 pandemic to transform its fortunes. It simplified its "war without boundaries" doctrine against the US to the "three Fs": foment weakness, foment chaos, and foment destruction. Or to make the US "fail, frail, and fall", according to some interpretations.

Even, in 2019 and 2020, the Government of India had also taken advantage of the global distractions and quietly abrogated its own Constitution — thereby damaging its claim to being the world's largest democracy — when it sent about a million of its own troops to invade an autonomous state in its own Union, Jammu & Kashmir. A million troops! That's 6.4 times the number of troops the Allies threw against the heavily-fortified shores of Normandy on D-Day, during Operation *Overlord*, on June 6, 1944; against a trained and determined military force.

The world slept through the Kashmir events of 2019 and 2020, because the Indian Government ensured that all media and foreigners were removed from Kashmir before the invasion occurred in the name of Hindu nationalism.

That was the kind of information dominance war which had been perfected by the early 21st Century. Warfare had evolved. The targets were total and indiscriminate: commoditized; often within societies. The forces which engaged in these glacial struggles were themselves "total" and often indistinguishable from humanity as a whole.

The Kashmir invasion was only one example of many diverse skeins of warfare underway and developing as the Century unfolded. Apart from the change in normal warfare, "total war" truly had become more total than the great wars of the 18th, 19th, and 20th centuries. And less easily defined than ever before; less controllable; less immediately perceivable as lethal or kinetic ... and yet ultimately more transformative and destructive.

The perceptional uncertainties surrounding these diverse strands of warfare — and our inability thus far to see "total war" of today as a unified field of action because it embraces more "civil" aspects than military — only make more urgent the need for an understanding of the pervasive conflicts of the 21st Century.

The 21st Century sees the culmination of the "mass movement", the ultimate face of the 20th Century. At some point in this 21st Century, with the decline of population mass, we will see, again, the cyclical dominance of hierarchies. That will once more change the nature of warfare.

But if, at the end of the day, it is freedom we seek, then we had best understand what it is and what it should be. And how concepts of freedom can be mobilized as a defense against the creeping conscription of humanity into an ongoing, mob-led shadow drama.

The new form of total war embraces many inter-related operational aspects of governance, military actions, and society, including:

> **Information dominance warfare,** including all the social aspects of psychological strategies and cyber warfare, big data and the progress of quantum computing and artificial intelligence. This must — unlike the latter part of the 20th Century — be firmly rooted in the context of sociology, history, and geopolitics, if it is to be meaningful in an age of decreasing budgets and declining populations;

> **Population and economic warfare,** including currency strategies; food strategies (and therefore water and agriculture); trade channeling (including new funding approaches and tariffs); the construction of new trade and technology *blocs*; and the ability to resist or utilize mass movements of peoples, while understanding and coping with the hostile strategies to stampede, impede, or destroy population groups;

> **Force projection and military operations** in the new economic and technological frameworks, which include a greater reliance on innovation and creativity to offset declining operating, procurement, and research and development funds.

Within even these spheres, as we will discuss, it is anything but business as usual.

The irony, meanwhile, was that ongoing cry of the urban globalists that "the state" must save them, but that the state should be forbidden from saving itself.

I

A New War Dawns

AR HAD BECOME amorphous by the 21st Century. Electrical. Amorphous because it had pervaded every phase of almost every human life. Electrical because the entire conduct of war and peace was no longer practicable without a constant flow of electricity.

It had become impossible to see where warfare began and ended.

Impossible to see where glittering military capabilities were any more to be construed as the primary tools of war, or merely the punctuation carronades of strategic theater.

Impossible to see where the power of nations could any more be clearly identified and used.

And war, it seemed at first glance, had lost its sting.

In fact it had merely become insidious, transformed. It favored as its form of cratocide — the murder of nations — the more slow strangulation of societies rather than their abrupt dispatch with a bullet to the back of the head. And war had become its own thing, self-sustaining, and over which national leaderships held only tenuous sway.

World War III, if anyone wished to call it that, had no apparent beginning. It evolved and progressed as a hollowing of the seven decades or so of unparalleled growth and wealth which had followed World War II.

All the world had become the stage. And literally all the men and women merely players. First, the early 21st Century political dynamic had sucked the oxygen from freedoms in a way which differed from the 20th Century. Then it held the prospect of chaos.

Warfare, like electricity, had become the tool of *all* society.

There was to be no escape from it. Unless electricity itself ceased to flow. And that was possible. Probable in some areas, where economic pressures caused interruptions to electrical services. Then those areas could become deliberate or collateral targets and victims in this insatiable and organically-evolving process.

It was this ubiquity, this pervasiveness, which had made it become true "total" war; in which keystrokes and consumer choices — even consumer panic — could move bigger outcomes. Outcomes which could not be predetermined. This had fleshed out as a new type of warfare.

Chinese strategists Qiao Liang and Wang Xiangsui also saw this phenomenon coming in 1999 in their book, *Unrestricted Warfare*, noting: "When we suddenly realize that all these non-war actions may be the new factors constituting future warfare, we have to come up with a new name for this new form of war: Warfare which transcends all boundaries and limits, in short: unrestricted warfare."[7]

They continued: "If this name [unrestricted warfare] becomes established, this kind of war means that all means will be in readiness, that information will be omnipresent, and the battlefield will be everywhere. It means that all weapons and technology can be superimposed at will, it means that all the boundaries lying between the two worlds of war and non-war, of military and non-military, will be totally destroyed, and it also means that many of the current principles of combat will be modified, and even that the rules of war may need to be rewritten."

Total war in the 21st Century was, as all total war is, the realm of grand strategy, but in a grand strategic context heavily driven by grassroots factors.

Formal and semi-formal warfare is the province only of military strategy. There has always been tension between grand strategy and military strategy because each represents a different approach to — and a different level of — national security.

But the change in the global context of the 21st Century meant that grand strategy was becoming something which needed to be most urgently addressed.

7   Qiao Liang and Wang Xiangsui, Senior Colonels, People's Liberation Army, PRC: *Unrestricted Warfare* (the Mandarin title literally translates as "Warfare Beyond Bounds"). Beijing, February 1999: PLA Literature and Arts Publishing House. Subsequently translated and published by the US Foreign Broadcast Information Service (FBIS) in 1999. It is significant that this book has consistently been upgraded and developed as the strategic playbook — the operating grand strategy doctrine — of the Communist Party of China. Moreover, the original English-language translation by FBIS — done very rapidly after the original was issued — was not as clear and true to the original as later interpretations.

So, at a time when most of those in the cities had largely forgotten or mis-remembered their history, the entire world now found itself immersed in a form of war. Not like the world wars of the 20th Century. Even those wars are now only remembered in the images of iconic, set-piece battles.

How can we compare this amorphous "thing" in which we are now engaged with the great wars of the past century?

Is what we are now embarked upon really "war"?

Tanks are rarely in the streets; uniformed armed forces are static or declining as a proportion of societies' numbers; and the sporadic kinetic warfare we see around the world is nothing like the charnel battlefields of the 20th Century.

It is a war, however, which envelops all of human society, because everywhere there are existential challenges to societies.

There have been challenges growing since the end of the 20th Century from *within* societies, as urban-utopianist city-states once again rejected — as inferiors and vassals — their fellow countrymen outside the major population concentrations.[8]

There are challenges *between* societies as the global strategic architecture of nation-states predictably and logically collapsed following the end of the Cold War. There, the formal mechanisms of states still come into play, and we will address that.

---

8   See again, for example, Copley, Gregory R.: *UnCivilization: Urban Geopolitics in a Time of Chaos*; op cit.; and *Sovereignty in the 21st Century and the Crisis for Identity, Cultures, Nation-States, and Civilizations*; op cit.

But in the overall matrix of societal engagement and state realms, there are challenges on a scale never seen before, as an unprecedentedly large human population faces dislocation across the spectrum of demographics, economics, and security.

So "total war" in the 21st Century looked very different from the fairly rigid and formal confrontations of uniformed troops of the previous century. Yet the very survival of many societies and nation-states in their existing forms was already clearly open to question as the 2020s arrived.

We will not see an end to formal military confrontation in the 21st Century. It will continue, but increasingly — *no matter how serious* — it will form only part of the continuum of conflict. Such conventional inter-state warfare is rarely likely to be decisive by itself in the long-term. Armed conflict, because it has become so circumscribed, may subdue, but it rarely resolves. It can nudge trends toward specific outcomes, but only if all other instruments of change are appropriately played.

The ancient maxim applies: Do not take your armies to a war before you have already won it.

In some instances, the very act of going to war in the traditional military sense opens paths to political, social, or economic decline within the initiating power. That was evidenced with the second Gulf War by the US against Iraq's Saddam Hussein Government (2003-11). There was never truly a plan in that engagement beyond the military aspects of war.

In any event, "total war" of the 21st Century has moved well beyond the clash of armies.

The phrase "total war" was coined by German General Erich Ludendorff[9] to describe — after the event — the great supply chain engagement of World War I. That, however, was nowhere near the "constant global war" which now transcends the formal military conflict and logistics of 1914-18.

Gen. Ludendorff did not grasp the full extent of the concept, even by then-current standards. The greatest contribution he made to thought on it was in the *title* of his book, *Der totale Krieg* (*The Total War*).

Viennese-born US grand strategist Dr Stefan Possony (1913-95) dramatically updated and fleshed out the perspective of "total war" in 1938, embracing the economics of war and an understanding of war-economy.[10]

Even Possony's ground-breaking study could not encompass the point we had reached by the 2020s, given the transformation which was to come after 1938 in the technological and sociological complexity of societies, and the reality that the late-maturity phase was

---

9   Ludendorff, Erich Friedrich Wilhelm. 1865-1937; Prussian; general of infantry. Achieved fame first in 1914 as the victor of the battles of Liege and Tannenberg. On being appointed Quartermaster-General of the German General Staff, he then became a central figure in the military leadership of Germany until the end of the Great War. His failure to win the major Spring Offensive for Germany in 1918 saw him forced from office by October 1918. He published *Der totale Krieg* (*The Total War*) in 1935, in which he posited that war required the entire moral strength of a nation, and also that peace was merely an interval between wars.

10   See particularly, Possony, Stefan T.: *To-morrow's War: Its Planning, Management, and Cost.* London, 1938: William Hodge & Comany Ltd. It was particularly important with its original German title, *Die Wehrwirtschaft des totalen Krieges* (*The Economy of Total War*).

to emerge for Western Civilization[11]. But a combined reading of Possony and Oswald Spengler's *Decline of the West*[12] should have given the world an understanding of where the concept of total war was heading.

Had Adolf Hitler's German General Staff leaders read and understood Possony's *To-morrow's War*, they would have known from the outset that the metrics of their war could have led them only to disaster. They did not comprehend the long-term equations of population and resource reserves which were the foundation of the total war in which they were to become engaged. Moreover, Hitler allowed himself to be drawn toward a series of unimagined and unintended consequences in an unstable chain of events.

Truly, no plan of campaign survives the first volley. Third and fourth order effects are so numerous that some form of unanticipated impact is certain, regardless of planning.

And that era was nothing compared with the brittle intricacy of the world of the early 21st Century: a time of socio-technological, electricity-driven super-complexity, coupled with concurrent socio-economic deterioration, social media magnification and distortion, fragmentation, and fissiparous splitting and churning of societies into the swirls of chaos.

---

11 Bearing in mind the historical tendency for civilizations — as expressed by the existence of empires — to last an average of only 250 years, as Sir John Glubb outlined in *The Fate of Empires and the Search for Survival*, published in Edinburgh, Scotland, 1976-77.

12 Spengler, Oswald: *The Decline of the West* (originally: *Der Untergang des Abendlandes*). Vol. I first appeared in 1918; Vol. II in 1922. See also, Copley, Gregory R.: *UnCivilization: Urban Geopolitics in a Time of Chaos*. Alexandria, Virginia, 2012: The International Strategic Studies Association.

Today, largely as a result of that second great war, we are in yet another world, and it is a world immersed in conscious and unconscious conflict, embracing literally all aspects of all societies. It is a world in which formal military conflict and the use of the icons of military power for prestige, deterrence, and persuasion represent only a narrow component of the framework.

At their essence, we still do not understand even the 20th Century's two great wars.

By not understanding the two world wars and the Cold War, we cannot therefore understand the dynamics which guide our present dilemma, with all the underlying demographic currents.

We do not even comprehend the inevitable, primal forces which presently divide us *within* the borders of our nation-states.

And yet who could *not* have thought, as the 2020s dawned, that the world was already on the brink of massive, disquieting change?

Not the change which brings the guarantee of a better tomorrow for all, or most; but the change which reaches out and grasps us from the darkness.

All of this was foreseen. When no-one wished to contemplate the shape of the post-Cold War world in 1990, I spoke of the significantly new imperatives challenging every nation-state[13]. Even in 2008, with regard to the influence of global pandemics, I noted:

The unintended, or unforeseen, consequences of

13 Copley, Gregory: "Global Geopolitics in the 1990s: An Era of Instability", in *Defense & Foreign Affairs*, January-February 1991; based on a November 1990 speech to The Asian Council in Tokyo.

economic dislocation — as this writer has repeatedly noted — can be expected to lead to a rise in globalized (or at least regionalized) pandemic health challenges at a time when societies are weakened.

These will lead to wealthier societies becoming more nationalistic and isolated, in some respects, merely to protect themselves. Pandemics will be matched by similar anomic social responses, including rising crime, of which the new era of maritime piracy is merely one aspect.

Indeed, it is clear that the best avenue which nation-states can take is one marked by gaining as much control over their own destinies as possible. That requires a growing focus on domestic food self-sufficiency, and domestic market bases for manufactured goods and services. In other words: a return to a sense of the nation. The age of globalization is ending; it was a brief window in which the technologies which were created to fight the Cold War became the technologies of global social integration. Now, again, the luxury of internationalism is ending, and survival is based around the extended clan: the nation.[14]

A new pandemic did occur the next year, 2009: "influenza A (H1N1)pdm09", which was first noted in the US in April 2009 (and discussed later in this book). More than a half-million people were believed to have died from that virus in the first year alone.

With all of these manmade and natural evolutions, the global architecture of nation-states which had been evolving since the Peace of Westphalia in 1648 was already in tatters by about 2020.

14 Copley, Gregory R.: "Globalization is Dead; Nationalism Returns as the Bulwark", in *Defense & Foreign Affairs* **Strategic Policy**, 10/2008.

This was what the Victory of the West had wrought.

As usual, it was a legacy of unintended, unconsidered, and ill-considered consequences. It was wrought, above all, by the arrogance of victory and the dull, leaden pall of "unawareness" — narcolepsis — of post-Cold War wealth.

There was no longer a viable concept of war.

And the concept of peace was just a vision of sugar-plum fairies delivering a constant gratification of material distractions.

Even among the unshackled peoples, broken from the fetters of the rigid bipolarity of three-quarters of a century of the "superpower era", there was merely *ambition*. It was an understandable yearning for "their turn", a desire for hitherto unimagined consumerism, and for the restoration of imagined past glories.

What was happening after the false dawn of the first two decades of the 21st Century was that the world was in a very new place. The legacy of the wealth created by the 20th Century — the wealth of materialism, food for all; and technologies, the origins of which were unknown to their possessors — gave an ignorant sense of empowerment at all levels of almost all societies.

Forgotten was how the evolution of history had given structure to the viable functioning of societies. Not always their *efficient* orchestration, but enough efficiency to give symmetry and function to societies for their own wellbeing and self-protection. The world was like a clock with loosely-fitted parts; slipping sometimes, but regulating the place of all things in all places with a whimsical variety which assumed a workable form.

But all things evolve. All eras pass. It was natural that our earlier definitions of war, peace, wealth, security, happiness, and even fear, should present themselves for review and revision. If not now, then when?

The world ignored the inflection point emerging from Beijing, in September 2018, when the Communist Party of China (CPC) declared the start of a "New Thirty Years War" with the United States of America.[15]

It was a confident declaration — ignored by the population and leadership of the US — that the People's Republic of China (PRC), under the CPC, would be the "global hegemon" at the end of this "New Thirty Years War"; and that it would then be the CPC which determined the *new* "Peace of Westphalia"[16]. Thus would a "New Rules-Based World Order" be ordained, this time by the CPC. Beijing urged the US not to fight the inevitable, nor even to struggle militarily to resist the "unstoppable" rise of the PRC.

It was not that the US failed to hear the declaration.

Most Americans would, even hearing it, have failed to *understand* it. And Beijing itself, ringing with a righteousness that it was now "its turn" to dominate the

---

15 See, Bodansky, Yossef: "Beijing's 'New Thirty Years War'", in *Defense & Foreign Affairs Strategic Policy*, 10/2018.

16 The Peace of Westphalia describes the agreements reached in Westphalia in 1648, marking the end of Europe's Thirty Years War. It was far-reaching in its import, because it essentially, for the first time, codified a common understanding of the modern "nation-state" as a geopolitical entity, rather than just the "nation", which implied a human phenomenon rather than human populations tied to a specific geographic region. So the "Westphalian state" came to represent a recognized geographical area and the people it contained as the unit of sovereignty which commanded the recognition of other such entities.

world, also failed even to comprehend fully what it had declared. That is not to say that the CPC did not have a clear intent to be the "global hegemon" and to relegate the US into subordination. It did. But, in reality, it did not have a clear path to that objective, other than the *hope* that it could outlast the will of its principal adversary, the United States — perhaps even the West as a conceptual whole — to survive.

Frankly, the CPC did not intend the US to hear its declaration of war. It was meant for internal motivation within the Party and the People's Liberation Army (PLA). But over-zealous distribution of the new declaration leaked, despite the attempts of the PLA Political Department to claw back copies of the statement.

Perhaps it was a reliance on the historical reality that victory is not so much won by one side, but lost by the other due to its own internal weaknesses.

The question was whether the CPC mandarins, or even those within the US or Western political and security apparatus, fully understood how to move from their present positions to their envisaged goals.

There was no "grand strategy", nor even an understanding of the place and discipline of grand strategy. It was a term which had become meaningless. In this area, though, at least the CPC had plans to create or reinforce the internal weakness of the US and the West.

There was also, within the European Union (EU), literally no understanding of the underpinnings of power and survival required for the coming century.

The landscape of the EU now embraced the ancient

battlefields of the original Thirty Years War and the Peace of Westphalia which ended it in 1648, giving us four centuries of evolution of a nation-state-dominated geopolitical architecture. But the Westphalian nation-state was no longer understood.

As 2020 dawned — with the reality that the European Union itself was crumbling — there was a call by *its* mandarins for the EU to re-assert "moral authority" on the world through the suasion of "soft power"[17]. There was not even a hint of realism in the school of sophistry which arose within the EU's halls of academe, funded by the toils of now-disenfranchised farmers and workers, as to what they meant by "soft power". To EU officials, it represented a repudiation of the crude bluntness of the "hard power"[18] — which the EU bureaucrats could not match — of the United States, or the PRC, or even Russia.

There was little comprehension that "soft power" was not, in fact, a "third behavioral way of achieving desired outcomes", as the utopianists of the EU claimed. The term, "third behavioral way", implied

17 Soft power is usually defined as the projection of influence (or the imposition of will) by non-kinetic means, or by means which are not seen as overtly physically threatening. Economic, political, and psychological suasion all come into this realm, but soft power is by itself an incomplete aspect of the projection of societal will, just as hard, or military, power is an incomplete aspect of the "total power" matrix necessary for the achievement of long-term national goals and national security. And *soft power requires the existence of prestige in hard power capability.*

18 There is, in fact, no firm definition of "hard power", other than that it implies the use or credible threat of physical force by formal state formations, such as the armed forces. The consideration of a concept of constant total war implies that there is not even a blurred line separating "soft" from "hard" power; there is only a nuanced continuum in which a range of direct, indirect, and proxy effects are deployed to achieve national objectives. It is so in all forms of life: too much weight at either the "soft" or "hard" end of the scale leads to inefficiencies which can either invite hostility — to fill a power vacuum — or miss the opportunities to seize stability and prosperity.

that the EU's exercise of power would involve "nudging" friends and foes into behavior modification.[19]

"Soft power" exists, *and may be the most powerful element of power projection and survival,* but only if it is truly understood and wielded as a component of *an entire matrix* of the tools which societies must employ to survive and prosper. Similarly, "hard" or military power can only be viable if the concept of victory is understood and the military aspect married to the greater matrix of power and the purpose of power.

"Soft power" exists only as an aspect — perhaps the most important aspect — of *power* as an holistic framework. The engine may be the most important component of an automobile, but it is meaningless without the chassis, the drive train, the wheels, and so on. Certainly, the power of maneuver, moral influence, and sound economic and social policies can have an influence, but they fall before the sword if their prestige is thrown into doubt.

Prestige is the peak component of "soft power" *and* hard power, and it is prestige which dominates everything. A collapse of prestige makes the use of the sword inevitable. The essence of durable power is summed up in the word "prestige". Absent prestige, all is lost, or all is a struggle for survival. As Stefan Possony would say: "Prestige is the credit rating of nations"[20]; of us all.

19 Anne-Lise Sibony and Alberto Alemanno in "The Emergence of Behavioural Policy-Making: A European Perspective". 2015.
20 Contained in Possony, Stefan T.: "The Invisible Hand of Strategy" in *Defense & Foreign Affairs Digest,* 8/1975. He noted, in that article: "If Britain's prestige in 1914 had been as good as it was in 1878, World War I would never have happened. If, in 1939, US prestige had not been that of a distant and disinterested power —

And thus, the examples of the PRC and the EU cited in this chapter may themselves be of moot significance by the mid-21st Century. Even by early 2020 it was an open question as to whether the economy of the PRC would survive the challenges facing it. The entire bombast of the "inevitable" rise of "China" to global hegemony by 2049 — by which the Beijing leadership meant the hegemony of the Communist Party of China — seemed more likely to have been forgotten long before then.

But Xi's Beijing was compelled to fight for its survival and knew that 2020 opened what might have seemed like its last opportunity to reverse its fortunes.

Meanwhile, the carefully insinuated hope of the European Union leadership for an "ever closer union" of European peoples — in other words, abandoning their Westphalian home-states — seemed equally, by 2020, destined for early disillusionment.

Failure and collapse, as well as victory, are difficult to recognize. The geography and peoples of China will continue to exist, just as will the peoples and territory of Europe. We saw transformations in interpretations of what we even meant by "China" and "Europe" in the Cold War and post-Cold War eras, just as we saw the term "America" come to mean only the United States of America — and not the Western Hemisphere of numerous states — over the course of the 20th Century.

Part of our struggle is to know what we mean by our

with a penchant for rhetorical bluff and clowning about disarmament — World War II could have been avoided. A policy of strength and firmness would have prevented Pearl Harbor and its worldwide consequences."

language. Precision of thought leads to precision linguistically in defining and conveying our goals, understanding our context, and achieving our survival and prosperity.

That is the objective of this book: to define our *modus pugnandi*: how we face the challenge.

It will require a re-definition of economic models, of our views of currency, concepts of growth, and concepts of democracy, as well as our models of warfare.

* * *

A BASIC PREMISE OF THIS BOOK is that the "new total war of the 21st Century" began when the "last total war of the 20th Century" — the Cold War — ended. The Cold War, although total, was predominantly in the social, economic, and technological space, and had only moments of formal or informal armed conflict.

The Cold War resulted in the defeat of the USSR and the Warsaw Treaty *bloc*, partly because the West was able to split the People's Republic of China from the USSR. The PRC, undefeated, did not then become an ally of the West, but rather a key victor of the Cold War.

The PRC knows that to succeed in the new total war, it must continue to ensure that grand strategic maneuver dominates, and military *contact* is minimized and only used to nudge trends or deliver decisive culmination. In all this, military prestige must remain high.

US Pres. Donald Trump, like Xi, intrinsically understood that the actual use of military force in total war holds the greatest risk of strategic decline, rather than success. Comprehensive, total maneuver is the game.

II

The Premise of Total War in the 21st Century

TOTAL WAR IN THE 20th Century was governed solely by governments, and was between the formal entities of nation-states. But total war transformed beyond recognition in the 21st Century.

The beginning of the 21st Century began to reflect the loss of authority, control, and trust once held by the national hierarchies. Nation-states, which had become vitiated as to their clear definition, assumed the amorphous character of the horizontally-linked "total society", which believed itself as well-educated and well-informed as its leaders, and therefore had little need for hierarchy.

"Society", although blind to consequences and demanding in its need for gratification, came to drive governance and determine priorities. But that "triumph of society" was not in what could be called a democratic fashion. Rather, factionalized pressure groups began to congeal into politically-correct *blocs* which could dominate government.

But this in turn polarized societies and moved warfare into additional realms, including confrontations between societal groups (or sub-groups), as well as the traditional field of state-to-state conflict. However, the broader, technologically-flattened societies, had, by the 21st Century, become integrally-engaged elements which would become a major factor in 21st Century total war.

1. The State controlled the conduct of total war up to *the end of the 20th Century*

Total war as a concept galvanized into a clear, concise definition in the 20th Century.

That century saw total war as a concept in which the state took command of the entire civilian society in support of the conduct of military warfare against the entire society — military and civil — of an opposing state.

This concept included the co-option of entire allied, subordinate states which were often subsumed, *de facto*, into a neo-confederal framework to conduct war on a broader scale against enemies which may have been also linked in a neo-confederal fashion.

In the case of the 20th Century, it also embraced the conduct of the Cold War, which saw, essentially, the pattern extended to the creation of *a common war-economy* of one strategic-economic *bloc* of states against another (for example, the NATO/Western states *versus* the Warsaw Treaty states).

So total war in the 20th Century saw the state take

control — through a creeping process of intervention — of all the resources of the nation to wage war against other nation-states or their proxies. As a result, states used their formal, standing resources to wage war, and these centered around the legitimacy of military forces and legal declarations of war.

2. Society, not the State, dominates the conduct of total war in the 21st Century

The concept that the state controlled the conduct of total war had been overturned by default by the early 21st Century.

Civil society in Western democracies had effectively begun to co-opt the state (rather than the reverse), and through it the conscious and unconscious conduct of warfare.

Arguably, it could be seen as democratization, re-turning governments (and military) to become subject to the people. But which people? The majority? Or merely a particular segment of society?

One portion of "civil society"[21] — not to be confused with the overall, or general, civilian populace — no longer really supported a formal military structure. Rather, the military had become merely *a subordinate*

---

21 Civil society is the phrase usually meant to embrace groups outside the governmental structure of a nation-state, but not including the commercial sector. The phrase has come, in the late 20th and early 21st centuries, to be a deliberate formalization of a rôle for "non-profit" activist groups, including so-called "non-governmental organizations" (NGOs), which have assumed *de facto* power as "legitimate" voices of authority based solely on their activism and sometimes the power of their discreet funding. So the phrase, "civil society", has become psychologically loaded and no longer actually implies the civilian body of a population, which includes a wider range of individuals and organized bodies, whether they be religious institutions or corporations.

aspect of an ongoing confrontation in which one society or elements of a society impelled confrontation against another society or elements of a society.

In this case, however, the "total war" — particularly the aspect *within* Western democracies — was not conducted by a particular demographic grouping of a civil society initially or primarily against other nation-states. It began with the conduct of war against another demographic *bloc* within its own, supposedly-shared, nation-state. Interstate (ie: international) conflict was *a secondary consideration* for the offensive forces preoccupied with this kind of domestic war.

War, including total war *between nation-states* was usually considered as a primary means of power exertion only by those nation-states in which vertical hierarchies still retained dominance over their component societies, such as in the PRC and Russia.

So total war in the 21st Century was being envisaged or conducted asymmetrically. In the West, it became *primarily* war *within* societies with most domestic preoccupation focused on internal schisms[22].

In other areas of the world and in other circumstances, total war bore a similarity to an evolution of 20th Century warfare, which often coupled with governmental dominance of domestic society.

The legacy military establishments of divided Western societies retained as *their* primary objective the ability to conduct war solely against foreign nation-

---

22 See, Copley, Gregory R.: *Sovereignty in the 21st Century.* Op cit. Specifically Chapter XX, "World War III as a Global Civil War".

state entities and their proxies (including terrorist and subversive forces).

What became significant, however, was that those Western defense establishments were being seen as irrelevant by urban-globalist "civil society" elements of their own societies; elements principally committed to conducting war against the nationalist elements of their own nation-states.

"Total war" in Western nation-states now involved a churn *within* populations as elements vied for supremacy or even, as they perceived it, survival. This polarization within societies had the prospect to break up nation-states, as we saw in the 1861-65 US Civil War. Or the resurgence of Scottish secessionism in the wake of the UK withdrawal from the EU, or the Catalan, Biafran, and Western Australian secessionist moves.

Significantly, this threat of national break-up also applied as much (although differently expressed) in "democratic" societies as in authoritarian ones.

3. The initial war of urban-globalists in Western states in the 21st Century is against nationalists within their own state

War in the 21st Century is, then, "more total" than the "total war" thinking of the 18th, 19th, and 20th century concepts. It is now more driven by sociological trends which both impel governments and reinforce permanent or "constant total war" through what may be described as permanent or constant "war societies".

These transcend what had evolved as war-economies: formal state-dominated approaches which took on *aspects* of command economies, if not becoming comprehensive command economies.

The result could be described as the "democratization" of total war in which governments — particularly of Western nation-states — were reduced to subordination to large sociological segments *within* national societies, including segments *within governments*. Absent a perceived external threat, these segments choose to wage war by all means (meaning primarily political coercion) against other sociological *blocs* within the same nation-state.

This phenomenon has resulted in the "sub-vision"[23] of the state apparatus — the government — as the pinnacle of a social command hierarchy which once had supervisory power over all elements of a society within a state.

In many respects, the overturning of the state's authority to command both the war-economy and the military and society in the conduct of war against another state or against an informal non-state actor was the result of the global reality of urbanization.

Urbanization had tipped the balance by the early 21st Century.

By that time, urbanization had ensured that some 55 percent of the world's population lived in urban ag-

---

23 The concept of "subvision", or "supervision from below" was expressed first to this author by the 20th Century US author Miles Copeland as a description of how the US State Department operated: the inmates, he said, ran the asylum. Something which US Secretary of State Alexander Haig, Jr., confirmed to to this writer when he said: "When I became Secretary of State, I mistakenly thought that this meant I ran the State Department."

glomerations: cities writ large. But in "advanced economies", the urbanization levels were far higher. In the
US (by 2018), it was 82.3 percent; in Germany, 77.3
percent; in Australia, 86+ percent; in the United Kingdom, 83.4 percent, for example. In the PRC, the urban
portion of the population had risen from 13.3 percent
of a population of 582,603,417 for mainland China in
1953 (the first modern census)[24] to 58.5 percent of a
population of 1.3-billion in 2018[25].

4. Total war in the 21st Century is evolving to be strategically asymmetric in nature

It had become a decisive, although unstated, act of
many in the cities to wage political warfare against the
un-urbanized *blocs* of their national populations.

This meant war waged by the sociological *bloc* in
power against the rest of domestic society. This often
had the consequence of folding-in hostility toward an
external actor, which could often serve as a legitimizing distraction or excuse for the domestic conflict.[26]

But the process of this new form of "total war" was

24 Cheng-Sian Chen: "Population Growth and Urbanization in China, 1953-1970", in *Geographical Review*, Vol. 63, No. 1 (January 1973), pp 55-72.
25 Wu Zhiqiang, vice-president of Tongji University, in an article in (the official) *China Daily*, June 19, 2018.
26 Witness the insistence in the US and UK mass media of the 1990s through to 2020 that "Russia" was to be conflated with the Union of Soviet Socialist Republics (USSR), which had, in fact, been overthrown by nationalist, pro-Western Russians by 1990-91. Nonetheless, post-Soviet "Russia" was seen as the enemy of the US and UK. There was no recognition that the West had already achieved victory over the USSR and could have embraced the liberated Russians. Similarly, in the PRC, troubled domestic times after World War II have usually seen the Communist Party of China invoke the specter of the old enemy, Japan, in order to rally popu-lar support among the Chinese populace to distract from domestic problems. The theory, as old as history, invokes the threat of iconic external enemies to unify sup-port for a government's domestic control.

by no means complete or universal as of 2020. There were still nation-states which resisted this trend — particularly the Russian Federation and the People's Republic of China, where strong hierarchical control persisted — and which continued to insist that the process of warfare would remain in at least one key respect in the 20th Century image: warfare would remain under absolute state control. By that definition, the state alone determined how the civil sector would be utilized to support the military in the conduct of formal armed conflict, or support the State in informal total war.

This, then, became the larger, "international" and asymmetrical picture of the "urban globalist *versus* nationalist" polarization. *Clearly-defined* nation-states were in conflict — informal and formal — with *loosely-defined* nation-states. It could be argued that this was merely a distinction between authoritarian societies *versus* democratic societies, but, on closer inspection, it became one of authoritarian societies *versus* neo-anarchic societies. Or strongly hierarchical societies *versus* flat structure societies. By any perspective, the confrontation became strategically asymmetrical.

Authoritarian societies, or nation-states where hierarchy remained dominant, were preoccupied with the view that conventional military forces and operations were a decisive, visible tool of power projection, not necessarily *warfighting*. [Weaponized non-kinetic actions were the primary warfighting tools.] "Democratic" and flat-structure societies would tend to use the conventional armed forces as a secondary tool (albeit the most iconic and visible) of strategic projection. The clear representation of the latter form was, by 2020, the European Union *bloc*. Regardless of its expenditure on military spending (outside of the UK which departed the Union in 2020, and France), it remained unable to seriously project military power.

One aspect of the 21st Century framework still to be determined by 2020 was how and when could unstructured but nonetheless solid sociological *blocs* go to war against their own or foreign governments, or other sociological *blocs* of their own society; or how and whether more traditional nation-states could conduct war in their own defensive or offensive need.

In short, warfare in the 21st Century assumed many forms, including:

- ➤ Amorphous conflict, which occurs in waves of activities of varying intensities within and between societies, and often engages market forces, transnational crime, and all the tools of information dominance, as well as proxy, hybrid, and conventional (state-run) warfare;
- ➤ Nation-state *versus* nation-state (or *blocs* of states against *blocs* of states);
- ➤ Societies (sub-groups of national populations) against other elements of their own society and against social elements of other nation-states;
- ➤ Governments against segments of their populations;
- ➤ Population groups against their governments; and

➤ Variations or combinations of these themes.

From a doctrinal or warfighting perspective, all of these types of conflict could involve conventional warfare (ie: formal military engagements, including special weapons, such as nuclear); proxy and hybrid warfare engaging irregular and terrorist forces; psychopolitical warfare (including information dominance operations, which can engage terrorism); economic warfare; and, often implicitly, population warfare.

Accompanying this is grassroots-driven warfare which is essentially sociological and part of the amorphous warfare set: mobilization of identity groups using demographic dynamics. This force may act independently of state structures; it may act as an insurgency, revolutionary, or terrorist[27] force; or it may act as a high-pressure force which causes state structures to bend to "the street".

---

27 Terrorism is, as its designation implies, a tool or doctrine within the framework of psychological warfare, and within what the Soviets, during the period of the Union of Soviet Socialist Republics (USSR: 1917-1990), called "agitprop": agitation propaganda. It uses physical actions to create psychological and political outcomes. It should not be confused with guerilla warfare and subversion, which, like all forms of human behavior, also induce a psychological result, but which have physical warfighting goals as the primary objective. Terrorism is designed specifically to have psychological impact, in turn inducing a socio-political response. Specifically, by using actions which induce fear or terror in the target audience, the target audience becomes either paralyzed, or moves politically in a direction which suits the perpetrator's objectives. However, direct practitioners of terrorism may also have as an objective merely the perpetuation of the importance of their own societies which the terrorist fears may be crushed and destroyed forever by an overwhelming hostile force (the target of the terrorism). So terrorism is a weapon of asymmetric response to a formal adversary which cannot be challenged in any other way by the weaker society. Terrorism, then, is seen by its practitioners as a doctrine or weapon of last response. As a result, those willing to sacrifice themselves in terrorist actions are often susceptible to patronage by a hidden, sponsoring power which sees advantage in using the sacrifice of the terrorist against a common foe. Sustained terrorism, therefore, is usually only possible when it is supported deniably (in black, or at least grey operations) by a state power. It is, then, a tool of proxy warfare.

Clearly, broad-form amorphous warfare forms, including information dominance warfare, require closer engagement between skill-sets — military, intelligence, economic, police, psychological, political, and technology specialists — than narrow-form warfare.

It is difficult to say which form of warfare would be dominant at any given time, and certainly no single form would remain constantly dominant. Of principle concern will be to determine who is in real control of the process at any given time.

The 21st Century has already become complex and interactive to a degree never before seen on a global scale. To a strong degree, it will mean that leadership — to ensure control of situations — will require demonstrations of visceral appeal in a period when mere institutions alone may not suffice or be trusted.

Trust in institutions, generally weakened by valid or invalid media and social media over several decades, will take time to restore. That trust may be difficult to restore at all unless external threats galvanize social structures and/or unless, or until, hierarchies are restored naturally. Restoration of hierarchies can only occur with a restoration of trust in governance and leadership, equating to a rebuilding of their prestige. And that must be earned.

Meanwhile, the new doctrines of warfare had not been resolved as the first quarter of the 21st Century ticked away. Even by 2020, clear formulation of amorphous warfare doctrine or psychological strategic doctrine appeared not to have been even considered.

III

Continuity as Illusion, Continuum as Reality

WE LIVE IN A WORLD OF ILLUSION. We unconsciously transform the meaning of things. We
gradually adapt words and phrases, so that, at
different times and places, they have evolved
to help us justify to ourselves our behavior and our
situation.

The English writer, Lewis Carroll, said it well in his
nonsense novel, *Alice Through the Looking Glass*[28].

> "When I use a word," Humpty Dumpty said in a
> rather scornful tone, "it means just what I choose it to
> mean — neither more nor less."
> "The question is," said Alice, "whether you can
> make words mean so many different things."
> "The question is," said Humpty Dumpty, "which is
> to be master — that's all."

To be master. The use of language defines our ability
to set goals, structure command, and, above all, to impose will. So if we are to master our environment, we
had best first define it. That is not only the function of
intelligence (in the strategic sense), which gives us an

---

28 Carroll, Lewis (Charles Lutwidge Dodgson): also known as *Alice's Adventures in
Wonderland.* London, 1865: Macmillan and Co.

understanding of our context. It is the function of our ability to define and comprehend what we see, what we wish to achieve, and how we wish to achieve it, while communicating those factors in ways which enables us to achieve mastery: the ability to deliver Victory. And that includes mastery through the building of social cohesion and the ability to destroy cohesion in other societies.

Egyptian Pres. Anwar as-Sadat is famously quoted to have said, during a heated war planning meeting during the start of the October 1973 War with Israel: "Speak English; this is no time to use Arabic." His point was that he needed linguistic precision — not emotionally-loaded language — to convey his commands, and English afforded that more comprehensively than Arabic.

And yet, in all languages, the meaning of words and phrases transforms over time based on context and experience. We often take words and phrases from the past, yet interpret them through the lens of our current morality and broader context. We also pointedly adopt and "load" words and phrases with new meanings. We weaponize them. This is part of our unconscious defensive gathering into "political correctness": language is the first weapon of choice. Loaded words are the principal weapon of culture warfare.

The phrase, "Total War", originally brought into popular usage just before World War II by German Gen. Erich Ludendorff, had a specific meaning to him at the time. We use the phrase today with little regard to what Ludendorff originally meant (or thought he meant), and with even less regard to what it means in the context of the 21st Century, a hundred years or so after it evolved as a concept. Yet it is a valuable phrase, worthy of being redefined to accommodate an entirely new world of social complexity. Moreover, it is a concept which has now subsumed all of 21st Century society and means much more than when it was coined, perhaps without deep thought, by the Prussian material directness of Ludendorff.

He only published *Der totale Krieg* (*The Total War*) in 1935, by which time he was witnessing, encouraging, and shaping the re-birth of (nazi) Germany to fight new wars. By that time, 17 years after the end of World War I, he arguably should have advanced his thinking even more profoundly. The world had changed beyond measure with and after the Great War.

As we have discussed, one young Austrian scholar at the University of Vienna, Stefan Thomas Possony, understood what had happened and where it was leading, and more succinctly stated his theories in *To-morrow's War*, in 1938.

His German-language first edition, *Die Wehrwirtschaft des totalen Krieges*[29], was quickly translated into French, and then into English. By 1939 it was in the United States, but by then Possony had been forced to flee Vienna because of the 1938 nazi annexation of Austria (*Anschluss Österreichs*), and was in Paris advis-

---

29 Possony, Stefan T.: *Die Wehrwirtschaft des totalen Krieges*. Vienna, 1938. This title, which translates directly as "The defense economy of total war", far more explicitly addresses Possony's approach.

ing the French Air Ministry and Foreign Ministry.

The old soldiers, like Ludendorff himself, did not come suddenly, nor alone, to even the Ludendorff theory of "total war". Ludendorff, and the world, had, before the Great War, been sobered into the modern age. They had absorbed the lessons of the Russo-Japanese War of 1904; not just the naval aspects, but also the land warfare scramble by Japan and the European powers to secure territory in the loosely-defined Asian Pacific region.

They also learned from the US Civil War of 1861-63. That conflict saw the immense power of the urbanized North's industrial wealth and infrastructure nearly defeated because it clung to antique military tactics, leading to vast casualty levels. [There were Prussian military observers present during the US Civil War, and they learned much.]

But ultimately, as the US Civil War showed, it is strategic industrial depth which ultimately always prevails as long as political ineptitude does not squander this deep resource before it can gain preponderance. The Franco-Prussian War of 1870-71, which followed close on the heels of the US Civil War, merely showed that France did not gather its inherent advantages into strategic form before superior and decisive Prussian planning and execution decided the day, even drawing on France's own resources in the process. The Prussians heeded Napoleon's and Sun-tzu's rule of living off captured lands. That rule has modern applications.

Similarly, the Anglo-Boer Wars (1880-81 and 1899-

1902), also after the US Civil War, showed that industrial might and material preparedness could still fall prey to the erosion of power caused by distance and geography.

German military philosophers knew all of this before World War I. And yet when war is left solely to generals — as we are warned that it is too important to be so entrusted — thoughts always return to narrowly-viewed "military arts". In short, military thinking is most often constrained to battles, rather than wars; and wars, rather than "total war" (much less to Victory[30]) in the grand strategy sense.

So when Ludendorff (by the late war period dominating the German General Staff) raised the thinking level to "total war", he had to some extent already moved outside the military mindset of his time and military class. But not nearly far enough.

When retired Prussian cavalry Gen. Friedrich von Bernhardi completed his study, *On War of To-Day*[31], in 1911, he was already aware of how warfare had transformed. In his opening chapter, "The Secret of Modern War", he *almost* grasped the fact that the coming war would be decided by something beyond the force of arms.

He noted: "Whole nations are called up to take the field against each other." But he then reverts to purely military factors, albeit acknowledging that "The

30 For a concept of victory in the grand strategic sense, see Copley, Gregory R.: *The Art of Victory.* New York, 2006: Simon & Schuster's Threshold Editions.
31 Bernhardi, Friedrich v.: *On War of To-Day.* Translated by Karl von Donat. London, 1912: Hugh Rees Ltd.

course of events at sea may mean starvation for the population. In short, a future war will reveal to us a series of seemingly incalculable forces, One might almost come to think that success in war will be more or less a matter of chance, and could in no way be influenced by foresight or to any extent be forecast." Cautiously, he went on: "I think it is not so, after all."

Yet he returns merely to the debate in military terms, because — by the turn of the 20th Century, a time when nation-states had returned to standing professional armies — military power was the most visible and legal arm of warfare and of the state.

The reality was that Emperor Napoleon I (who reigned 1804-14 and 1815) had already come closer to comprehending "total war" because he had the grasp of his state and his military power together in a single fist. His great strength was that he comprehended, above all else, *the weakness of his opponents*. It was *this* which he sought out. Until he could no longer choose his opponents or his field of battle. But he stumbled upon an unwitting aspect of success: he fed his armies on the resources of his opponents, as Sun-tzu had instructed. He preyed psychologically on his enemies' weaknesses, as Tamerlaine had done. And as the PRC was doing in the 21st Century

The Franco-Prussian War of 1870-71 saw the Prussians heed Napoleon's lessons and feed off — as von Bernhardi says — "opulent France" as they invaded.

So what we must conclude is that the study of battle is not the study of war; and that the study of warfare is certainly not the study of "total war".

Généralissime Ferdinand Foch quoted in 1918 in his *The Principles of War*[32], published before the end of World War I, Napoleon I's remark: "We are not more numerous, we are not better armed, but we shall beat you because by our planning we shall have greater numbers at the decisive point; by our energy, our knowledge, our use of weapons we shall succeed in raising our morale and in breaking down yours."

Napoleon Bonaparte implicitly understood "total war", and all of its socio-economic and psychological aspects, but his age was one of substantially less technological (and even social) complexity than the early 21st Century. It was understandable, then, that he did not feel the need to explain the concept of "total war", even in the terms of reference of the late 18th and early 19th centuries. Indeed, Napoleon's concept of total war was his most powerful secret.

By 1938, however, Possony had not only grasped where the world was going, he was also steeped in the Viennese school of economics and knew some of the great economists who created that school of thought. In this regard, then, he was well in advance of Ludendorff's 1935 view of war, and far more attuned to how Western powers could combine the economics of war

---

32 Foch, Ferdinand, Gen.: *The Principles of War*. Translated by J. de Morini. New York, 1918: H.K. Fly Company. Foch was made Marshal of France on August 6, 1918, just before the war's end; in 1919, he was made a Field Marshal of the United Kingdom, and in 1923 a Marshal of Poland. However, it is far more important to read and understand the works of Georges Clemenceau (Prime Minister of France from 1906 to 1909 and from 1917 to 1920). It was he who said: "War is too important to be left to the generals." He better understood grand strategy and total war than Foch.

with the evolution of market societies. His 1938 book earmarked the US as the socio-economic entity which, above all others, had the balance — depth — of capabilities, resources, and geography to adequately manage the coming "total war": World War II.

But Possony was also fearful of the unholy alliance of economics and conflict. "Most systems of war-economy are built round a skeleton of planned economy," he noted. This, he felt, was a problem, because "no completely planned economy or partially interventionist system has worked properly".

This begs the question as to whether, in fact, a planned economy, or a heavily interventionist economy, is, or becomes, a *de facto*, war-economy.

The Soviet economy in the USSR (1917-1990) clearly functioned as a perpetual war-economy, as did (and does) the economy of the People's Republic of China (PRC) since the takeover of mainland China in 1949 by the Communist Party of China (CPC). In these societies, literally all economic and social life was subordinated to and in support of the great goal of domination of their own and all other societies. This was their *modus pugnandi* and their entire *raison d'être*.

Indeed, by definition, the CPC *must* maintain a philosophy of "constant struggle" to justify continual, divisive paranoia within its own society to ensure the continued rôle and primacy of the Party.

Today, as I write this in 2020, the Soviet Union has long given way to a substantially more market-based economy in the Russian Federation. Clearly, the proportion of defense or war orientation of the Russian economy is dramatically less than that of the old Union of Soviet Socialist Republics, which arguably devoted some 80 percent of its economy to defense. As a result, the more that Russia moved away from a war-economy, the more that it prospered ... and the more it has actually become capable of sustaining war.

At the same time, the economies of the major Western powers were — particularly with the new economic interventionism of the 2020 crisis — becoming more "planned" and interventionist. Does this propel them toward *becoming* "war-economies"?

It could be argued that the European Union (albeit not a sovereign entity in the Westphalian sense) has functioned so poorly in the context of military preparedness that it could *not* be construed as becoming a war-economy society. However, as we discuss "total war in the 21st Century", it is clear that today's total war is not your grandfather's total war.

And so perhaps the EU *had* evolved into a perpetual war-economy, not to fund military actions specifically, but to use *weaponized political-economic strategies* to subdue its own member states to suppress their sovereignty, but also to fight, for example, the US and the ungrateful Britons who had defied it.

So, as a result, the interventionism of the European Union had, in fact, transformed the EU economy into an inefficient kind of war-economy, believing it could use this weapon to prosecute a "third way" of war in order to dominate Europe and to project power. Despite the kind of short-term coercion by the dominant EU power, Germany, of Greece, Cyprus, and Italy, and the use of economic levers to attempt to prevent Britain's departure from the EU (Brexit; eventually successful despite the EU in 2020), this use of economics as "soft power" was ultimately likely to prove unsuccessful.

We were, by 2020 then, in a war environment in which formal, direct military coercion had become dramatically less visible than in the 20th Century. And yet, even with less direct military presence, it was war nonetheless, because we saw forms of behavior which would either save or destroy entire societies.

The limitation of Greece's options to remediate its sovereign debt crisis and failed economy, starting in 2009 following the worldwide recession in 2007-08, was solely due to the fact that the Government and nation of Greece had abandoned the nation's ability to sustain its own currency. The abandonment of the Greek currency, the *drachma*, in favor of the *euro* in 2001 meant that Greek sovereignty had essentially been usurped by, nominally, the European Central Bank (ECB), or more realistically by the German Government as the power behind the ECB.

The ECB effectively forced Greece into line with German strategic requirements in a way which, during World War II, would have taken the uniformed forces of tens of divisions of German, Italian, and Bulgarian troops. The outcome after 2009 was not satisfactory for Greece or Germany, but, then, neither was the military occupation of the country in World War II.

But had Greece maintained control of its money supply — in other words, had it regarded its own sovereignty as something of value — then, despite its economic mismanagement, it could have mitigated the savage assault on the welfare of its population in the 2009-18 timeframe far more satisfactorily than it did. Germany had, in essence, in the decades following 1990, turned much of Europe into the start of a planned economy: a patchwork of unconscious satrapies. In this it had power over many states which a century earlier would have required military action.

Is economic domination more humane than military occupation or military action? Perhaps, but in the case of Greece, for example, there was still loss of life and deprivation caused by economic weakness and subordination. It was, whether called that or not at the time, "war by other means", to invoke the Clausewitzean image. And Greece did not even know it was in a war at that time.

That is one aspect of the transforming nature of 21st Century conflict; it is most commonly indirect, using non-military means, and it is conducted to dominate "friends" and foes alike. But even when war bursts into the stark imagery of traditional conflict, it is often now through the guise of proxy forces, which — apart from the fact that many such proxies have an actual war to fight on their own account — have taken on the rôle of the mercenary forces of the Middle Ages. And news of their actions scarcely raises political concerns in the electorates of their sponsoring societies, because the comfort of those sponsoring peoples is undisturbed.

A significant part of total war in the 21st Century is the reality that most of it is not conducted as "something apart"; as set-piece dramas on foreign shores. Much of it occurs within our own societies, or at least within our umbrella societies, the nation-states. And within that concept we must consider that *most of today's nation-states would have been considered empires a century or two before.*

[The collections of states which today comprise the United States, Canada, Australia, Russia, Germany, Italy, Ethiopia, India, Nigeria, and so on, have all evolved from separate, sometimes confederal or satrap, entities into unitary or semi-unitary states. The reality is that it is merely the word "empire" which has become unpopular and tainted; it has become a "loaded" word.]

Most conflict centers around the issue of identity. Anything alien to us is threatening, especially at times of crisis or polarization. Sometimes, conflict is deliberately engendered, not only inter-state warfare, but domestically, to gain or consolidate power.

Once again, the great strategist, Stefan Possony, showed how he remained the deep observer of human social trends.

* * *

POSSONY, IN 1976, IDENTIFIED A phenomenon of the deliberate destruction of entire cultures, tribes, civilizations, and social groupings; a conscious program which was particularly attached to the urban globalist movement of Soviet communists.[33]

It was a process mirrored, but distorted, by the maoists of the People's Republic of China. But it is also a phenomenon promoted in the 21st Century by the "universalism" of the post-Cold War, urban-dominated phenomenon of globalism.

Possony called it ethnomorphosis, but preferred the German term, *umvolkung*: the root *volk* (people); the prefix *um* denoting change; and the ending *ung* refers to action. Ethnomorphosis or *umvolkung* would occur naturally as tribes and groups merged, and lost their original identity, but "In real life, *umvolkung* does not happen without bloodshed and the violation of most human rights". He noted that "deliberate *umvolkung* is a major crime or set of crimes against humanity which have remained hidden only because the process may be spaced out over several generations".

Possony's study highlighted the lasting impact of the loss of identity, cultures, religions, and bloodlines as a result of conquests and migratory usurpation of territories. Most of this *umvolkung* was the scarcely-considered outcome of predatory conquest. But what he highlighted was the fact that the Communist Party of the Soviet Union (CPSU) and the Communist Party of China (CPC) attempted to eliminate troublesome ethnicities and bring them into a morphed new "nationality", such as "Soviet man". Both the Soviets and the

---

33 Possony, Stefan T.: "Ethnomorphosis: Invisible Catastrophic Crime", in *Plural Societies*, Autumn 1976, Vol. 7, No. 3. Published by the Foundation for the Study of Plural Societies.

CPC spent inordinate attention and funding on developing and applying the "response conditioning" works of Russian scientist Ivan Pavlov[34].

But it was more than merely the brainwashing or conditioning of subordinate societies. Deliberate programs of economic and political dispensation were — and are — used to divide (or "split") or eliminate nationalities, even while appearing to venerate cultures within an homogenized society.

The phenomenon of deliberate — even unconsciously-applied — ethnomorphosis is an overwhelming feature of 21st Century urbanist thinking. The projected belief that all humanity is, or should be, the same in its thought processes and values (and those values and processes are those dictated by urban materialism) has taken on the power of an ideology which implies that all resistance to it must be crushed.

Nothing explained early 21st Century "global civil war" — a subset of global total war — more clearly than this innate commitment to *umvolkung* by urban societies which feel threatened by the resistance and rebellion of traditional identities. The revival of various Celtic or Norse dialects over the past century has been typical of the resistance of remnant identities to the domination of their conquerors.

Few movements since the collapse of the Soviet Un-

34 Ivan Pavlov (1849-1936). Russian physiologist known for his work in achieving conditioned responses in subjects. His research results were, unwitting to him, used by the Communist Party of the USSR (CPSU) and the Communist Party of China (CPC) to attempt the conversion of target subjects through mind control, either individually or *en masse*, to create "new Soviet man" and a society which would be completely obedient to the ruling party. See, among other works: Babkin, B. P., Dr: *Pavlov: A Biography.* Chicago, 1949: University of Chicago Press.

ion in 1990 have exemplified deliberate *umvolkung* like the European Union movement. And that movement, too, has been experiencing significant pushback, not just with the Brexit momentum to remove the United Kingdom from the EU, but also in Scotland's attempt to preserve its Gaelic/Celtic identity by attempting, ironically, to utilize the EU as a means to extract itself from the UK.

Deliberate *umvolkung* was used in Ethiopia, too, following the coup and regicide against the 3,000-year-old Solomonic supra-identity of the empire in 1974. The two successive communist movements which seized the country attempted to use regional ethnicities as a means to "divide and conquer" Ethiopians, in a clear — and almost certainly conscious — process advocated by the Soviets in Moscow. That process collapsed in 2018 with the appointment of a new Ethiopian leader, Dr Abiy Ahmed Ali, who not only attempted to restore the over-arching Ethiopian identity, but did so in a way which aimed to preserve and honor the component historical ethnicities, languages, and beliefs.

The Soviet and People's Republic of China governments successfully reduced the number of "nationalities" in their empires since their conquests of the Russian and Chinese empires in 1917 and 1949 respectively. Many ancient languages and cultures were gradually manipulated out of existence.

A similar process was underway in 2019-20 by the Government of India, which deployed about a million troops to literally invade the constitutionally autonomous Indian state of Jammu & Kashmir. One object was to eradicate the separate Kashmiri identity so that it could never again thwart Indian geopolitical control over the strategically vital terrain of the Vale of Kashmir. Kashmir's constitutional autonomy had been negotiated as part of the state's accession to India, not merely to preserve the rights to its mainly Muslim and Buddhist religious practices, but to preserve its distinct Kashmiri identity.

It was this which had stopped the Indian Union Government from controlling the headwaters of the Indus River — which rise from the Vale — which forms the spinal chord of Pakistan. And it thwarted access *through* Kashmir, the Western part of which was occupied by Pakistan, to Central Asia. It was the Pakistan-occupied portion which also gave the People's Republic of China an overland route to Pakistan, and through it to the Indian Ocean.

So Kashmir's ancient identity and culture were to be sacrificed in New Delhi's campaign, just as the identity of the ancient sovereign state of Deccan Hyderabad, in central India, was sacrificed with the Indian invasion of 1948. In 1948, with so much confusion attending the creation of independent India and Pakistan, the loss of Deccan Hyderabad went unchallenged by the world. In 2019-20, the invasion of Jammu & Kashmir also went largely unnoticed, this time because the Indian Government of Prime Minister Narendra Modi ensured that all foreigners and media were absent from the state when the troops entered.

The success of this operation owed as much to information dominance warfare as to military action.

A similar process is underway by default with modern urbanism which links the great super-city-states of the 21st Century, driven by a deliberate process to eliminate history and cultural logic and replace it with short-term materialism. This process, emphasized by a flat hierarchical approach, has become xenophobic, and justified by the legitimizing appeal of "progress".

Little wonder that the concept has been experiencing push-back from societies which fear for their continued existence and validity. We see it among the peoples of Persia (Iran), Egypt, Ethiopia, Europe, and the recent societies of, for example, the United States (and within its constituent North American tribal and "first nations"; similarly with Australia's "first peoples").

We have insufficient documentary evidence to know whether this push-back is yet extending to the many nationalities within China (although we see the resistance of the Uighur Turkic people of the Xinjiang region, and the Tibetans). But we can assume that it is affecting numerous peoples of China, as it was in the Russian *Pamyat* (memory) movement which helped in the 1980s to bring about the collapse of the USSR.

The "re-discovery" of Possony's study brings a startling clarity to the current "global civil war". And it reminds us that, *to a society under threat, all war is "total".* It is for that reason that societies which feel that their existence is existentially threatened will resort not only to terrorism to project their cause onto a larger stage, but particularly to "martyr terrorism" or martyrdom on a visible stage, to make a dying identity blaze into the future.[35]

Understanding the evolution of total war: We need to understand how the phenomenon of "total war" evolved, because it certainly emerged before recorded history, even if we failed until the 20th Century to have a label for it.

But some aspects of it, such as the demand of confident assailants for the "unconditional surrender" of their opponents, retained very specific meaning until the mid-20th Century. Arguably, when the Allies began demanding the "unconditional surrender" of the Axis powers, particularly Germany and Japan, in World War II, the meaning of the phrase was distorted and rendered almost meaningless — except as a symbol — in the halls of power of Washington and Whitehall. It was not so misunderstood in Berlin and Tokyo where "unconditional surrender" meant the total subjugation of the conquered. They were to become slaves if they were allowed to live, and all of their properties and rights forfeit.

That was not exactly what Winston Churchill and Franklin D. Roosevelt had in mind for the Germans and the Japanese. But the phrase expressed a sense of resolute confidence to Churchill's and Roosevelt's own *domestic* populations. The unfortunate ramification,

35 Hoffer, Eric: *The True Believer: Thoughts on the Nature of Mass Movements.* New York, 1951: Perennial Library, Harper & Row.

however, was that the Germans and Japanese also heard the demand and interpreted it through a lens which would have been understood by Genghis Khan or Tamerlaine.

Already, then, in the mid-20th Century, there were significant nuances as to the meaning of "total war". Moreover, in the Allied camp, the engagement of all of the nations' resources in the conduct of formal war was meant to be temporary; in the Axis powers and the USSR it was meant to be permanent.

To a degree, after World War II, the Western Allied states surrendered most of the control over their economies back to the market. However, sociological changes, such as urbanization and the introduction of women into the workplace required to create the appropriate war-economy, meant that the transformation of Western economies had already been irreversibly begun.

So how did "total war" evolve?

It is possible that tribal struggles for survival in pre-historic times necessitated the eradication of everything which threatened a group's access to food and water, and the land which sustained that bounty. This was, of necessity, a life of brute resistance to all people and things which took away the security of food supply. At best, conquest required, where possible, the permanent elimination of rivals and, at its most lenient, the seizure of women to increase the breeding stock and slaves to perform productive work. It was total war, and the reality was that defeat and unconditional surrender were usually synonymous.

The allocation of specific rôles of armed security and warfare to dedicated members of a society was a natural evolution of whole-of-society offensive and defensive operations. Such dedicated capabilities were not only for the protection of a society and the further-ance of its objectives, but served as the protection and perpetuation of a leadership. But at that point, warfare often took a less-than "whole-of-society" aspect.

The evolution of standing armies became a critical element in creating the default condition of a perma-nent war-economy, and standing armed forces be-came, then, very much the focus of national prestige.

It was a logical step, as World War I — the Great War — erupted to move from standing armies to mass con-scription, engaging a broad swathe of society, and then to the creation of national- and international-level supply chains to support formal military operations. This not only included the production and supply of defense equipment by what came to be called the "mil-itary-industrial complex"[36] — a standing defense in-dustrial capability — but also the production, supply, and transportation by the non-defense sector of raw materials, food, and non-weapons goods for the con-duct of war.

US Pres. Dwight D. Eisenhower, without specifically seeing the rise of "the military industrial complex" as part of the evolution of the total war pattern into the

---

36 By US Pres. Dwight D. Eisenhower, in his farewell speech before leaving the Presi-dency on January 17, 1961.

Cold War, *did* see that the evolution of a war-economy could lead to the creation of a planned economy. And a planned economy was exactly what he saw in the USSR. So his warning about the military-industrial complex on January 17, 1961, noted: "We must never let the weight of this combination endanger our liberties or democratic processes."

By 2020, it was difficult to see that his warning had been heeded, or, more importantly whether it *could* have been heeded. The world, because of the two World Wars and the Cold War of the 20th Century was moving closer to the framework of constant total war, because governments' interventions in economies — and the social consequences they provoked — had become part of the global, amorphous process. It began to become difficult to determine where "the government" began and ended; it had become ubiquitous in daily life in advanced economies.

To fight the ideology which it so vehemently opposed, the US and the Allies were forced to take on many of the characteristics of their foes.

Those changes remained with the West well into the 21st Century.

IV

Warfare as a Natural State

W AR IS NOW THE NATURAL STATE of us all. Perhaps it always was. Certainly life has always been a competition for the means of survival and dominance.

War is not aberrant; nor is its conduct any longer confined to governmental bodies. It is a river which flows perpetually, sometimes openly to our door with vengeful fury. Sometimes silently leeching through subterranean aquifers.

It is — has again become — omnipresent and inexorable. The horizon between underworld and overworld has become blurred. And it has disguised the reality that 21st Century total war had become the cure for the fatal disease of "normal war", with its high mortality rate. Amorphous total war, which has subsumed "normal conflict", had fewer direct fatalities but a more pervasive, and often more indirectly fatal consequence.

The cure for war, then, was a different war. A new war.

War masters us unless we master it. War is life: it is the imposition of our will upon our surroundings, or our subjugation to the will of others or of nature.

But these rivers of war have come into a new confluence in the 21st Century. War has become something which cannot be assigned to specialized detachments of warriors.

We progressively, after World War II, sought a society of horizontal — or flat — communication and consensus as a technologically-powered form of democracy. Well, this is what it has brought us: a world *without* hierarchy, or a world opposed to hierarchy, and with only fettered leadership.

At best, fettered leadership is just management, but *management with power.* But that does not create a forward-oriented structure; most management hierarchy is about supervision of the *status quo,* which is, in reality, just a snapshot of the past.

At some point, with a "horizontal hierarchy"[37] society, there is nothing and no-one to impose order except political correctness (the self-imposed inclusiveness/exclusivity of a society). And neither is there consensus as to what order *should* be.

Without structure there is chaos. In chaos there is war. A *world* in chaos is a world in total war, even down to a microbial level.

So total war is just that. Total. It engages, willingly or

---

37 "Horizontal hierarchy" is an oxymoron of a term; hierarchies are by definition vertical. "Horizontal hierarchy" explicitly opposes leadership, but tolerates "social management", and therefore implicitly vitiates the concept of specific direction for a society.

otherwise, every element of a society down to an individual, unitary level to organize for its own protection and furtherance against the interests of all other individuals or societies. That does not preclude — in fact it demands — alliances and mutual interests with other individuals and societies, but not to the point of complete sacrifice to the interests of another society.[38]

Given that it is total, total war is not therefore focused around any single discipline or aspect of society. It is difficult to see, therefore, where total war begins or ends.

Given that it is total, total war demands an integrated and holistic approach to its defense, and to the creation of goals, strategies, and doctrine.

Ultimately, total war demands and conjures up something — including leadership — which can create order out of the chaos. Without specific goals, total war becomes interminable. Sun-tzu said: "There is no instance of a country having benefited from prolonged warfare." But sometimes, as with the Thirty Years War ending with the Peace of Westphalia in 1648, or the Cold War's end in 1990 providing temporary relief from communism, there are occasional benefits for society as a whole, even if the combatant governments suffer from protracted war.

Total war requires, then, an understanding of the nature and totality of the society and its relationship to its

---

38 As I say in *The Art of Victory* (2006) in the chapter on alliances (Chapter 19: "Loyalty and Survival"), only junior members of alliances are loyal (above all to the senior member), but alliance leaders rarely show consistent loyalty to junior alliance partners.

space: its geography. The definition of society is an amalgam of both the objective and tangible with the subjective and intangible components — the secular and the sacred symbiosis — of an historically-bonded group of individuals. But the achievement of victory for a society is dominated by its imposition of collective will upon any others who would stand in the way of, or could be dragooned to assist in, its victory. And such a victory — being subject to a constantly shifting global context — is ephemeral and must be constantly shifting in its own goals.

The grand strategist and the leadership, of necessity, commit themselves to intellectually bedouin lives. They are in perpetual motion across the undulating sands of time and the mind.

The articulated concept of total war has been evolving since the 19th Century, although it has been practiced sporadically throughout all history, with the examples of Genghis Khan and Timur — Tamerlaine — and Napoleon I at the forefront of modern thinking. We could see Gen. Ludendorff grasping to comprehend the scope of total war during the Great War, but he scarcely scratched the surface. Dr Stefan Possony took it further into perspective in 1938 with *To-morrow's War.*[39]

As Possony said in the introductory note to his 1938 study (originally published in Vienna, in German): "The expression 'total war' was first coined by General Ludendorff to express his view that in the next war it

---

39 Possony, Stefan T.: *To-morrow's War;* op cit.

will not be a question of armies but of nation to nation, since the ramifications of warfare have grown so much that the entire population will have to be mobilized in one way or another."

He went on: "This ... has given birth to a new science, that of organizing the economy for war, the science of war-economy. In reading this [Possony's] book, which is the first comprehensive work on the subject, the reader must distinguish between war-economy, *which is the organization during peace-time* [italics added], and the economy of war, which is the actual state of a country's economy during the war itself."

If the condition of war evolved from the Great War concepts articulated by Ludendorff to the extensive national planning for military capabilities, as envisaged by Possony in his prescient view leading to World War II, then Possony's writings continued to evolve through the 20th Century. Today, it is impossible to say exactly where any element of society is either engaged in, or exempt from, the conflict for security and survival, or, indeed, where war or peace begin or end.

Carl von Clausewitz said that war was the continuation of politics by other means.[40] Today, politics *is* predominantly war, and war is predominately politics.

So, to reiterate, the evolution of organized warfare has seen the demise of the principle that warfare is solely the province of structured military units.

---

40 von Clausewitz, Gen. Carl: "War is not an independent phenomenon, but the continuation of politics by different means." in *Vom Kriege* (*On War*), in 1832.

"War" — if we think of the phenomenon as an episodic or periodic activity rather than as a sustained event — is almost always pre-determined as to its outcome by a complex array of other factors, whether we are fully conscious of these factors or not. And its principal actors are not necessarily or primarily the girded, resplendent warriors who must strut their piece upon the stage only when the strategists have failed. Indeed war, while it may show highly-visible peaks, is not, in truth, episodic, but an aspect of the continuum.

Possony took the concept of "total war" into the realm of national economic planning, by considering — as he did in some detail — the ongoing costs in raw materials (iron, steel, energy, etc., and their products in weapons, ships, vehicles, and aircraft). From this, and the manpower requirements to conduct conventional warfare and such issues as geographic differences, he could adduce requirements for strategic preparations and strategic targeting.

By 1949, almost a decade after *To-morrow's War*, and after World War II had proven the wisdom of his theories, Possony was able to address the impact and potential of transformed battlefields which resulted in the creation of long-range air power, nuclear weapons, and ballistic missiles.[41] But even at that stage, war was primarily considered a formal event, conducted between nation-states.

Possony certainly grasped the evolution of the con-

---

41 Possony, Stefan T.: *Strategic Air Power: The Pattern of Dynamic Security.* Washington, DC, 1949: Infantry Press.

cept when he created the notion of space-based, anti-ballistic missile capability to defeat the threat of nuclear war. His creation of the Strategic Defense Initiative (SDI) concept in the early 1970s (and introduced by US Pres. Ronald Reagan in 1983) showed his awareness that conflict could not be constrained to old models. Nor even to the earth itself.

To counteract SDI, the Soviets turned to information dominance techniques as their primary defense. It worked. And SDI became known by its Soviet propaganda epithet, meant to belittle it as a "Hollywood" strategy: "Star Wars".

But the end of the Cold War in 1990-91 had obscured the Soviet constraining of SDI, and saw the beginning of a gradual, but near-total restructuring of the global strategic architecture. This did not engage merely an end to the rigid framework of nation-states and their relative strategic positioning — as a pre-requisite for an eventual realignment — but an even more profound transformation of the *social* hierarchical structure of the global human population.

This transformation of demographics and attitudes I attempted to outline in two earlier studies[42].

Essentially, the change was the result of a 21st Century near-global end to population growth (which had begun at the end of World War II) and the start of rapid population decline; the acceleration of mass urbanization (which had also begun its rapid rise with

---

42 Copley, Gregory R.: *UnCivilization,* op cit.; and *Sovereignty in the 21st Century,* op cit.

World War II); and a new and transformative wave of mass transnational migration.

Now, the concept we must consider is not merely "total war", but "constant total war", because the 21st Century has become a century of constant change *across all spheres of humanity.*

That implies constantly changing threat, and constantly emerging opportunities.

Constant total war should not — particularly in the 21st Century — imply constant and overwhelming military confrontation, or, more specifically, military contact. Indeed, military confrontation is often — but not always — the epitome of failure of a society, as Sun-tzu avers[43]. And yet the *symbolism of credible military capability* remains at the core of the prestige needed to prevail in 21st Century total war.

We will address the different values of *latent energy* and *expended energy* in military and strategic terms. [See Chapter VII: "Conducting Total War".]

* * *

So where do "private sector" organizations fit into this framework?

Modern interpretations of the rôle of organized bodies in civilian societies — and particularly corporations — require that, as with individuals, they identify with their society of origin.

They must declare their loyalty, even if not in a manner which unduly fetters their performance, so that

---

43 To fight and conquer in all our battles is not supreme excellence; supreme excellence consists in breaking the enemy's resistance without fighting.

loyalty may be reciprocated to them by their own society, by either protection, formal trade support, tax benefits, and so on. This will become increasingly a feature of 21st Century social structuring, given that the uncertainties of the century can only be addressed through the careful return of societies to national identity (even if new nation-states are created when old ones fail). This emerges as a response to the uncertainties of a world which had drifted, because of wealth, into indefinite and therefore vitiated borders and identities.

It is important to make that point, because the brief era of ideological "globalism" (not the mechanics of international trade itself), of, say, 1945-2010 meant that individuals and corporations could take temporary leave of their traditional requirement to identify strongly with their nation-state of origin.[44]

There are always times and places in history for borders to be more porous, and when identities retreat from the forefront of our thinking. Those are times of wealth and security, such as we saw for some seven decades or more after World War II. That was a time

---

44 The Communist Party of China's "Belt and Road Initiative" (BRI) was created not so much as a practical economic framework (although it was that, too, with the PRC at the hub of economic and political activity) but as an *ideological* weapon to overturn the power of sovereignty of states which needed to be bent to Beijing. It was a definitive expression of globalism. It was maoist marxism put into transactional, materialistic terms to bind adherents to Beijing. The BRI has been called a form of "predatory capitalism", but, in fact, it is not based on market capitalism in any way, or on capitalist cost-benefit thinking. It is based on political cost-benefit thinking, using cash as a replacement for intellectual or philosophical appeal. The BRI, in essence, is *financial maoism*. The ideology of the European Union "visionaries" is similar; it is not based on economic or market reality. *Globalization*, on the other hand, is the infrastructure and process of the actual mechanisms of trade.

when we were not required to think of who we were. Or how we became who we were. We could afford to concern ourselves less with the future, and the future of our children. Wealth enabled us to think only of today and to gratify all our demands (but not necessarily our needs).

So we lost ourselves not in a shining city on a hill, but in a nursery of self-indulgent thoughtlessness.

But that was yesterday. Today, our wealth began to crumble and dissipate because our systems peaked along with human numbers, and our economics transformed. We are looking toward a new economic framework, which is *not* the model of constantly growing market size and constantly increasing demand.

Rather, it is the reverse.

And this reversal is not only the break of the trend of growth which had moved steadily along an upward path since, possibly, the 13th Century. *This* reversal also began the challenge to the domination of the human population by urban agglomerations.

We have, however, no new economic methodologies or concepts to cope with a world in decline and volatility of human numbers. And without that new economic model, we will fail to fund our lives of plenty. We will still, of course, fight for our survival with whatever tools we have at hand. But these tools may be less than we imagined we would have.

Already the scent of danger is everywhere. Already, and unconsciously, human society moves to re-assert its identities, even identities supposed or somehow dreamt from a past which may be imperfectly recalled.

The human race — entirely, perhaps for the first time, because this is a time when we have all become connected consciously through technology — has begun its retreat into the *laagers* of identity. And no-one is immune from the fear, and therefore the responsibility, to fight for survival.

It is a time of great volatility, and volatility brings opportunity. New societies will emerge; prosperity will eventually be reasserted upon the land, and we will once again greet strangers without fear.

But not yet.

This is the start of the constant total war. Those who will impose the stamp of their will upon their world are those who see the challenge holistically and consciously engage every fiber of society in the prosecution of its interests.

It is probable that those societies which draw the best from their members are those which will give most freedom to thought, speech, and action, for they will throw forth leaders, inspiration, and the intellectual confidence to exude prestige enough to cast their will upon the earth.

But it is equally possible that societies coerced, deceived, or used without their conscious knowledge or informed consent may be effectively utilized in a global war. This is at the heart of population warfare. We will discuss that in more detail in Chapter XIV: Global Movement in a World at War: Population warfare meets the new age.

V

The Rôle of Grand Strategy in Total War

H AVING A LEADERSHIP WITH grand strategic vision is the most vital asset a nation can possess in time of war. This is particularly true because war is never entirely (or even mostly) kinetic; never entirely, or even mostly, about set-piece military operations.

And it is particularly the case that all wars actually begin long before the shooting starts.

The "grand strategist", therefore sees *when* wars are brewing, likely, possible, or even desirable; ideally even before the rest of the world is aware of the reality.

Grand strategy knows that achieving victory — which is durable — is more important than winning wars; and winning wars is more important than winning battles. As Sun-tzu avers in *The Art of War*: "To fight and conquer in all your battles is not supreme excellence; supreme excellence consists in breaking the enemy's resistance without fighting."

What has been forgotten is that Sun-tzu's *Art of War* is not about tactics or military engagement, except in peripheral ways. It is about being above, before, and beyond warfare. Reading Sun-tzu as a grand strategist, then, is the key to deriving the most benefit from him.

Tactics is about the immediate in time and space. Single-theme strategy takes a broader view of the terrain and a slightly longer view of time and space. But grand strategy embraces the total warp and weft of terrain and time from all history to the farthest imaginings of the future.

Did People's Republic of China Pres. Xi Jinping, who clearly planned on a global and long-term scale, risk defeat, then, when he began his protracted war in about 2012 against the US? Or when he declared it — as his "new Thirty Years War" — to his followers (if not directly to the target of his war) in September 2018? Or could he perceive no other viable options? Sun-tzu told us: "In war, let your great object be victory, not lengthy campaigns."

Deng Xiaoping, when he assumed authority in the PRC after Mao Zedong, made it clear in about 1990 — as the USSR was collapsing — that Beijing's strategy should be to avoid war; to bide its time, and be patient, hiding its strengths and highlighting weakness in order to avoid arousing enemies. Deng understood Sun-tzu; he was a grand strategist, while Xi — despite following the practical, overarching grand strategic doctrine of *Unrestricted Warfare* — emerged as an operational strategist.

What, then, *is* "grand strategy"? The phrase had become essentially meaningless in a world in which urban societies believed that everything was transaction-ally based, materialistic: tactical, and apparently with-out the need for hierarchy; rudderless.[45]

History, however, tells us that no society can protect itself without a central hierarchy when instability or threats arise. Neither, without the hierarchy which specifies a leadership at its pinnacle, can it project power in its own interests.

Prosperity allowed the creation in the late 20th Cen-tury (and increasingly in the 21st) of the concept of a "horizontal hierarchy", or, more accurately, a "flat [or-ganizational] structure". The word hierarchy is, unsur-prisingly, derived from the Greek *hierarkhia*: "rule of a high priest". It is implicitly vertical and top down.

How quickly and easily the flat society reverted in some ways to the hierarchical structure when the 2020 fear pandemic struck. The question was, then, how much longer what remained of the flat structure — lit-erally the "flat earth" utopianism — would persist be-yond 2020.

Strategic success emerges from the appropriate use of flat structures to enable creative peer-to-peer (or free form) competition for the brewing of ideas, *and then* for those ideas to be applied with the discipline of vertical hierarchy to ensure efficient operational exe-cution and decisionmaking.

The challenge lies in finding the appropriate balance in the mix of flat, free-form creativity — freedom —

---

45 A comprehensive view of grand strategy is presented in *The Art of Victory*. op cit. A further definition can be found in the Glossary at the end of this book.

on the one hand, and, on the other, respected hierarchy for operational performance in organizations and societies. But what is critical to accept is that grand strategy requires a leader (the pinnacle of a hierarchy) to envisage and implement.

Grand strategy, in essence, is a vision; an all-encompassing view of the total world: past, present, and future. And using that vision to set goals and command their fulfillment. Grand strategy, then, requires subsidiary "implementing strategies" coordinated by a leader who must give appropriate weight to the disciplines required to be orchestrated in harmony. French *Général d'Armée* André Beaufre (1902-1975) created the concept of "total strategy" to address what would later be called "hybrid warfare". But he was a great proponent of psychological strategy, along with his contemporary and friend, Stefan Possony.

Beaufre once noted: "The game of strategy can, like music, be played in two keys. The major key is direct strategy, in which force is the essential factor. The minor key is indirect strategy, in which force recedes into the background and its place is taken by psychology and planning."

In the 21st Century, however, amorphous warfare, dominated by psychological strategy (imperfectly translated as information dominance strategy) is the essential factor, with the use of force as part of direct strategy as the secondary doctrine. Unless it fails, which then calls forth the necessity for direct application of force.

It goes without saying that goals cannot be achieved if they are never set. "If you don't know where you're going, every road will lead to disaster."[46]

Can overarching, grand strategic goals be set and achieved by a flat-structured society? It has never seemed so in history. Goal creation and implementation, then, are embodied in the symbolism and, ideally, the wisdom and decisiveness — and the secrecy — of leadership. That is a characteristic of grand strategy.

Electronic communications meant, as we have discussed, that the early 21st Century became a time of largely flat social structures in Western societies.

In other words, the early 21st Century saw grand strategy struggling for air. The very concept (as nebulous as it has always been) of "grand strategy", associated as it was with "nationalism", was everywhere vilified. But "Where there is no vision, the people perish: but he that keepeth the law, happy is he."[47]

Overwhelmed (vertical) hierarchies were unable to exert sufficient leadership by the early 21st Century. This imbalance — as it has occurred cyclically in most mature, wealthy societies through history — creates vulnerabilities which threaten national stability and security. That *is* the cyclical nature of history.

It is reflected in the polarization of societies into urban globalists, who have prospered under no-threat wealth conditions (and who, essentially, feel that the nation-state is no longer important), and regional na-

---

46 Copley: *Art of Victory.* op cit.
47 Proverbs 29:18 of *The Bible*, King James Version.

tionalists, who feel that they have not prospered under those conditions which gave wealth to the urban globalists.

In the 21st Century, flat social structures were not evenly balanced or partnered with hierarchies, and therefore the flat structures did *not* represent freedom. They reflected brittle, self-organized *conformity* which lacked leadership and goals. Threats and insecurity, however, cause spontaneous flight to the safety of hierarchies.

The societal segment which feels most threatened reacts first and seeks to ameliorate the threat by taking control of its context and restoring or strengthening vertical hierarchy and reinforcing traditional identity (which provides the security of known practices and common cause). This activity is disruptive of the wealth and privilege of the sector which has not yet felt threatened, creating alarms which in turn causes it to react by punishing or attempting to contain the first group.

When this occurs within a nation-state, the disharmony cannot usually be resolved until and unless both groups equally feel sufficiently threatened by a common external challenge, or by internal conflict (civil war). What is significant is that civil war rarely leads to a resolution of the internal schism, but merely allows the triumph of the dominant sector in suppressing into dormancy the grievances and fears of the weaker.

We saw this exemplified by the civil wars which marked the break-up of the former Federal Socialist

Republic of Yugoslavia (FSRY) in the 1990s and in the US Civil War (1861-65).

Peacekeeping without conflict resolution is rarely durable, and is always economically and socially damaging. There is a definitive process or life-cycle for societies to overcome internal schisms at the civil war level[48], after which they have the flexibility to formulate truly national (in the nation-state sense) grand strategies.

The conception and execution of durable grand strategy usually requires national consensus. This is not in the sense that the entire society directly participates in formulating national goals, but in creating the general trust of the society in the leadership which creates definitive grand strategic goals and methods.

That "general trust" can be either earned or coerced. It cannot occur easily in Western "democracies" until domestic schisms are resolved. Schisms — short of civil war or separatism — can allow *some* normal functioning of the overarching state apparatus to enable the maintenance and creation of a grand strategic capability. We saw this in the US during the Donald Trump Administration (2017-), in the UK during the Boris Johnson Government (2019-), and in Australia with the Government of Scott Morrison (2019-). But internal schisms hamper the creation and execution of a substantive national grand strategy, let alone give scope for any public discourse on national objectives. A natural return to vertical hierarchy has not yet oc-

---

48 We know that there is a fairly predictable life-cycle for revolutions, which often display the characteristics of civil war. See *The Anatomy of Revolution*, by Crane Brinton. Published by Vintage, London, 1938.

curred in such circumstances.

It requires a catalyst.

Trust does not necessarily equate to affection. It implies that the hierarchy has earned a reputation for a certain level of reliability of performance which can amount to prestige. This becomes, within geopolitical nation-states, part of Rousseau's "social contract".[49]

More nationally-cohesive societies in the 2020s (such as the People's Republic of China, the Russian Federation, and the like), whether their cohesion is artificially coerced or not, can and do exercise authority through an imposed or natural vertical hierarchy.

Other societies began, or attempted, to return to cohesion by natural means (in this timeframe, we could include Egypt, Greece, Ethiopia, Iran[50], etc.) and were therefore more able to gradually restore normal, vertical hierarchies and the ability to formulate national visions.

49 Rousseau, Jean-Jacques (1712-1778): *The Social Contract or Principles of Political Right*; Paris, 1762.
50 Iran, by 2020, was still seen by its clerical leadership as a post-Persian, Shi'a state. As a state which used Shi'ism as its vehicle to project influence. But Iranian society was moving separately back toward a Persian — even Zoroastrian — historical identity. What had been clear in the early 21st Century was that the clerical leadership was embracing Persian historical geopolitics while attempting to sustain the legitimacy of its siezed control (in 1979) of power in the name of Shi'a Islam.

VI

Why Leadership Differs in the 21st Century

NATIONAL SOCIETIES *DEMAND* LEADERS — the pinnacle of hierarchies — only in times of crisis; times of "clear and present danger". Or at least times when danger is suspected. When fear seeps into the marrow.

At all other times they *prefer* managers, regardless of whether they actually need leaders.

Leaders cause unease. They disrupt. They galvanize and polarize.

It is what they are built to do. To show courage and nobility, which, by its very solitary example, causes either shame or inspiration in the populace. Shame and anger among those who are craven; inspiration among those seeking a destiny beyond themselves, beyond immediate self-interest.

Leaders deliver non-linear outcomes. This, by definition, breaks the *status quo*. Not just in physical transformation, but in the self-perception of entire peoples. On the battlefield, the courageous general who shares danger with his troops creates a bond of loyalty which

is forever unshakeable. For a nation-state, the enduring iconography of symbols, but also the stoic courage
and loyalty of a crowned head or a single leader who
transcends his time by the ability to share challenge
and yet demonstrate courage and inspiration: this is
what builds a great society.

Yet when danger has passed, crisis averted or overcome, the qualities of leadership are no longer comfortable. A manager is then sought; someone to ensure
that wealth is maintained and expanded. The Julius
Cæsars, the Winston Churchills — perhaps the Donald Trumps — having strode their hour or two upon
the stage are invited to retire from the scene.

So if we are in a condition of "constant total war" in
this century of unrelenting challenge, then it will not
always be a state of *visible* crisis, where the adrenalin of
fear creates the demand for leaders. There will be times
when the crisis will be smouldering deep in the
peat-bog of normal life, beneath the surface. So then
the alarums will not be sounded; tocsins will not be
called for a man on horseback to heed. It will be a *time*
for leaders, no doubt, but not a time when that leadership can perform best. The time for leadership to perform best would be when there is a visible, iconic, and
disruptive call to arms.

But the alarm may not be evident; the crisis disguised by the chaos and smugness of something which
masks itself as normalcy.

The challenge, then, will be for leadership to guide
from the shadows, and cloak itself in the grey of man-

agement.

What we are witnessing, as the complex framework of the 21st Century evolves, with its combination of high technologies and abstract economies, is the need for leadership which can manage a whole-of-nation response capable of delivering something like unity of action. The threats and opportunities are not always direct; not always obvious; and present themselves as a combination of compromised options.

We are then — each society — facing a hybrid threat/opportunity matrix which will call for a hybrid response. Not in the 2020 definition of "hybrid warfare", which is merely, often, about facing differing forms of kinetic threat, but a response to challenges which are domestic as well as foreign. Economic and sociological even more than conventional or even quasi-military.

Such threat and opportunity response will require — already *does* require — a carefully balanced symphony of divergent cultural and physical capabilities in leaders. At present, it is difficult to see any society in which conventional military structures work seamlessly with domestic security forces as well as economic and social agencies.

To show courage and leadership within the monastic framework of military structures can draw upon ancient and visceral examples. But what we saw during much of the 20th and 21st centuries was the evisceration even of this nobility of inspirational courage of leadership. Technology and management by generals remote from the dangers of their troops produced a diminution of brilliance, inspiration, and loyalty at the battlefield.[51]

Within the realm of national leadership, it is courage which is the most significant quality to see exhibited, second only to the ability to share that inspiration with the great spectrum of society.

So what national leaders or managers do we see who easily blend courage and empathy with operational capabilities across a spectrum of information dominance (ID), military projection (and capability *presentation*), economic maneuver, and socio-political galvanization?

Can the same leader, in order to guide society in times of overt crisis, transform into a "disguised leader" — a leader disguised as, or bringing to the forefront, the skills of a manager — in times of apparent calm? After all, the practice of politics invariably sees managers assume the mantle or *claim* of leadership, often failing to comprehend the real and separate isolation and vision required for true leadership.

---

51 Politician and soldier alike should reflect on the pocket volume of great wisdom written by Maj.-Gen. J. F. C. Fuller: *Generalship: Its Diseases and Their Cure.* Harrisburg, Pennsylvania, 1936: Military Service Publishing Co.

VII

Conducting Total War

The Offense and Defense

ENGAGEMENT IN THE TOTAL WARS of the 21st Century is not optional. The ramifications of war are thrust upon most of global society. "Opting out" implies choice which does not exist, just as Zulu King Cetshwayo kaMpande discovered when confronted by the British in 1879.

King Cetshwayo did not seek war, but it was thrust upon him. The Zulus were not defeated at the Battle of Isandlwana, but their fortunes were forever changed.

That is the crucial point: war is often thrust upon us.

Sun-tzu said that "in war, the victorious strategist seeks only battle after victory has been won, whereas he who is destined to defeat first fights and afterwards looks for victory". Therefore, having been drawn into *war* — as we have been in the 21st Century — be careful in choosing *battles*. And recall Sun-tzu's admonition: "In all fighting, the direct method may be used for joining battle, but indirect methods will be needed in order to secure victory."

The great total war of the early 21st Century had

reached an inflection point with the strategic impact on economies of the 2020 aspects of the global coronavirus health crisis.

As with the localized impact of the Anglo-Zulu war in the late 19th Century, things were forever changed for the global community — but particularly for the US and the People's Republic of China — by the way key players managed their strategic status with relation to how they handled their societies during the 2019-20 coronavirus crisis. [See specifically, Chapter XII: Fear.]

The outcome was that the way in which warfare would be conducted after the fear pandemic of 2020 would be changed substantially.

> ➤ Firstly, the model of new-form total war would continue to expand and be refined, and
> ➤ Secondly, it would be conducted in a climate of diminished and often fragile economic resources.

It had already become clear that the operational tempo of the amorphous wars of the 21st Century waxed and waned, and fluctuated between (often concurrent) direct and indirect warfare; between conventional, proxy, economic, informational, and psycho-political. Each form of warfare requires specialist skills, and yet, given the interwoven nature of warfare in this century, warfare also requires a comprehensive understanding of the overall tapestry.

It would obviously be unviable or inefficient (even counterproductive), in such a multi-dimensional conflict framework, to have military solutions applied to situations which have predominantly sociological components. Or the reverse. The recipe rarely calls for a single ingredient, but the skill of the chef is in knowing in what proportions to mix the elements, and when. Or to use only soft power when hard power is required; political when military components are required.

Our age of educational, skill, and geographically-determined specialization means that we favor the application of our own particular skill-sets whether they are appropriate or not. To a hammer, everything looks like a nail.

Already, the US military had learned from the Somalia fighting in the early 1990s against warlord Gen. Mohamed Farrah Aideed. As the Chinese strategists Qiao Liang and Wang Xiangsui noted: "The most modern military force does not have the ability to control public clamor, and cannot deal with an opponent who does things in an unconventional manner."[52]

Who, then, in this age of chaotic interaction, takes the lead organizing rôle in a society's or nation's offensive and defensive operations? And it is rarely the case that it is either offensive or defensive capabilities which are required, but a concurrent mix of both, viewed from constantly evolving and nuanced perspectives.

Stefan Possony made a convincing case that a national leader — a president or prime minister — must be the society's chief intelligence officer and strategist.[53] This is inescapable — and has been proven

52 *Unrestricted Warfare.* Op cit.
53 Possony, Stefan T.: *Waking Up The Giant: The Strategy for American Victory and World Freedom.* New Rochelle, New York, 1974: Arlingon House.

through history — and yet there is a persistence in the belief that those skills are somehow not acquired by education, but are, rather intrinsic, solely intuitive, and tangentially acquired.

What types of war should society, the government, and the armed forces anticipate? And what are the resources to be employed? We have grown accustomed to career military officials taking the view that they would tell us when we were at war, and define what war was. But that clarity has become vitiated.

The major operational theme of total war in the 21st Century will be how governments — the formal arm of states — can capture or re-capture command of the global battlefield and orchestrate "whole of society" offensive and defensive operations *without permanently distorting the nature of their societies.*

To be forced to assume the characteristics of an adversary, in order to defeat it — in other words, to become that which we oppose — nullifies or taints any victory which is attained. Thus, for some societies, a pre-requisite part of the process must be that the state — the government and the armed forces — actually comprehends the nature of their own state, even though they function as a separate part of it.

This should be a precondition of evolving the national grand strategy: knowing one's own society as well as knowing the context of international competition. However, the fundamental characteristic of total war in the 21st Century is that *everything is weaponized.* The 20th Century communist movements all operating from fundamental positions of weakness, recognized this because they often lacked parity in formal military and economic capabilities. But it is now the law of the jungle that everything is to be viewed as a weapon; every thought, deed, and asset.

The Russian Government of Pres. Vladimir Putin had begun by 2013 to formulate a plan for the transformed nature of conflict.

By late 2019, a Presidential decree — *Questions of the General Staff of the Russian Federation Armed Forces* — was about to be finalized, giving the Russian General Staff a central and supervising rôle in developing, integrating, and coordinating the national concepts and doctrine for the total security of the state, by having the Armed Forces act "in conjunction with public authorities".[54] Pres. Putin recognized the need for a national command authority and capability, and could see no better home for it than the General Staff.

Significantly, the plan to give this authority to the General Staff was resisted by many in the Russian bureaucracy as well as in the General Staff itself. According to *Izvestia*, "sometimes it was necessary to overcome the resistance of local officials, to fight against the unwillingness to obey the instructions of the General Staff. Now [November 2019] the vast majority of these issues have been resolved."

The decree gave the General Staff coordinating and command authority to integrate many aspects of op-

54 See: "At the center of defense: General Staff appointed senior among security forces", in *Izvestia*, November 26, 2019. The Presidential decree was due to be finalized and issued by "Summer 2020"; around mid-year 2020.

erations by not only the Armed Forces, but the Federal Security Service (FSB: *Federal'naya sluzhba bezopasnosti Rossiyskoy Federatsii*), the Federal Protective Service (FSO: *Federalnaya Sluzhba Okhrany*), *Rosguard* [The National Guard of the Russian Federation: *Rosgvardiya*], the Ministry of Emergencies[55], the defense industrial sector, and other "law enforcement agencies and authorities at all levels". Pres. Putin referred to this collection as "the Military Organization", a new term to embrace the cultures and institutions which had hitherto been stovepiped.

This reflected the fact that the General Staff had already come to the conclusion that non-military actions comprised 80 percent of contemporary conflict. The new authority would make the General Staff responsible for combating crime in the Armed Forces, executing punishments, agreeing on the parameters for the export of sensitive equipment, and issuing certificates of keys for verifying electronic signatures. Indeed, the decree also gave the General Staff "coordination of and interaction with" the federal Russian agency responsible for communications on issues relating to joint operation (and protection) of a unified telecommunications network. It would also control the protection of key state facilities.

Thus the General Staff was to become the "leading

---

55 It was appropriate to view the Ministry of Emergencies as part of "the Military Organization". Such ministries in former Soviet states have been a key to controlling domestic populations as well as in managing national-level disaster response. The impact of wars, including amorphous wars (and particularly the cyber wars which immobilize cities), are analogous to great disasters caused by earthquakes, *tsunamis*, volcanoes, and hurricanes. Wars and natural disasters wreak equal havoc on the viability of nations.

body for the development of a national security strategy". All of this was decided at a meeting of the Russian Security Council on November 22, 2019. Theoretically, or legally, none of this expanded the powers of the General Staff over its structure authorized by Presidential decree in 2013, but it did clarify and project it onto a new contextual framework.

This was a major step in creating a "whole of government" responsibility for a unified defensive, offensive, and general societal preservation capability. But did it go far enough (albeit acknowledging that it was far ahead of any other such structured approach in the world)? Or did the proposed format actually limit thinking and operations on the matter of total war and total defense to the "formal" approach of a military structure?

Russia analyst Mark Galeotti, writing in his blog in 2013 — before the new Kremlin approach had been formally adopted — saw how Russia's approach was emerging. He called it "non-linear war", developing under Russian Chief of the General Staff, Gen. Valery Gerasimov. Non-linear thinking is crucial to the conduct of all-source, all-asset amorphous warfare.

Essentially, Russia's approach was a logical next-step beyond the creation of unified command and warfighting structures which had their origins largely — in the modern sense — in World War II. This was not just with Russia under Stalin, who brought every strand of governance and warfighting under his orbit. After Stalin, and particularly after the communist period ended in 1990, Russian governmental entities gradually stovepiped to a degree again, as they did elsewhere in the world.

But this concept — in some respects pioneered by Evgeny Messner but also the concept of survival necessity required by the communists — of *myatezh voyna,* or constant "rebellion war" continued. This became termed as "hybrid war" as Russia supported an indefinable war in Ukraine in the early 21st Century culminating with the re-annexation of Crimea back under Russian sovereignty on March 18, 2014.

Arguably, however, the new Russian changes of 2020 moved strategic warfighting doctrine well beyond the mere adoption of "hybrid warfare". It began to prepare for true total war, albeit not yet at the level of comprehensiveness of the PRC. Russia still left operational matters in the hands of the General Staff.

And as France's seriously literate Prime Minister (1906-09 and 1917-20) Georges Clemenceau noted: "*La guerre! C'est une chose trop grave pour la confier à des militaires*" (War is too serious a matter to entrust to military men). As major power leaderships in all previous total wars have seen, the prosecution of an all-asset war draws the strings back into the hands of a single national figure. Indeed, it blurs the lines as to what is military and what is not.

But Russia's movement beyond the premise of "hybrid warfare" — which still fascinates Western observers — became clear in 2019. And this showed that it was thinking at least that hybrid warfare or *myatezh voyna* was what it claimed to be, "rebellion warfare", and not sufficient for the conduct of total war.

US writer Rosa Brooks in 2016 wrote a book entitled *How Everything Became War and the Military Became Everything: Tales from the Pentagon.*[56] It demonstrated how the US had adapted to the high-fever, low-kinetics of the so-called brief "hybrid war" period. But it showed that the US at that time was not preparing for "total war in the 21st Century".

Significantly, by 2017, US Pres. Donald Trump was, in fact, attempting to move the US back to a total war capability, within the 21st Century meaning of the concept. Despite his efforts, there remained considerable pre-occupation in the US Defense Dept. with "special operations". Indeed, for a period, it seemed that the US military was being transformed into an entirely "special operations" force.

The history of the coalescing of formal war operations into "jointness" — the combined overview and management of conflict — began with the creation, for example, of Britain's Combined Operations Headquarters, under Admiral of the Fleet Sir Roger Keyes (later Baron Keyes) in 1940. Under wartime strategic governance, of course, UK Prime Minister Winston Churchill, no less Stalin or Hitler or Franklin Roosevelt, saw his function as being at the center of all aspects of national strategic decisionmaking.

But in the sense of military operations, "jointness"

---

56 Brooks, Rosa: *How Everything Became War and the Military Became Everything: Tales from the Pentagon.* New York, 2016: Simon & Schuster.

gradually began to reveal itself in unified command structures of an overarching structure.

In Australia, for example, there was a move to a more integrated command under a Chief of Defence Force in the 1974-76 timeframe (as a result of its Vietnam War experience, among other things). There was a similar unification of operational command under the Ground Force commander in Egypt, evolving out of the October 1973 war planning and experience.[57]

The Indian Armed Forces only began this level of integration at command level in 2020.

All of this, however, assumed that, as the 21st Century progressed, governments could bring the bulk of their security capabilities within the formal disciplines which the military and security services offer. This became critical when it was realized, even by Russian thinking in the 2019 timeframe, that 80 percent of contemporary (let alone anticipated) conflict was non-military in nature.

What was significant in the 2015-19 timeframe was that the Communist Party of China began re-ordering the People's Liberation Army (PLA) to wage the amorphous total war of the 21st Century. There was a definite understanding in both Moscow and Beijing that

57 See, Copley, Gregory R.: *The Defense & Foreign Affairs Handbook on Egypt*, 1995. London, 1995: International Media Corporation. In the chapter entitled "The Operations Authority and the Army", it notes: "The Minister of Defense is, in direct and practical terms, the Commander-in-Chief of the Armed Forces. The Chief of Staff of the Armed Forces is the day-to-day 'chief executive' of the Egyptian Armed Forces. Beneath the national command authority lies the Operations Authority. ... It is essentially the office of the Land Forces commander, and yet it is also the combined services coordination, command, and control center. The post of Chief of the Armed Forces Operations Authority is therefore extremely powerful and yet constrained by the need to make all force elements work well together."

warfare was changing, and that new structures must be created to handle it. But there were, equally, sufficient differences in the responses by Beijing and Moscow to show that there was no collusion, or the creation of a joint approach or close alliance between the two.

My colleague, Yossef Bodansky, brought much of the PRC thinking into perspective in a report on February 12, 2020.[58] He reminded us that the concept of broad strategic warfare, including non-military operations, was deeply embedded in Chinese communist strategy, dating back to the Gutian Conference of the Fourth Army of the Chinese Workers' & Peasants' Red Army in 1929, two decades before the Communist Party seized power on the Chinese mainland. The CPC highlighted the prescience of this event in 2019, 90 years later, as it unveiled the extent of its approach to fighting the total war of the 21st Century.

Bodansky noted:

Mao Zedong asserted that "the Chinese Red Army is an armed body for carrying out the political tasks of the revolution" in order to "establish revolutionary political power". Implementation is undertaken in the context of the "Three Warfares": the broad umbrella definition of political warfare.

---

58 Bodansky, Yossef: "The PRC's Strategic Support Force: Key Focus of US Concern", in *Defense & Foreign Affairs Strategic Policy, 2/2020*. He also noted that, for general background on the PLA Strategic Support Force (SSF) and its wartime rôles, it would be desirable to reference: (1) Elsa B. Kania and John K. Costello, "The Strategic Support Force and the Future of Chinese Information Operations", *The Cyber Defense Review*, Spring 2018; (2) John Costello and Joe McReynolds, "China's Strategic Support Force: A Force for a New Era", *China Strategic Perspectives No. 13*, Center for the Study of Chinese Military Affairs, Institute for National Strategic Studies, National Defense University Press, Washington, DC, October 2018; (3) Adam Ni and Bates Gill, "The People's Liberation Army Strategic Support Force: Update 2019", *China Brief*, Volume 19, Issue 10, May 29, 2019, The Jamestown Foundation, Washington DC.

The first of the "Three Warfares" is the struggle to influence media and public opinion; the second is influencing foreign decisionmakers and their China policies; and the third is shaping the legal context of Chinese actions and intentions. More recently, the PLA embraced the "Unrestricted War" concept, introduced in early 1999, which includes wreaking havoc on the Internet among the instruments and methods of "semi-warfare, quasi-warfare, and sub-warfare, that is, the embryonic form of another kind of warfare".

Presently, the PLA SSF [Strategic Support Force] is the combat arm most adapted for the conduct of the non-kinetic elements of the "Three Warfares" and "Unrestricted War" concepts.

He went on:

The PLA Strategic Support Force was established in the second half of 2015 as an outcome of the 2013 decision on the profound reforming and modernization of the PLA in order to meet the challenges of future warfare, particularly against the US and its allies. The SSF was defined as a "new-type combat force", responsible for addressing all challenges emanating from the emerging "strategic frontiers" — space, cyber-space, and the electromagnetic domain — as well as conduct and/or support the conduct of wartime operations in these domains.

The SSF was created by merging and markedly expanding the pertinent units of the PLA and a few intelligence and counter-intelligence elements. It was declared operational by the end of the year.

Presently, the SSF is answerable directly to the Joint Operations Command (JOC) under the Central Military Commission (CMC) which is chaired and run by

Xi Jinping. The raw data the SSF collects is analyzed by the Intelligence Bureau within the PLA's Joint Staff Department. For the conduct of their routine operations, the SSF also has direct links to specific departments of the Communist Party of China (CPC), the Ministry of State Security (MSS; that is, PRC Intelligence), the National Cyberspace Administration of China, etc.

The most efficient form of defense or projection of a nation-state is built around the hierarchical organization and command of forces, including (but not limited to) standing formal military and security structures. But, as we have outlined, that is no longer sufficient to the whole task in a comprehensive threat and opportunity environment.

So, *à priori*, the state itself must first be reclaimed from a passive globalist social condition where that exists. And operational hierarchies will need to be in a constant dynamic of evolution to meet emerging threats and opportunities.

That is not to say that governments claiming a globalist agenda cannot organize hierarchically to conduct efficient warfare. Globalism as an ideology works for its sponsor as an hierarchically-directed, predatory weapon, but not for target states which see their hierarchies (and therefore their defenses) broken.

We saw that the two great powers of the 20th and 21st centuries claiming a globalist agenda — the USSR and the People's Republic of China — developed comprehensive, large, and capable instruments of warfare across the spectrum of formal conflict, psycho-political warfare, and economic warfare.

In contrast, *democratic* societies which profess a globalist agenda (ie: urban globalist political *blocs* within societies, or actual governments, such as the US Administration of Barack Obama) tend to become essentially passive, or at least selective, in warfighting approach, largely because they mirror-image their threat perceptions. They think that if they do not seek conflict, then they will not be the target of it.

They have essentially succumbed to the psychological conditioning of the autocracy-driven globalist ideologies.

The difference is, in reality, that the declared globalist powers such as the USSR and the PRC were — like Germany in the nazi era (ie: until 1945), and, to a degree, fascist Italy — nationalist-globalist, or, in their own parlance, nationalist-socialist. They believed (and the Communist Party of China continued to believe) that sovereignty was only valid for themselves, and that all other societies' rights to sovereignty were invalid and illegitimate. This general approach has applied in varying degrees to earlier globalist powers, from Rome to Britain to the US.

To a degree, fundamental belief systems are less critical to efficient projection of national interests (ie: strategic warfighting) in the modern, amorphous war setting than whether the power structure of a society can clearly organize a new command and control hierarchy to meet an entirely new strategic context.

By automatically assigning strategic warfighting capability in the 21st Century to the armed forces leadership, it was possible that the grand strategic capabilities of a nation-state or society could be overlooked or could under-perform in circumstances outside formal kinetic operations.

Clean-sheet evaluation of the current and potential operating context — the strategic terrain writ large — should determine which skill-sets are required and how they should be coordinated. Information dominance (ID) capabilities, which include many aspects of cyber operations and signals functions, engage the broadest spectrum of the operational terrain, and thus cannot be allowed to automatically become subordinate to kinetic operations.

Kinetic capabilities remain critical and visible, however, and must *be seen to be* effective and confident. But once committed to war, their prestige, and therefore their deterrent value, are immediately degraded or impacted. At that point, these capabilities must be used rapidly and with absolutely unquestioned success, or their influence will decline consistently. Thus, keeping the capabilities of armed forces highly visible and within perceptionally-significant range of the target is critical, but success is jeopardized in almost direct proportion to the proximity with which the forces are moved to the point of contact.

Israel, by late 2019, had become conscious of the amorphous nature of the evolving threat environment it faced. by late 2019, was beginning to move toward a far more integrated military capability. The Israel Defense Forces Chief of Staff Lt.-Gen. Aviv Kochavi on October 23, 2019, outlined a multi-year plan — called *Momentum*, or, in Hebrew, *Tenufa* (*Tnufa*) — to restructure Israeli defense to meet emerging threat and conflict scenarios. He noted: "In the northern and southern arenas the situation is tense and precarious and poised to deteriorate into a conflict despite the fact that our enemies are not interested in war. In light of this, the IDF has been in an accelerated process of preparation." The planning essentially involved a major restructuring of the IDF General Staff, which comprised 24 brigadier and major generals.

Plan *Tenufa* would see huge investments in developing the IDF's arsenals, including increasing its collection of mid-sized unmanned aerial vehicles, obtaining large numbers of precision-guided missiles from the United States and purchasing additional air defense batteries. The IDF would also focus its training exercises more heavily toward urban combat, as it believed that its troops were more likely to fight in cities and towns than in the open fields where many drills were currently held. The plan formally began operational life on January 1, 2020. *Tenufa* was to be heavily intelligence-oriented, and would also, operationally, outfit individual troops for even more urban combat than had previously been the case. A multi-agency task force, involving Military Intelligence, the Israeli Air Force, and the three IDF regional commands, would finally come together on target selection, utilizing increased artificial intelligence (AI) and "big data".

The restructuring was not expected to be complete with the basic Plan *Tenufa*. A new Force Design Directorate of the IDF was unveiled in February 2020, replacing the Planning Directorate, and a new Strategy and Iran Directorate was created to specifically deal with the threat from the Islamic Republic of Iran. Essentially, the Israeli model was to designate a command-level (two-star) officer to address each major threat area: Northern Command countering *HizbAllah* and Iran; Southern Command against HAMAS.

The Commander of the Military Colleges would, under the reorganization, serve simultaneously as the head of the IDF Depth Corps, which was responsible for the military's operations beyond Israel's borders.

There would also be a greater emphasis on infantry in the Ground Forces. Lt.-Gen. Kochavi noted in January 2020: "It was decided that the IDF needs more infantry and that the infantry needs to be more lethal."

Israel's *Tenufa* Plan, however, was confined to the military attempting to address changes in the "visible spectrum" of kinetic threats. The Force Design Directorate attempted to make the formal IDF structure more responsive to an increasingly amorphous threat.

*   *   *

Latent Energy Versus Expended Energy

THE DETERRENT, INFLUENCING, intimidating power of military and political-economic structures is usually of strategic effect only if they have prestige.

Prestige is a latent energy but with the power to

cause dynamic outcomes.

Prestige is psychological power embodied in, and radiated from, visual (physical) and intellectually-constructed symbols implicit in demonstrable capability (including prowess), historical performance (reputation), unifying mysticism, implied capability, and the stored will of wealth and technological accomplishment.

It is a perishable commodity which must be nurtured and accumulated, but it evaporates with either a successful challenge to its credibility or with the physical use of the symbol as it descends from its iconic mountaintop to conquer. In other words, the latent energy of the strategic symbol, when used, becomes *expended energy.*

It can also atrophy or degrade through neglect.

Thus, the cost-benefit ratio must be determined before the expenditure of prestige. The latent energy, to retain value, must achieve an outcome measurable in tangible terms. The years and treasure expended for a strategic symbol to acquire prestige can be spent in an instant. So its use must be decisive.

Was it strategically wise, then, for the US to use high-potency strategic symbols, such as its aircraft carrier strike groups, its B-1 and B-2 strategic bombers (strategic because they were meant to deliver nuclear payloads in formal war situations), and the like to achieve tactical objectives in the wars in Afghanistan and Iraq in the first decades of the 21st Century? Their deterrent powers evaporated once the weapons were used.

Could not the same (or better) effects have been achieved using dedicated tactical platforms? The iconic strategic capabilities could have been left to prowl like watching male lions on the periphery of operations.

Niccolò Machiavelli (1469-1527) favored the medieval Italian word *sprezzatura* to embody his concept of doing the impossible or very difficult with grace and apparent ease. *Sprezzatura* is part of prestige, and a vital tool in the projection of power or the imposition of will.

All Space Activity is Either Part of the War, or is Strategic in Nature

SPACE, FROM THE TIME OF the first ballistic rockets which probed the stratosphere in the 20th Century, and from the first terrestrial use of the stars as tools of navigation, has been part of the existential human competition — war — and will remain so through the 21st Century.

The 2020s saw the beginning of private sector engagement in space activities, but all remained under significant state oversight and international regulation. The use of space would continue to expand as long as economies can be sustained. Moreover, regardless of the undoubted economic and commercial benefits of space activity (indeed, including that activity), space remains primarily a field of strategic competition.

What happens to that carefully-balanced strategic

competition, however, when the balance of nations is disrupted on earth? By 2020, the risks of disturbing the wellbeing of an adversary's national assets in space were clear: any significant attack on a space-based asset would exact retaliation or response.[59] All space-based assets were, more-or-less, equally vulnerable, and equally vital to the conduct of economies and military power on earth.

Only a nation-state with no reliance on space (if there is still such a state) could afford, for example, the luxury of damaging the near-earth space environment. To use space-detonated weapons in the area of low earth orbit (LEO) assets to damage fragile, orbiting sensors or communications platforms would risk damage to all. And by the time, for example, the Democratic People's Republic of (North) Korea obtained the ability to inflict damage on the space terrain it had also built a degree of reliance itself on space-based assets.

Dr Stefan Possony, advising Ronald Reagan before (and after) Reagan became US President in 1981, created the concept of the Strategic Defense Initiative (SDI) in order to utilize space-based platforms to detect, and subsequently neutralize, the launch of ballis-

59 French Armed Forces Minister Florence Parly on July 25, 2019, announced France's commitment to creating its Space Command, in a move given urgency by the fact that French space assets were already under attack. Minister Parly indicated that in 2018 the Russian *Luch Olymp* satellite had moved in close proximity to the *Athena-Fidus* Franco-Italian satellite used for secure military and police communication, and attempted to intercept signals traffic through that satellite. She said that the *Luch Olymp* also "left a business card to eight other satellites belonging to various countries". [*Athena-Fidus* is a geosynchronous EHF/Ka-band wideband communications satellite capable of data transfer rates of up to three Gb per second.]

tic missiles. The technologies capable of achieving Possony's vision — which were supported with variations, including the codenamed *Brilliant Pebbles* approach of nuclear warfare pioneers Lowell Wood and Edward Teller of the Lawrence Livermore National Laboratory (LLNL) in 1987 — were clearly within reach even when Possony proposed it in the early 1970s.

Significantly, when the USSR could not match the SDI technologies, its psychological warfare leaders under CPSU International Section leader Boris Ponomarev deployed their anti-nuclear "crowd" assets in the West to oppose SDI (calling SDI by the demeaning fantasy name "Star Wars") on the grounds that it would give the US a monopoly on the deployment of nuclear weapons, when Reagan, in fact, had offered the Soviets joint-control over SDI to ensure that *no* state could launch nuclear weapons using intercontinental ballistic missiles. And in a parallel move, the Soviets empowered their friends in the *seemingly*-authoritative *Bulletin of the Atomic Scientists* to say that the technology to achieve SDI would never be feasible. But it *was* eminently feasible, as history was to demonstrate.

What was clear by 2020, however, was that space was once again becoming not only a strategic area of maneuver and technological importance, but that it was a direct battlefield on its own account, and was imminently kinetic.

Individual space assets — by now vital for surveillance, communication, and navigation — were, within the first quarter of the 21st Century, able to be targeted without concurrent risk to the broader near-earth space terrain.

Space warfare, in the direct and kinetic sense, including cyber and electronic warfare, was becoming viable. This meant that the military — as opposed to broader strategic — war in space required a constant program of countermeasure development. This implied that the existing fleet of space assets would need to be replaced by hardened, defensible systems before major conflict could be considered. But it was likely that "the war in space" — an integral part of total constant war — would begin to become dynamic before the legacy assets in space could be replaced with hardened and defensible systems.

Indeed, given the reality that the more advanced a society the more critical its reliance on space-based capabilities, it was likely that any move from amorphous, terrestrially-based indirect warfare to direct kinetic, formal strategic action on earth would, *à priori*, require pre-emptive action in space.

The creation of the United States Space Force on December 20, 2019, absorbing the existing US Air Force Space Command, was a belated response to the acceleration of space warfare operations by the People's Republic of China and the Russian Federation. It was no surprise, then, that on July 13, 2019, Pres. Emmanuel Macron of France announced the creation of a space command within the Air Force, which would eventually become the Air and Space Force (*Armée de l'Air et de l'Espace).*

The United Kingdom, in early 2018 and anticipating separation of the UK from the European Union, had already begun a program for more extensive, hardened military space operations, including the option to revive its own launch capabilities for satellite systems. The new British generation of space assets, including its own navigation systems, were being developed in cognizance of the reality that space warfare was becoming direct and physical.

Cyber and Information Dominance as the Decisive Weapons of the Amorphous Warfare Age

WE HAD, BY THE FIRST QUARTER of the 21st Century, reached the prospect of a "mutually-assured cyber destruction" (MACD).

Cyber would prove to be of overwhelming capability when coupled — via electronic media and "social media" and messaging — with psychological warfare-driven message content.

The cyber phenomenon rendered obsolescent the 20th Century doctrine employed by the Soviet and Western *blocs* of "mutually assured (nuclear) destruction" (MAD). But being rendered obsolescent did not necessarily mean that MAD thinking was no longer considered or applied.

MAD required a sense of mutuality which accepted a rationalized mutual-hostage scenario which, in the 21st Century, was difficult to achieve in most competitive strategic situations. A continuation (which was accepted as a *de facto* condition) of the US-Soviet MAD balance extended to a US-Russian situation would not have realistically allowed either party to address broader, and perhaps more deep-seated concerns about a strategic balance with the PRC, for example.

That cyber had helped transform the conflict space into one which embraced all segments of society became apparent when, by 2020, cyber crime — that is, outside the government sectors — was responsible for some $2-trillion in losses per year. It was expected to rise to some $6-trillion a year within two to three years after that. This meant that cyber crime had an economic power greater than the GDP of, for example, Australia.

It was clear that cyber countermeasures were a long way from being able to constrain the level of private-sector warfare, let alone provide security for assets defended by a national government. Moreover, the nature of cyber warfare was that it transcended normal boundaries, and — perhaps most significantly — comprehended the reality that the most important strategic targets included non-governmental economic assets. And private sector criminal resources in the cyber realm were as advanced as those of states.

As a result, even private sector actions could result in strategic level damage being done to the national economy which was home to the target of criminal cyber action. So there was, through the first quarter of the 21st Century, no hope of "cyber security"; only "cyber resilience", even though system hardening and countermeasure capabilities meant that the cost of cyber actions and defenses was escalating.

But the exponential, or linear, extrapolation of this situation depended heavily on the continued stability and progress of the economic framework. Cyber warfare prospered only as a direct result of the electronic interconnectivity of society and the total dependence of society at all levels (including military operations) on the unbroken delivery of electricity.

As long as electricity was utilized by society, whether linked by landlines or not, then society was vulnerable to hostile cyber operations.

What could stop this hostile cycle?

Only a decreasing dependency on electricity *and/or electrical vulnerability.* After all, we had, by 2020, only been existentially dependent on electricity for just more than a century, and even in the total wars of the 20th Century we had not been existentially vulnerable to cyber warfare. Certainly the path to cyber dominance was evidenced in the importance of encrypted, electronically-based intelligence dissemination and interception from World War I onwards, but by 2020 all life — particularly urban life — could be held in the balance by cyber warfare.

Economic decline in societies would mean, at some point, a declining ability to produce consistent electricity. Even the transitional disruptions caused by attempting to move abruptly from one form of electricity production to another threatened economic dislocation and political repercussions. Certainly, the threat to increase the cost to voters of electricity, because of a promised switch to non-fossil fueled electricity generation, lost the Australian Labor Party its chance to win power in the Australian elections of May 18, 2019.

So there were many ways that electricity had become weaponized, physically and politically (or socially), by 2020. It begged the question, then, as to whether in the future there could exist a form of power and security which would not involve dependence on electricity. And if so, then when could it be developed, and at what stage could it achieve mass adoption by societies? The petroleum economy came into overwhelming acceptance over a period of, say, a quarter century; the electrical economy also took only, say, the same amount of time. And both forms remained concurrently utilized as the world moved toward the mid-point of the 21st Century.

In the meantime, can some goals of power projection or defense be achieved without dependence on electricity? Nuclear weapons had become of overwhelming strategic significance, largely as the default pinnacle of the weapons hierarchy, in the second half of the 20th Century. They became dormant within decades, however, because they were expensive and because they lacked political and warfighting utility (in many respects).

By the 21st Century, nuclear weapons had begun to achieve a degree of military utility partly *because* their iconic stature had faded. The emotional constraints on their use also loosened, but by then they had been eclipsed as the premier strategic tool by cyber. This enabled nuclear weapons to be considered as actual (rather than symbolic) warfighting tools at a theater or tactical level.

So, too, will cyber weapons eventually be eclipsed. Not by countermeasures, but by newer forms of power projection. No weapon remains forever symbolically or practically potent, and each new weapon builds upon its predecessors.

The significant challenge of the first half of the 21st Century is how, within the structured war-fighting realm as well as in societal war, nations will be able to devise capabilities which circumvent electricity. Or adequately ring-fence the use of it while guaranteeing levels of protection against its vulnerabilities.

But given this pervasive (and, in some senses, seemingly intractable) electronic dependency across the entire social spectrum, how do structured military forces maneuver going forward? Particularly in times of perceived relative peace?

The Rôle of Force Projection in 21st Century Total Amorphous War

FORCE PROJECTION, OR power projection, is the physicalization of strategic prestige, meant to accomplish domination or intimidation, or the strengthening of pride and confidence in the holder.

Force projection is, almost by definition, asymmetrical.

The worldwide tour of the British battleship, HMS *Hood,* and its Special Service Squadron in 1923-24 — the "Empire Cruise" — was apposite in the context of rebuilding British and British Empire faith and prestige after World War I. The United Kingdom's build-up of aircraft carrier battle groups in the 2020s became a modern equivalent of the *Hood's* Empire Cruise. Both were power projection instruments — essentially psycho-political in nature — designed to comfort allies, caution potential adversaries, and rebuild confidence at home.

The United Kingdom's fleet of nuclear-powered, nuclear missile-carrying submarines (SSBNs), which had been maintained to embody Britain's "seat at the table" of nuclear powers — the equivalent of the marshal's baton of the victors of World War II — had, by the 21st Century, become tired and visibly less potent as a symbol of power projection. For a start, they were, in fact, "less visible" because their mission was outside the public purview, and no longer could be — or was — symbolically powerful. Their prestige had faded.

The new (in the 2020s) *Dreadnaught*-class, *Trident* submarine-launched ballistic missile (SLBM) carrying SSBNs had declined in terms of strategic warfighting importance. This was largely because — for the UK to a greater degree than the US — the "strategic warfighting importance" was most significant in their symbolic, iconic representation.

The end of the Cold War, plus the development of newer weapons, had diminished the prestige of SSBNs.

But not their cost.

Aircraft carriers — whether or not they were surviv-
able in outright, peer-to-peer kinetic warfare or in the
face of ballistic or hypersonic weapons — were, in the
2020s, re-emerging as viable, more flexible, and more
visible elements of global power projection and influence.

This was because they carried the seeds of the past,
and partly because they could perform a range of military and civil-military functions which an SSBN could
not. Some of this also reflected the "tacticalization" of
nuclear-weapons in the early 21st Century. That was,
to a degree, the result of the rise of cyber as the premier
strategic weapon, and the recognition that nuclear
weapons at a theater level were more viable because
they were now more politically acceptable to use in
some circumstances.

Even so, the de-mysticization of nuclear warfare required an operational first-use example to unleash the
political viability of tactical nuclear weapons.

VIII

The Rôle of the Economy in the New Total War

And why economies — and economic theory — of declining scale may be decisive

ECONOMICS HAS ALWAYS been a subjective art. Economics is a psychological or intellectual construct and by no means a science. Attempts at reducing it solely to numerically-based formulæ have invariably fallen short.

Economics is a psychological response to a physical need.

But, in the 21st Century, as societies became technologically and sociologically more complex, so, too, did economics. Economics, indeed, became the Gordian knot of modern, urban societies, binding them into delicately-balanced frameworks dependent on totally notional values and therefore notionally-derived measurements of wealth. Unraveling this Gordian knot, then, throws societies into chaos.

And yet the knot's binding was fraying by 2020 or so. And the great dislocation of 2020 and beyond meant that new economic tools must arise.

The move to predominantly credit-based — or abstract — economies was almost universally complete in the more powerful nation-states before the end of the 20th Century, and physical cash — which was *always* a psychologically-based symbol for value and prestige — approached a declining utility. This was especially so as government intervention in economies increased to the point where state control of money supply became the critical tool in constraining or motivating one's own and foreign societies.

If trust, the implicit essence of the value of currency, could not be sustained through the prestige of the government, then the government would attempt to sustain "value" by interventionism and constraint.

Credit-based economics fueled the surge in Western societies' wealth and power in the 20th Century, while cash-based societies — such as most of those in sub-Saharan Africa — languished. Credit in various forms dramatically expanded money supply and wealth well beyond governments' abilities to effectively control it.

The real growth in wealth and power in the PRC began in the late 20th Century with the notion of individual entrepreneurship. This was, of course, contrary to maoist-marxist ideology, but was seen by Deng Xiaoping, who gradually assumed authority in 1976, as the only way to extract the PRC from what would have been — had it been allowed to continue — the terminal economic decline caused by Mao Zedong.

Deng saved the PRC and, more importantly, saved the Communist Party of China from the roiling revolts which began with Mao's so-called "Cultural Revolution".

In other words, the CPC having destroyed the Chinese economy and killing as many as 85-million Chinese people in peacetime, was given a reprieve by Deng, and the resilient Chinese people. That the CPC, because of Deng, *allowed* the Chinese people enough freedom to kick-start their economy through their own efforts does not mean that it was the Communist Party of China which lifted hundreds of millions of people out of poverty. It was the CPC which had ensured their poverty in the first place, and it was the Chinese people who *on their own* reclaimed their right to as much prosperity, dignity, and freedom as the autocratic party would allow.

The irony was that, by the second decade of the 21st Century, Pres. Xi Jinping — who modeled himself and his ideological approach on Mao — effectively curbed the free market and the credit opportunities available on a commercial basis. Absent credit; absent power. And absent the prestige of a government and its currency, power evaporates.

Africa and the Central Asian states had, however, begun moving toward more credit-based economics by the 2020s, but credit to an even greater extent than "cash" is based on prestige: faith, trust. So the failure of the PRC to achieve a "trust lift-off" for the *renminbi* inhibited Beijing's ability to expand its credit exponentially in the way, for example, the US did in the post-World War II era. Even the US had difficulty coming to grips with various credit mechanisms which basically became a seemingly limitless money supply. This was perhaps only begun to be understood by economist Maxwell Newton in his profound 1983 book, *The Fed.*[60]

But the means of measuring "creditworthiness" in such a framework did not keep pace with the complexity of social and strategic realities, even for the US. The growing use through the second half of the 20th Century of the measuring yardstick of Gross Domestic Product (GDP) to determine the performance of national economies had, by 2020, become a totally inadequate reflection of the economic health of nations, or their growth or decline.

So GDP statistics, the notional perspective as to how well or poorly an economy performs, became a totally inadequate tool to understand the strength or fragility of a nation-state. GDP had become part of the witchcraft of economics, and brought it no closer to science.[61] Even so, in the post-GDP era of the first half of the 21st Century, GDP was nonetheless a white cane by which to feel into the darkness.

---

60 Newton, Maxwell: *The Fed: Inside the Federal Reserve, the secret power center that controls the American economy.* New York, 1983: Times Books.
61 See, for example: Fioramonti, Lorenzo: *The World After GDP.* Cambridge, UK, and Malden, MA, USA, 2017: Polity Press. ISBN-13: 978-1-5095-1135-8.

Basing the value of a national defense capability on a notional percentage of a notional GDP given to a formal military capability is highly subjective, and potentially meaningless.

This, then, begs the question as to the place and rôle of economics in the exercise of power as the global complexity begins to approximate chaos in the 21st Century. That is not to deny that wealth is intrinsic to the exercise of power; it is. But how we measure and deploy wealth in the 21st Century would need to transform.

Economic factors have always helped to determine the rise of urban populations (concentrations of wealth) and therefore have been the primary driver of urban globalism ideology. But it is security factors which have always largely driven an historical sense of identity and nationalism in regional or rural communities. That may be an over-simplification to achieve perspective, but it helps to understand the fundamental difference in the primary drivers in the "global civil war" between globalists and nationalists in the 21st Century.

It also helps in understanding why urban globalism is geared around the "logic" of wealth and therefore open borders and short-term materialist transactionalism, while regional nationalism is geared around the restoration of identifiable horizons of identity, geography, and security. The cynicism of urbanist politics lies in the belief that the answer to *all* challenges is economic, or the provision of material reward.

The paradox of globalist philosophy is that, in order to perpetuate instant material gratification at the lowest cost, it favors "free trade". This is a similar mantra to libertarians and some conservatives.

In reality, however, *there is no such thing as "free trade"*, any more than there is truly "free love". All actions have consequences and responsibility.

As we saw in the late 20th and early 21st centuries, "free trade" resulted in most economies becoming subordinate to, and/or dependent on, the PRC for their vital — and desired — manufactures, including lifesaving pharmaceuticals. That meant that "free trade" ensured that dependent states lost their sovereignty: their ability to make independent decisions for their own security, survival, and way of life.

Of course, the perception of solutions and problems are usually *weighted toward economic factors* in urban areas, and *weighted toward identity factors* (including traditional beliefs, such as organized religion) in the regions. Either way, it is *the weight of beliefs* (rather than absolutes) which drives differences.

G.K. Chesterton, the author, is often quoted as having said: "When men choose not to believe in God, they do not thereafter believe in nothing, they then become capable of believing in anything."[62] It matters little whether he or someone else said it, but the expression has resonance, but not because it appears to

---

62 Chesterton did, however, write: "You hard-shelled materialists [are] all balanced on the very edge of belief — of belief in almost anything." That was in Chesterton's collection of eight stories, *The Incredulity of Father Brown*, published in 1926, in the tale of "The Miracle of Moon Crescent".

champion the cause of traditional religion. Rather, with what we have seen with the rise of urbanism and material wealth — which in many ways has paralleled the decline of organized religion in the late 20th and into the 21st centuries — is that there has been a commensurate rise in a tendency to only trust in visible materialism.

That sense of materialism has been ascribed to the gradual rise of the Age of Reason[63] (or the Age of Enlightenment) in the way in which colonial American activist Thomas Paine saw it in the late 18th Century.

It was, in a sense, an appeal to reason in suggesting a reliance on verifiable truths rather than "the bribe of heaven". And Paine's work, and the work of others of his mindset, *coincided* with the rise of what we call science in the modern sense, but was not entirely synonymous with it. With some justification: science *did* have answers or the promise of answers. At least some answers. It was tangible and material.

But not all people had the ability to understand science, particularly not the science of all disciplines. In any event, what resulted with the rise of science and materialism was the consequent rise in the *belief* that democracy — which was *theoretically*, or hypothetically quantifiable (ie: scientific) — could evolve to answer all questions. That "the will of the people" was paramount, whether or not it was based on an understanding of reality. Or whether or not democracy

---

63 Paine, Thomas: *The Age of Reason*, published in the US in two parts in 1794 and 1795, and then Part III in 1807.

could, as it became more rigid in its interpretation, also represent inequity or injustice.[64]

Belief once again became sufficient for the contentment of the urban electorates. And the secular belief was: "I believe I want more." In the absence of the promises of traditional religion, the "more" could only be more material reward. In other words, "democracy" became reduced to a short-term, transactional materialism, replacing long-term, transactional etherealism. The Rationalist Society of Australia, which began in a meeting of "freethinkers" in the University of Melbourne in 1906, epitomized the trend well, with its creed: "Spurn fear of hell and bribe of heaven."

So where has all this led in the 21st Century?

It is not reasonable to say that urban globalism, or utopianism in material terms, equates to a new, essentially anti-nationalist society, while nationalism and identity emphasis equates to the old "society of equal regions". There is a clear overlay, however, in the patterns, and therefore a more irreconcilable aspect to the division of societies within large nation-states than can be ignored.

Is that a sign that modern societies have gradually

64 The two Chinese strategists, Qiao Liang and Wang Xiangsui, both then senior colonels in the People's Liberation Army of the People's Republic of China, in their prescient 1999 book, *Unrestricted Warfare*, noted: "Stirred by the warm breeze of utilitarianism, it is not surprising that technology is more in favor with people than science is. The age of great scientific discoveries had already been left behind before Einstein's [20th Century] time. However, modern man is increasingly inclined to seeing all his dreams come true during his lifetime. This causes him, when betting on his own future, to prostrate himself and expect wonders from technology through a thousand-power concave lens. In this way, technology has achieved startling and explosive developments in a rather short period of time, and this has resulted in innumerable benefits for mankind, which is anxious for quick success and instant rewards."

transformed empires into increasingly centralized nation-states — often only barely disguised as federal states — to the breaking point? Were "empires of common interest and identity", which allowed component members (whether sovereign or satrap) more flexibility, better able to address localized beliefs and needs?

What became evident, particularly during the 20th Century, was that the overarching needs of the "empire" — which became federations or consolidated nation-states — were placed well ahead of localized needs of component societies. Super-consolidation of state power, with total prosecution of state intervention in economies (to the point where they became real or *de facto* command economies), produced powerful, short-term, war-winning powers.

This became particularly evident with World War II, where the United Kingdom became every bit as much a command economy as did, for example, Germany or the Soviet Union. The US was not far behind.

British researchers Stephen Broaderry, at the University of Warwick, and Peter Howlett, at the London School of Economics, in a 2002 chapter of a book on total war, noted that in the United Kingdom in World War II, "just over half of national expenditure was devoted directly to war and … the working population was divided roughly equally between on the one hand the armed forces, the munitions industries and other industries essential to the war effort, and on the other hand the less essential industries."

"Given the level of development and the structure of

the British economy (and given the strategic imperatives) this represented a total war economy."[65]

World War II may have represented the last opportunity to measure the actual proportions of *Western*
economies engaged in "total war", although the USSR
and the PRC remained in perpetual total war economies after World War II. Western economies —
whether in the US, UK, Western Europe, Canada, or
Australasia — attempted to revert to pre-war democratic freedoms after World War II, but were unable to
do so to the extent of restoration of the *status quo ante*.

For the USSR in 1945 and the PRC, when it assumed
power on the Chinese mainland in 1949, the emphasis
remained on a permanent war-economy, only relieved
by the fact that there were subsequent periods when
the killing of its citizens by foreigners diminished over
World War II levels. [Although this allowed the respective communist parties, acting through nominal governments, to then embark on purges of their own populations in one-sided, constant "civil wars", with losses
of lives of their citizens at even higher levels than
World War II. For the populations of the USSR and
PRC, the era of external Cold War was also a period of
domestic "total war", or "total civil war".]

The *relative* release of the Western Allied economies
from their command status of actual World War II
military operations afforded them a return to economic growth at far higher levels than the complete

---

65 In a chapter entitled "Blood, Sweat and Tears: British Mobilisation For World War
II" in Chickering, R. and Förster, S. (eds.), *A World at Total War: Global Conflict
and the Politics of Destruction, 1939-1945*, Cambridge: Cambridge University Press.

command economies of the Soviet *bloc* and the PRC. As a result, the liberation of economies from "total war-economies" actually enabled a greater warfighting economic capability than permanent, full command economies on constant war footing. Indeed, the perpetuation of a fully intervened economy (by the State in the USSR) proved that such economies are, in fact, as Possony has indicated, not suited to waging permanent total war.

The USSR collapsed by 1990 under that weight of perpetual militarism and constant war-economy. The PRC economy — a war-economy in which the principle enemy remained the Chinese population — under Mao Zedong (1949-1978) performed even worse than the Soviet economy. It would have seen the PRC reach political-economic implosion before the USSR had it not been for the death of Mao and the assumption of a leadership position by Deng Xiaoping in 1978.

Deng immediately liberated a small part of the non-state sector to grow food. That was the beginning.

The result was that, by the beginning of the 21st Century, the Communist Party of China (CPC) had become the beneficiary of a vastly-expanded national economy which, in fact, better enabled it to wage war, or prepare for direct warfare, than any of the earlier communist administrations in China. However, the release of a significant portion of the mainland Chinese economy also empowered a level of societal independence which challenged the CPC's control, so the "war" against the PRC's own citizenry began to be resumed by about 2012, when Xi Jinping began his rise to power.

By late 2018, when Xi and his administration declared the start of a "New Thirty Years War" with the United States, he had already begun to resume *de facto* interventionism in the PRC economy. Limitations on the private sector economy began to re-appear, along with policies favoring the massive state-owned enterprises (SOEs), which had contributed not one jot to the "Chinese economic miracle" which had actually made the PRC a globally-competitive power.

As well, the CPC began, in the 2010s, quietly seizing control of major private sector corporations.

These policies of economic and social intervention and centralization of Beijing's authority also brought about a revolt in 2019-20 in the autonomous region of Hong Kong, further hurting the PRC's economy.

On balance, and for reasons which also included population demographics, water supply, and food production, Xi's policies of a return to a permanent war-economy were set in stone by 2020 to begin a reduction in the PRC's strategic competitiveness.

Some of that may have been beyond the control of Xi. The population of the PRC was getting ready to begin a significant decline in numbers, just as population reduction was impacting much of the rest of the world. The 2019 outbreak in Wuhan of coronavirus — COVID-19 — was just another indicator in the declining traction of the PRC economy.

The question was whether the demographic transformation — which, as with Western societies, involved a period of ageing populations reducing productivity and increasing social costs — would, within a decade, "save" the PRC and the CPC, or not. Certainly, the Xi Government welcomed the reality that population reduction — particularly among the older, seemingly less-productive demographic — would reduce the challenges of food and water supply shortages.

Nonetheless, the era of the PRC being an attractive destination for foreign investment and a source of low-cost manufacturing was ending.

The next question, given the emerging almost global pattern of reduction in population size — and therefore market size — was whether new economic models could empower viable war-economies based on smaller market size. Or whether smaller market size was a lesser factor for war-economies than for peacetime economies, other than the reality that labor pool size may be a factor in sustaining war operations.

All of that must be taken into the perspective that the "constant total war" environment of the 21st Century would be less committed to military production and the support of military operations than the total wars of the 20th Century, and would be geared more to economic and information dominance warfare. [See Chapter XI: Information Dominance in a Total War World.]

The 21st Century may best be represented by the reality that it became "the post-growth era", and not just because of the 2020 crisis. It was to become the era of post-economic growth except in key areas. This coincided with the post-population growth area (again, except in a few areas). And, in some ways, with the post-technological growth period. These "post-growth" trends were all, of course, interrelated.

This view, by 2020, was almost universally unacceptable or unpalatable, but it had become at least open for discussion, whereas at the turn of the 21st Century it was ridiculed even as a possibility.

One more word on Beijing's plans leading up to, and during, its own 2020 crisis. This was to be the pivotal point for the Communist Party of China: if the PRC could not compete economically with the US under the terms of the existing, Western-created "rules-based world order", then those terms of engagement, those "rules", would have to be changed.

If the PRC economy could not grow in terms defined by the West, then the West's economies would have to be reduced by whatever means possible. So 2020 set in train the dynamic which would potentially "level the playing field": flattening the terrain of strategic engagement.

As a by-product of this, however, was the reality that the tipping point of the 2020 world crisis also lowered the global demand for energy, particularly fossil fuels which had come to be the primary energy driver of global economic growth. Oil had been the great underpinning of 20th Century growth.

As a result of the lowered demand for oil and gas, those states which were primarily dependent upon the export of fossil fuels would see — as 2020 proved — a sustained reduction in market demand and therefore a reduction in the value of their exports. This meant that the first casualty of the crisis — and Beijing's determination to transform the "rules-based world order" — would be some of the states which depended predominantly on the sale of oil and gas.

That included most of the state members of OPEC, the Organization of Petroleum Exporting Countries. But not all. And for as long as Beijing was able to halt or change the Western-defined "rules-based world order" those affected states would see their golden ages eclipsed. But, again, not all: ancient and entrenched societies such as Persia (Iran) and Russia, although damaged, would retain viability because of historical social patterns and because of a level of diversification of economic survival patterns.

For Beijing, this in particular meant that Russia could possibly be humbled to true supplicancy to the PRC; to become a tributary state of the Middle Kingdom. If Beijing's strategy was successful, Russia would be unable again to strategically compete with the PRC.

This era of "cheap oil and gas" — unsustainable for producers — could arguably have been seen as the removal of one impediment to the cost of economic growth ... unless the economic unsustainability of fossil fuel production meant that it was no longer readily available. That situation would, of course, and under normal circumstances, automatically impel a cyclical rise in the price of oil and gas.

... Unless demand remained low because of Beijing's success in continuing to depress global economic growth for its own strategic reasons.

There was no question, even in 2020, that the short-term economic depression would be partially overcome and that some revived energy demand would be evident in the near-term. Prices would start (as they did) to haltingly rise a little, albeit not enough to restore the economic fortunes of Saudi Arabia, Kuwait, the United Arab Emirates, Venezuela, Nigeria, Angola, and so on. *Their* fates would, to varying degrees, become parlous once their sovereign wealth funds and finances became depleted.

But at what cost to the world?

My old colleague, mentor, and partner, Stefan Possony, told me in 1972 — and I am sure wrote it somewhere in the pages of our *Defense & Foreign Affairs* publications — that all great powers (and notably Rome) were hallmarked through history as being the most profligate users of energy in their respective eras.

It was this "waste" of energy which enabled the creation of strategic advantage. From the cooking of healthier food diets to the creation of sufficient light by which to extend the hours of learning and production. And certainly to forge better metals, from the creation of bronze from copper and tin, to the smelting of iron to the creation of steel, and so on.

What, then, docs this "new rules-based world order" promise to us if its first order of effect is to ensure a decline in the economic levels of the world merely so that

Beijing could emerge at the top of the heap — not even a soaring mountain — of human growth?

Beijing's maxim as it entered and passed through the crisis of 2020 was that to succeed all others must fail.

The lesson to be taken away from this is that there are times for freer trade, and times for more nationalistically-based, channeled trade. Times when trust is less important; times when it is not.

At its core, *nationalism saves societies; free trade makes them wealthy.* But wealth and security or survival are not always synonymous. It is appropriate to be a free trader when the times are right, but with that caveat that there is no such thing, in the end, as "free trade". There is no free lunch.

For free trade to work, it must be seen not as an abdication of responsibility, but the assumption of it. And that responsibility is to see that free trade should not be seen as the surrender of control over the vital requirements of sovereign self-reliance in order to gain short-term material satisfaction.

Rather, free trade should be seen as the stimulus to achieve the efficiencies which are the result of competition. If one area competes through lower costs, another must compete through greater efficiency, productivity, and innovation.

IX

The Sociology of Constant Total War

Nationalism, fear, and the return of leaders

ONSTANT TOTAL WAR WAS VISITED upon the 21st Century because of the combination of sociological, technological, and wealth growth factors of the 20th Century.

Given that all aspects of history are essentially cyclical, however, we saw an end to the *underlying conditions* which gave such significant stability, prosperity, and levels of technological integration through the age of the Cold War and immediate post-Cold War (say, 1945 to 2010).

We witnessed the end of Eden.

We saw a world transitioning to "the age after growth", and the 21st Century would be initially an age of dislocation. Societies were moving from more than a half-century of linear growth in average global *per capita* wealth, caloric intake, lifespan extension and live birth rates, and technological progression.

Virtually all of these advances were generated by the galvanizing necessities of World War II, which caused a dramatic uptick in urbanization among industrialized states (both to create a mobilized defense economy and when returning troops mostly elected to settle in cities). This helped compound advances in wealth, productivity, technology, and health (including improved live birth rates).

But the post-World War II generation — which had been enabled to live longer and better than any generation before it — failed to replace itself in almost all areas of the world. Population numbers, and therefore market size, began moving from growth to decline, almost overnight, by the first years of the 21st Century.

This began as an erratic process — and some areas, such as Africa and India, were late entering the population decline phase — but one which had become significant by 2020, and would become profound by 2030. It would, inevitably, be accompanied by a slowdown (at least temporarily) and a change in the pace and direction of technological evolution, and by the failure of existing economic models which were based on perpetual growth of market size and wealth.

It is a cycle which has occurred before in history, but which, in its 21st Century iteration, was more vast in its scale than anything before it.

We have already discussed how the growth of urbanization, electronic communications, and wealth contributed to a "flat societal model", or, more accurately, an anti-hierarchical state in societies. What emerged was an almost contradictory situation, particularly in urban areas, of obsessive, self-imposed conformity in societies coupled with an almost anarchic sense of revolt against some forms of hierarchy.

After the first view of the contradictory nature of this new society, however, it becomes clear how compatible or logical was this approach to the threats to the social condition.

The obsessive conformity of views — political correctness — was, along with the revolt against hierarchy, often expressed in seemingly self-destructive terms (for the society as a whole), based on (a) fear of change, and especially a fear of changing a condition of "prosperity without responsibility"; and therefore (b) a rejection of the arrival of leadership, given that leaders emerge only in times of crisis and *demand* change or cause it.

It is rarely recognized by seemingly self-contained bubbles of societies — which is what many urban geopolitical entities become — that change will occur regardless of their wishes, and that cycles of growth and wealth end.

They reject change. They reject that which they, in fact, have no power to reject.

So the social condition in most nation-states was, by about 2020, becoming artificial, fragile, and yet galvanized into mindsets which could hardly be more separate than had the different peoples — though living as citizens of the same polity — been of totally different origins, with different languages and customs.

How, then, does a "national government" retain or re-assert authority and create sufficient unity so that it can prosecute the national interest in a global environment? This becomes a particularly difficult question when an element of the society essentially sees that what is necessary to be done (or what is happening) means, or reflects, the end of its stability. That social *bloc* will reject such change, even placing short-term self-interest above the continued existence of the larger society. It is in a state of denial.

By 2020, the *status quo bloc* had become avowedly anti-nationalist, and decried nationalist or sovereignty movements as being retrograde. In fact, the nationalist or sovereignty segment of society is the segment looking to safeguard the future, by pushing the nation-state (the larger geopolitical entity beyond just the cities) to its traditional rôle of embracing security of resources and geography to survive and prosper.

The cyclical swing toward nationalism, often imperfectly described as conservatism, is natural and inevitable when the prosperity of a globalist world is shaken by security, economic, or demographic change. This was well underway even as the 21st Century began.

At the same time as this phenomenon occurs, some of the population remain in denial: it wishes the prosperous *status quo* to continue, and sees no reason to change. So thought the peoples of the Eastern Mediterranean and Levant about 1,200 years before the Common Era. They refused to see that change had already been thrust upon them.

The old order changeth, for good or ill.

And at that point, too, momentum builds toward a stress on *sacro egoismo*: the sacred self-interest of the nation. Ironically, the urban globalists had practised *sacro egoismo* at an individual level: the sacred self-interest at the expense of others within their own society.

Italy defined the terms of its entry into World War I on a policy of *sacro egoismo* at a national level. That is how societies gather around their national interests in times of threat, fear, and opportunity.

But the schism between the *status quo bloc* and the nationalist *bloc* had — with the 2020 fear pandemic — become more defined than it had been before 2020. The fear pandemic caused the *status quo bloc* — the urban globalists — to *embrace* self-imposed conformity and massive top-down control and surveillance of society, while the nationalists opposed such surveillance and control.

The urban globalists in the West, then, began advocating cellphone-based tools to surveil and track the movements of almost all members of society in order to achieve or coerce conformity. And this was not a government-initiated approach, but it was avowedly statist by design. Indeed, it paralleled efforts in the PRC to achieve as near to total surveillance of all members of society as possible.

The question, then, is how governments can do what is necessary to ensure the survival of the state without the destruction of society.

Some governments do not, in fact, consider the "survival of the state", but, rather, pander to short-term electorate demand to merely deliver the continuation of the *status quo*. That, too, is a condition of denial. It keeps politicians in power, even if it demands *more* intervention in the economy and society to transfer the dwindling prosperity of the productive sector into the hands of the larger voting sector (or, in reality, into the hands of the group which *claims* to speak for the larger voting sector).

It is clearly a process which leads to an inevitable conclusion: collapse.

But not "collapse in my time". Well, that is the hope.

Thus we see the contradictory combination of authoritarian state behavior coupled with a willingness to let mobs free in the streets. They are mobs which are no longer faceless and nameless, however, if the new surveillance technologies can be brought to bear.

Thus do we see the decline of great cities, and the standards of life therein, at the same time as the power of the governance increases.

Roger Bacon, the 13th Century English philosopher and advocate of the empirical method of Ibn al-Haytham, in writing *Of Empire*, is attributed with the words: "Nothing destroyeth authority so much as the unequal and untimely interchange of power pressed too far, and relaxed too much."

How, then, to manage a society in which power is often pressed too far and yet relaxed too much at the same time? That was the immediate question following the impact of 2020.

"A gigantic technological race is in progress between interception and penetration and each time capacity for interception makes progress it is answered by a new advance in the capacity for penetration. Thus a new form of strategy is developing in peacetime, a strategy of which the phrase 'arms race' used prior to the old great conflicts is hardly more than a faint reflection.

"There are no battles in this strategy; each side is merely trying to outdo in performance the equipment of the other. It has been termed 'logistics strategy'. Its tactics are industrial, technical, and financial. It is a form of indirect attrition; instead of destroying enemy resources, its objective is to make them obsolete, thereby forcing on him enormous expenditure ...

"A silent and apparently peaceful war is therefore in progress, but it could well *be a war which of itself could be decisive.*"

**— Général d'Armée André Beaufre (1902-75),
French creator of the concept of "Total Strategy". His comments, above, have distinct application in the 21st Century, not merely to the war of hypersonic offense and defense, but also in other spheres of technological competition.**

X

The Technologies of the New, Constant, Total War

VICTORIES IN THE 21ST CENTURY may not be the result of the possession of the most advanced technology. Technology, like formal military strength, counts for only a portion of strategic strength, depth, and capability, and therefore for only a portion of outcomes.

It contributes barely a jot to the creativity of surprise, maneuver, and will, although it is a servant of all.

In the 21st Century, more than in the 20th, it was likely to be true that *other* factors, combined with the command of *appropriate* technology, would be the determinant of strategic success. "Today," as the Chinese strategists Qiao Liang and Wang Xiangsui noted, "the independent use of individual technologies is now becoming more and more unimaginable".[66]

---

66 *Unrestricted Warfare.* Op cit. They continued: "The situation of loud solo parts is in the process of being replaced by a multipart chorus. The general fusion of technology is irreversibly guiding the rising globalization trend, while the globalization trend in turn is accelerating the process of the general fusion of technology, and this is the basic characteristic of our age."

And, "In the history of war, the general unwritten rule that people have adhered to all along is to 'fight the fight that fits one's weapons.'" But noted that the demarcation between traditional and future warfare was that the future should demand that warfighters rather should "build the weapons to fit the fight" than the traditional tendency to develop doctrine, tactics, and strategies around the weapons they have.

The 20th Century saw most states squander their resources on inappropriate technologies. South Africa's development and deployment of nuclear weapons (1960s to 1989) wasted scarce resources to create a capability which had no viable strategic purpose, *other than prestige/deterrence.* It was also a reflection of misplaced threat/opportunity perception.

South Africa succumbed in the end to an inability to make the appropriate non-military decisions at a time of complex psycho-political pressures wielded by a more globally-capable Soviet psychological warfare force. To be fair, the South African Government at the time recognized its primary adversary, the USSR, and its capabilities. But it did not fully recognize the extent to which the USSR's psychological operations had turned the West against South Africa.

By the 21st Century, for the first time in modern conflict, critical strategic weapons were in the hands of both nation-state and non-state actors down to the level of the individual. Clearly, this had not usually included general access by smaller powers and non-state actors to strategic-level kinetic, traditional weapons, but — far more importantly — they could now readily obtain weapons which could bring down electrical grids, banking and commerce centers. And, through the manipulation of words and imagery on various media platforms, whole governments or individual people or institutions could be targeted.

By the 2020s, the power of state wealth had begun to see the development of cyber countermeasures, effectively shrinking to a degree the rôle of non-state actors in strategic cyber warfare. The primary difference between the state actors and non-state actors, however, was that their objectives were differently delineated, if often overlapping.

Cyber crime had become a c.$2-trillion industry annually by 2020, and was expected to triple in scope within three or so years after that. In other words, by 2020, cyber crime was considerably greater in transactional value than the GDP of Australia. It automatically, then, had the capacity to undermine substantial portions of the economies of target nations.

To what extent could cyber criminal enterprises, then, be utilized as proxy warfare combatants? And to what extent was this already evident?

Cyber *proxy* warfare had already, by 2020, become as strategically significant (if not more so) as the use of terrorist proxies.

Again, as with terrorism — little understood as a definitive form of psychological warfare — cyber proxy/criminal activities blurred the social and perceptional strategic battlefield.

Meanwhile, the definitions of terrorism, criminality, and transnational (and therefore largely unregulated) political actions became blurred, overlapping, and, in some respects, meaningless.

And as with all forms of proxy provocations, the question of plausible deniability of operations was key to avoiding conflict escalation to the point of formal kinetic operations.

Direct military confrontations carry a high risk of defeat or downstream penalty of mostly unforeseeable impact, and must therefore be undertaken reluctantly.

But there is more to the empowerment of supposedly inferior forces[67] than access to cyber warfare tools, crypto-currencies, 3D printing (additive manufacturing), robotics, and possibly access to "big data". The overwhelming use of wealth-enabled advanced weapons, it is worth remembering, failed to give the US victory in its 21st Century wars in Iraq or Afghanistan. This was largely because Washington had left the door open to its adversaries for a variety of reasons:

➤ 1. Washington failed to define its strategic and grand strategic goals, and therefore failed to develop milestone objectives and the means of achieving them;

➤ 2. Washington failed to comprehend the true nature of the strategic context of its adversaries;

➤ 3. Washington used strategic weapons to achieve tactical outcomes, thereby degrading the prestige

---

67 Whether they are smaller states, violent extremist organizations (VEOs) or super-empowered individuals (SEIs).

of those weapons and therefore the holder of them;

➤ 4. Washington prioritized process (largely centered around logistics) over outcomes, because the desired outcomes were never specified.[68]

By the turn of the 21st Century, in contrast to the US approach to warfighting, the PRC had embraced the view "that there is nothing in the world today that cannot become a weapon".[69]

Qiao Lang and Wang Xiangsui noted, even in 1999 (in *Unrestricted Warfare*), how information technology (IT) enabled force size reductions. They further, to the question "where is the battlefield?", answered "everywhere". Even then, the PRC's People's Liberation Army (PLA) shared this recognition, and enabled the capabilities of the PLA to grow in inverse proportion to the decline in military manpower numbers.

And the most cost-effective "soldier" had become the hacker. Like terrorists, *ad hoc* insurgent groups, and cults, the hacker can function inside or outside the realm of state sponsorship. And as Qiao and Wang noted: "Compared to these adversaries, professional

---

68 That, as far as the US war in Afghanistan was concerned, changed in late 2019 when US Pres. Donald Trump made a pointed effort to conclude the Afghanistan war — after almost two decades of waste and destruction — in such a way that a stable post-conflict Afghanistan would give access by the five Central Asian states to its north to the Indian Ocean via overland links through Afghanistan and Pakistan. That would automatically free the Central Asian region from its historical dependence on Russia and the People's Republic of China, presenting a geo-strategic opportunity for the US as well as the Central Asian states.

69 *Unrestricted Warfare*. Op cit. It went on: "A single man-made stock-market crash, a single computer virus invasion, or a single rumor or scandal that results in a fluctuation in the enemy country's exchange rates or exposes the leaders of an enemy country on the Internet, all can be included in the ranks of new-concept weapons."

armies are like gigantic dinosaurs which lack strength commensurate to their size in this new age."

Little wonder, then, that professional armies began absorbing these irregular skills into their frames of reference.

The US had by that stage also recognized the transformed battle-space, focusing on (1) information warfare; (2) precision warfare; (3) joint operations; and (4) military operations other than war (MOOTW).

What this highlights is the reality that the dominant aspects of 21st Century total warfare remain, still, outside the realm of the professional military. The scope of economic warfare (including trade war), grand strategic-level maneuver (such as that employed by US Pres. Donald Trump to bring North Korea and the PRC to negotiations in the 2018-19 timeframe), population warfare, and so on remain outside the scope of "military strategy", or even the expertise acquired in the course of military careers.

The commoditization of intelligence: Electronic communications, surveillance and sensor systems, and artificial intelligence (AI) had, by the end of the first quarter of the 21st Century, essentially commoditized operational intelligence within governmental and military operations. To all intents, removing the human element had automated both the battlefield and the precursor intelligence processes.

Wisdom acquired over ages was deemed subjective and unquantifiable, and was therefore largely viewed as suspect and disruptive of the intelligence process.

Throwing vast quantities of expensively-acquired "data" at threats, often fed to automated response systems, was the 21st Century equivalent of throwing vast quantities of humans against threats in the manner of the Napoleonic wars or the US Civil War of the 19th Century. So there was a question as to how efficacious this modern equivalent of commoditization could be in the conduct of conflict operations. Clearly, given the human-generated increase in the complexity and amorphous nature of the 21st Century battlefield, computer assistance and supportive algorithms would be necessary.

But at what point did experience-based human wisdom become an input of supposedly diminished value?

The capability in the 21st Century to automate the collection of data — not to be confused with finished intelligence — had reached unprecedented levels. This process promised to continue as long as funds were available; in other words, as long as economies remained stable, and research and development could continue. Moreover, the addition of machine learning, artificial intelligence, and quantum computing meant that data could be handled instantaneously and with increasing nuance and sophistication.

But did we see, in the early decades of the 21st Century, a commensurate increase in the achievement of strategic objectives, or even the achievement of decisive military successes, with the addition of high-volume, commoditized intelligence and data flow? Arguably, there was *no* improvement in the situation for most players: those decades saw a decline in true strategic situational awareness by key decisionmakers in almost all countries. Those who prospered did so through resort to wisdom acquired by policymakers — and, yes, in this instance we can call them leaders — from an acquired understanding of their own societies and the societies of the seas of nation-states among which they were required to navigate.

The problem which began to emerge on the strategic battlefield was not that the vast pipeline of "intelligence" — data and electronically-based imagery and sensor points, as well as finished intelligence — was not valid or accurate. Rather, it was the reality that the flow had become so overwhelming that it could not be prioritized and contextualized to assist in strategic decisionmaking. Certainly, particularly at tactical levels, automated management of data and responses to it could provide invaluable improvements in managing cyber or kinetic environments. But absent a broader contextual view of the strategic landscape, it was like playing tennis on a golf course.

Artificial intelligence was not moving toward artificial wisdom. So the imperative toward ensuring that decisionmakers had an uncluttered field of vision, undistracted by high-volume, low-grade intelligence, remained as critical as ensuring that they also had the benefit of deeply-rooted contextual, historical experience.

As Sun-tzu said: "If you know the enemy and know

yourself you need not fear the results of a hundred battles. If you know yourself but not the enemy, for every victory gained you will also suffer a defeat. If you know neither the enemy nor yourself, you will succumb in every battle."

Clearly, most formal decisionmakers in the world, as the 21st Century matured, failed to either know their own society, or their enemy's society.

Intelligence reporting may provide facts, but not the context to understand the global battlefield. It is like (paraphrasing Oscar Wilde) knowing the price of everything without knowing the value of anything.

What was significant as the 21st Century gained momentum was that one of the most important international alliance structures in the world — the UKUSA Accords, otherwise known as the "Five Eyes" — had been rendered increasingly inefficient because it sank beneath a vast flow of commoditized intelligence. Even before 2020, the exchange levels of "intelligence" meant that all parties to the Accords — the US, United Kingdom, Australia, Canada, and New Zealand — had been forced to create bigger and bigger intelligence communities to cope with the flow of "product".

At the same time, their actual ability to share common strategic goals and appreciations declined in almost direct proportion to the growth of traffic flow.

The societal and skill-set base for 21st Century warfare technologies: The social patterns, wealth, and technology of the second half of the 20th Century saw a transformation in how individuals and societies functioned. There was a growing specialization of skill-sets across a broader and often novel range of technologies. As a result, narrow specialization was required to cope with complex fields of technology, and educational processes needed to adapt to accommodate this.

Significantly, the educational base which had guaranteed the technological and social progress of Western societies in the 18th and 19th centuries and well into the 20th Century had, by the 1990s (and perhaps earlier), been abandoned.

Firstly, education which strengthened knowledge of history, geography, literature, and the evolution of wisdom was abandoned or distorted to meet short-term political agendas;

Secondly, skills acquisition to enable the work-forces of Western societies to be employed in emerging market and technology sectors meant increasing specialization of technological education. This, coupled with the reduction in the type of education which would lead to contextual awareness, contributed to a rise in strategic, historical ignorance, and contributed to the xenophobia or distrust of other societies by the early 2000s.

Even as short-term education commitment to ensure employment in stove-piped industries contributed to a "re-serfing" of societies, it was nonetheless insufficient to enable Western societies to compete adequately with emerging societies. Nonetheless, most Western, urban societies doubled down on so-called

STEM education — science, technology, engineering, and mathematics — while still either neglecting or radicalizing *contextual* studies, particularly the literacy which leads to self-learning. Indeed, to wisdom.

It begs the question as to whether wisdom can be acquired in the world which we have created: a world which is a vacuum of pure science or a singular devotion to "hard" studies. The contextual perspective has been lost.

Lacking completely was an understanding of *strategic financial maneuver*, and this became increasingly evident as the economic crisis of 2020 emerged. In reality, recovery from the economic carnage inflicted globally by the 2020 COVID-19 crisis would depend on a mix of political, economic, financial, and industrial skills at an order of magnitude never before seen. It would be addressed not just by advanced *technology*, but by entrepreneurial behavior.

Thus, while some material progress could be made in the West's capabilities, there was no comprehensible context to it: no direction. With it, too, came the implicit rejection of those with agricultural skills, and therefore the rejection of non-urban contextual factors.

The solutions included a renewed balance between the rural ability to sustain food production (and the vital logistics of food delivery) in a time of crisis with the urban ability to deliver financial mechanisms and credible instruments so that the production and delivery of food would remain feasible.

In *UnCivilization: Urban Geopolitics in a Time of Chaos*, in 2012, I highlighted the disenfranchisement of individuals or societies from their roots, their soil. Urbanization creates this schism between traditional and "modern" society. We may even see that the "war of *terroir*" actually creates terror and terrorism, as we see people clinging to their traditions — the *terroir* links of soil and geography to diet, culture, and beliefs, and therefore identity — as their world crumbles.[70]

That study further highlighted the emergence of an "urban *terroir*": a geographical frame of reference which guides the logic development of urban populations. We are all guided by our environment and experience, our sense of *terroir*[71], whether we are conscious of it or not.

Given the profound differences between urban and rural skill-sets and that differing sense of *terroir*, it was unsurprising that the issue of the "boundaries of the state" once again became critical in the 21st Century. The nation-state is a geopolitical construct, but, in a world dominated by urban societies, which societies and which geography should dominate? In other words, does the "state" become re-defined around the urban agglomerations? This has been a question which has arisen cyclically through history, and ultimately, at each cycle, the city-states succumb to the need of the broader definition of the nation-state, to include the

70 *UnCivilization*, op cit.
71 In its strictest sense, *terroir* is defined as the set of environmental factors which affect a crop's phenotype, including unique environmental contexts, farming practices, and a crop-specific growth habitat. Clearly, it has a cross-species application to mammalian life.

rural geography which provides the food, water, resources, and buffer to protect society.

By 2020, however, the shifting dynamic caused by core population declines in many countries and rapid urbanization had, with technology, caused such a dislocation of historical hierarchies that there was a growing trust deficit between societies and the instruments of governance. Not only was there a polarization of urban and regional societies; and rich and poor; but there was a polarization between governed and governors. Democracy in Western societies was clearly brittle and fracturing, resulting in a fundamental sense of hostility in and between societies.

Thus was the "war" total and pervasive, filled with a deepening lack of contextual understanding, and — in the absence of understanding — fear.

Masse und Macht

Crowds and Power: The Song of the Psychological Warrior.
With thanks to Elias Canetti for the title.

༄ GIVE ME PARCHMENT,
Give me pen;
Give me dreams,
I'll give you men.

Give me nations,
Give me peoples;
I'll give you hist'ry,
Hamlet and steeples.

Give me whirlwinds,
Give me schemes;
Give me the chance,
I'll make the dreams.

Give me masses,
Mindless and cruel;
I'll give you power
To seize and to rule.

Give me slogans,
Pack the square;
I'll promise each voice
Will fill the air.

Give me flags,
Dividing the storm;
I'll give you armies
To shape and to form.

Give me streams
From harmless clouds;
I'll give you the roar
Of the ocean crowds.

Give me the tinder
Of a parched mankind;
I'll set the blaze
Of the masses' mind.

Sounds and symbols
Mark my field:
Omnipotent sword
To flail and wield.

For I am the man
Who will play on the
mind
Of the unthinking masses
To 'slave and bind.

Gregory Copley
— Washington DC, August 20, 1983

XI

Information Dominance in a Total War World

Indirect tactics, efficiently applied, are inexhaustible as Heaven and Earth, unending as the flow of rivers and streams.

— Sun-tzu, The Art of War

War, like revolution, is founded upon intimidation.

— Soviet Minister of War Leon Trotsky

INFORMATION DOMINANCE — ID — became the over-arching strategic operational realm of the 21st Century. Technology is absolutely secondary to this.

Technology may help to *facilitate* some ID applications, but the driving force for ID and its parent, grand strategy, is human.

ID is particularly significant because it embraces a range of civil and military capabilities related to the sole purpose of power: the imposition of will on opposing *and* supportive societies.

It is far more than just information warfare (IW) or "media warfare".

This is significant, particularly given the reality that by 2020 no major power had given formal shape to the creation of an overarching authority to bring together the prosecution of the security of a nation-state in an age of amorphous warfare.

The opportunistic use of the COVID-19 crisis of 2019-20 as a vehicle for ID operations was particularly significant, employing offensive and defensive ID and political warfare to achieve overarching strategic outcomes. We discussed that in an earlier chapter. But it merely highlighted the fact that fear is the most powerful psychological motivational force, with its ability to be operationalized to achieve specific pressures on government.

Meanwhile, Russia's decision to assign responsibility in 2020 to the Russian General Staff for a "whole of government" approach to national security was based on Moscow's view that non-military actions comprised 80 percent of the character of contemporary conflict.

The reality is that the General Staff, while it may be the best tool available to Moscow to handle the technical complexity of such operations, may not have the ideal operational *culture* to see the task in grand strategic terms.

ID, which has traditionally not been understood as a comprehensive framework for a range of capabilities, had fallen into the category of "dark arts". This was largely because much of it is in the "black", or deniable realm; its targeting and leadership is of necessity discreet. It has its strategic and its tactical aspects, and it is more than merely psychological strategy, psychological warfare and propaganda, information warfare, and so on.

It must embrace *all* perceptional and informational aspects of strategic and tactical operations, *and also* the electronic control of data and weapon command functions, up to and including the hardening or denial of the means of transmitting and receiving all such messaging.

So, from a technical perspective, information dominance — an imperfect name for the over-arching doctrine — embraces cyber warfare, communications, electronic warfare (EW) and electronic countermeasures (ECM), imagery, AI-driven tactical decision-making and systems operational controls, and much more. Intelligence itself is part of the information spectrum, and therefore forms part of the framework.

Clearly, many of these areas of operations have specialist departments and expertise built over generations. This would embrace, for example (in the US parlance), the military's J6 and J2 joint departments: cyber, joint information environment, information technology, etc.; and joint staff intelligence functions. Today, in military and joint operations command, there are designated slots for the management of the "information environment" and the conduct of information warfare, functioning mostly quite separately from, for example, cyber, communications and signals security, or electronic control of systems such as aircraft, vessels, vehicles, and so on.

The key is that these vital non-kinetic functions

work most effectively when seen as part of an integrated offensive and defensive capability within 21st Century amorphous warfare. And this clearly does not even touch on the psychological warfare aspects of ID.

So is "information dominance", when viewed within the context of "total war" an exemplar of "soft power"? Or is it "weaponized soft power", or merely covert strategic warfare without the need to categorize it as soft or hard? Specifically, it is *integral.*

The Communist Party of China's methodological approach in the current (as at 2020) amorphous war against the US has also been sometimes summarized as "BGY", meaning "Blue, Gold and Yellow". Blue in general represents Internet and media control; Gold represents money and bribery used to buy influence; Yellow represents the use of honey traps to compromise espionage targets. It's all, in a sense, ID.

Diplomacy falls within the information and communications spectrum, but it would be difficult to categorize it even as "soft power" unless and until it is weaponized as part of the arsenal of tools in the (usually) "white" spectrum, and occasionally in the "grey" spectrum.[72] So diplomacy, if it is to play a substantial and meaningful rôle in information dominance doctrine, as part of a national grand strategy, must be there to project and enforce the prestige and will of hard power and other options of suasion in the military, po-

---

72 In psychological warfare or intelligence operations, the fundamental categories are "white", being totally open and attributable to the originating body; "grey", being assumed to be linked to the originating body, but with plausible ambiguity; and "black", being totally covert and deniable (by the originating body), with the prospect of the actions being false-flagged to be attributed to a third party.

litical, economic, and related realms.

Track II diplomacy — or "proxy diplomacy" — also deserves doctrinal development in terms of how it can be used and managed. Track II diplomacy usually falls within the "grey" operational spectrum, but it can be extended further into the "grey to black" spectrum — Track II.5 or Track III — requiring plausible deniability.

Formal state actors such as foreign ministries are often as reluctant to employ Track II-series diplomatic efforts as defense ministries are to employ proxy or mercenary deniable kinetic options. But the reality is that the conveyance of messaging must be developed around achieving the greatest receptivity in target minds.

Once again, to heed Sun-tzu, it is about understanding self and adversary; not just one or the other. And in 21st Century horizontal communications, the irony is that the social logic remains built around the assumption that our own larger society has views identical to our own, as individuals, and that the target society also has views or priorities which mirror our own.

The more electronic-only the communication, the more difficult it is to comprehend the nature of our adversaries, our friends, and our operating context.

The Strategic Importance of Self-Deception

NOTHING COULD BE AS STRATEGICALLY valuable in conflict than that the adversary should deceive himself. Self-deception is the path to defeat.

To win victory through skill and effort is a less efficient path to success. To receive victory through the failure of others is to attain success without damage and cost to oneself.

To accept that we are prone to self-deception is the first step in achieving the humility necessary to exploit the characteristic in our competitors and to minimize it in ourselves. The Lord Buddha said: "Your greatest weapon is your enemy's mind." The objective is to avoid becoming one's own enemy.

Four major clouds of self-deception constrained the players of the early 21st Century.

The first cloud of self-deception was that those in control of the Communist Party of China (CPC) appeared to believe their own propaganda which said that the rise of their power was inevitable, as was the decline of the United States.

Even recent history showed (as if all of history did not show) with the collapse of "the inevitable triumph of Soviet communism" that nothing is inevitable, and certainly nothing which is engineered on a reliance of a transformation of human society. The value of promulgating "the inevitability myth" is clear when target audiences (at home and abroad) believe it; but it is fatal if those who administer the propaganda swallow it.

Having said that, there was sound evidence, by 2020, that the PRC leadership itself was critically aware that it faced substantial challenges to the unchecked rise of its power. Notwithstanding that, however, was the perception that Pres. Xi Jinping of the PRC may not have grasped the depth and scope of his target audiences in the West (not just the US), other than his recognition by early 2017 that US Pres. Donald Trump himself represented a major disruptor to PRC plans.

The second cloud of self-deception was that almost half the population of the United States believed that the other half of the US population was either "the enemy" or insufficiently sophisticated to comprehend its own best interests, and that, in fact, the concept of the US as a sovereign nation-state was the enemy of the inhabitants of the major cities.

The function of deceiving oneself that other peoples or groups are somehow less than human (a process called pseudospeciation: the belief that others are of a species which do not deserve consideration as humans) is part of the trait which under-estimates opponents. The rabid belief, which began just before the 2016 US Presidential election that the eventual winner, Donald Trump, and his supporters were less than human ("deplorables"), led to the attempt to remove him from office before he even began serving in it.

This form of self-deception severely weakened the United States to the point where, for example, the CPC in Beijing could be forgiven for thinking that its rise *would* or could be "inevitable".

The third cloud of self-deception was the Western belief that the Russian Federation was still the Union of Soviet Socialist Republics (USSR) under the Communist Party of the Soviet Union. Russia today is led by nationalists; the Soviets were communist and globalist. Throughout the Cold War, this writer maintained an insistence that the Soviets should not be referred to as "Russians". The Soviets (many of whom *were* Russian, although, for example, Stalin and Khrushchev were not) were the enemy of the Russian nationalists who are now in power.

Conflating Russia with the USSR, and insisting that it remained the enemy of the West after the Cold War, created a self-fulfilling prophecy. Russia was again forced to become, in some ways, the enemy of the West, and was forced into the arms of the PRC. Significantly, to achieve an end to the Cold War, the successful discreet task of the West was to develop and exploit the "Sino-Soviet rift", which was why US Pres. Richard Nixon went to Beijing and met with then-PRC leader Mao Zedong.

The fourth cloud of self-deception was that "climate change" could be impacted by taxation and the redistribution of wealth. The deliberate attempts to equate environmental damage caused by humans with the *many* processes which affect *how* climate changes foster belief-driven xenophobia, significantly affecting economies.

Climate change of far greater significance has occurred routinely through human and pre-human history. Changing climate in the past 10,000 years has swallowed entire and extensive human settlements; it may do so again. Can we tax our way out of that? Or should we take a longer-term and more nuanced view of how we interact with nature?

All of these "self-deceptions", which have major strategic consequences, arise from the reality that we actually moved in the 20th Century away from the scientific age; the age of empirical knowledge-building. We moved back to an age of beliefs and superstitions, which lead only to "political correctness" on a scale so vast that the Salem witch trials of the US seem but an iconic reflection. And yet we saw the Salem witch trials being re-enacted with the attempted impeachment of the US President in 2019.

It became significant through 2019 — and dramatically reinforced in 2020 — that the politics of climate change became relegated largely to history by societies around the world. To be sure, political groups which had wielded the "climate change" agenda effectively before the 2020 crisis, attempted to raise it again, but the social response was substantially diminished.

I wrote in *UnCivilization: Urban Geopolitics in a Time of Chaos* (in 2012) how we had maligned the beautiful little mammals, the lemmings, for apparently committing mass suicide in some belief-driven action. But nature tells us that this was never so: the lemmings carefully manage their reproduction to ensure compatibility with nature.

Humans do not.

We ignore our strategic interests to favor short-term gratification.

"[T]he only thing we have to fear is fear itself — nameless, unreasoning, unjustified terror which paralyzes needed efforts to convert retreat into advance."

— Inaugural address of US Pres. Franklin D. Roosevelt, March 4, 1933.

"I would not spend another such
* night*
Though 'twere to buy a world
* of happy days —*
So full of dismal terror was
* the time!"*

— Clarence, in Shakespeare's *Richard the Third*

XII

Fear

FEAR IS THE MOST POWERFUL MASS SOCIAL force. It is capable of driving national and strategic outcomes, overturning entrenched positions in the historical blink of an eye.

The 2020 COVID-19 fears were a signal.

Mass fear is like a virus, often burning itself out rapidly, but after immense effect. That is the impact of irrational, exaggerated fear.

More rational fear — such as that in the United States (and other areas affected by the Great Depression of 1929-1940), with the real fear of hunger and want, which was the subject of US Pres. Franklin D. Roosevelt's 1933 "nothing to fear but fear itself" speech — is slower burning and filled more with growing despair and paralysis than irrational fear.

But so appealing is the force of fear that it is often weaponized with great effect, with real danger to those who incite it as well as to targets of it. When fear is not weaponized in a virulent sense, it is politicized. As a weaponized malignancy, fear is often only marginally more explosive and unpredictable in its contagion than the release of expectations in a society suddenly freed from suppression.[73]

But there are a range of "fears" which exhibit, or present themselves, in individual as well as in mass human societies. They can be immobilizing/paralyzing, or inciting, in varying degrees.

Fear, of course, regardless of its possibly physical origins in some cases, is a phenomenon of the psychological arena, and is therefore something to be studied, managed, and utilized by psychological strategists as part of an overarching information dominance (ID) environment. It was captured, or parodied, as a tactical or localized political force in the 2015 US movie, *Our Brand is Crisis,* featuring two (fictionalized) US political consultants advising rival Bolivian presidential candidates in the 2002 election.[74]

Recognizing the type of fear we face at any given time as Type 1 (viral and irrational) or Type 2 (more rational and slower-burning) is critical to how the manipulation or containment of the contagion can be handled. With more rational emotions, more rational and practical solutions can apply. With irrational, viral panic, all forms of suggestion — rather than practical solutions — are applicable, but the "suggestability" may be as unstable as the disease itself.

The force multiplier of fear is, of course, electronics. Fear pandemics of the 21st Century thus know no social distancing. They plunge into the darkness of every

73 See, Copley, Gregory R.: "Perception is Nine-Tenths of the Law: The Race For Perception Dominance", in *Defense & Foreign Affairs Special Analysis,* July 31, 2009. Also in *Defense & Foreign Affairs* **Strategic Policy,** 7/2009.
74 The film was based on a 2005 US documentary film of the same name, by Rachel Boynton.

heart at the flick of a switch.

Good strategic generalship lies in comprehending the psychological or psycho-physical terrain as clearly and swiftly as the physical terrain or context is understood.

It gets back, however, to the fundamental premise that all human behavior is psychologically driven, even when some physical conditions may stimulate certain psychological behavior. And *all* strategic outcomes — physical, political, economic, and otherwise — are psychologically driven.[75]

"Crisis" is one organizational or social manifestation of fear. Of course, crises can arise from a set of logical challenges to the *status quo* which do not necessarily depend on mass, visceral fear. But fear-borne crisis can be sudden, overwhelming, and seemingly irrational. It is a force which spreads virally, and needs to be managed by special skills and understanding.

The geographic spread of such mass, visceral fear is clearly enhanced by viral communications, which are now electronic in nature to a greater degree than at any time since the introduction of electrified societies in

75 Particular importance should be attached to the origins and outcome of the 1990-2000 war for the break-up of Yugoslavia and the integral, and particular, war against Serbia which evolved in several phases. What was a critical underpinning were the preceding decades of the 20th Century which led to the formation of Yugoslavia, particularly after World War I, and then the successful overthrow of Serbian leadership of Yugoslavia by Croatian communist Josip Broz (Tito) in 1945, coupled with the advance work of the Croation *Ustaše* movement in World War II. By re-defining "national" boundaries within Yugoslavia, the inevitable break-up of Yugoslavia in 1990 meant a return to, and rise of, paranoia as to the security of many national groupings of the Federation. This was in the early era of global communications, but still sufficient to see information dominance practices led by Croatian, Albanian, and Bosnian Muslim groups drive a worldwide suppression of Serbs and Serbia. This, however, was relatively "containable", geographically, in that the viral outbreak of fears for survival could be contained within the Balkans.

the early 1900s. So globalized fear pandemics are more likely to be a phenomenon of the 21st Century type of total war scenario than at any time in history.

Most such viral fear-bursts will be of relatively short duration, and most will be geographically constrained. Those which have global spread are likely to be based around a naturally-occurring or man-made threat to health, or around a force-multiplied economic panic, or because of a ubiquitous science (nuclear warfare, for example).

Hillary Clinton, when she was US Secretary of State in March 2009, told an audience in Brussels: "Never waste a good crisis."

Crisis exploitation, then, is opportunistic and, by definition, volatile and unpredictable. Handling must be partly reactive, and success is determined by how much control can be injected into it. Engineered crises and deliberately instigated fear can be more targeted and controlled. And in this regard, terrorism is one of the tools for the creation of irrational fear.

The way in which the 2008 global recession (called the "Global Financial Crisis" by some) occurred had the hallmarks of a "rational fear" crisis. It had real political-economic underpinnings, but once despair was transmitted to the marketplace, the economic impact struck global wealth indices. But that crisis was more rational in its fear-base and responded gradually to (often, frankly irrational) financial stimuli as a calmative.

It should have served, however, as a primer to understanding the perfect strategic crisis, with multiple dimensions in the global strategic arena, which emerged in late 2019 with the COVID-19 epidemic, which created an irrational fear pandemic by March 2020. [Again, there were precedents to consider in the social fear spread, such as the initial global contagion of HIV-AIDS in the 1970s, which became highly-politicized with social-political outcomes still reverberating in the 2020s. And the ebola viral hemorrhagic fever outbreaks in the 2000s (including the late 2018 occurrence), which had social, economic, and political consequences extending far beyond the physical disease.]

COVID-19, however, had indeed become, by March 2020, a crisis which was there to be wielded, or taken up, as the first example of a truly strategic information dominance weapon capable of determining outcomes on a global scale. It became a critical pivot or trigger in the existential competition between the People's Republic of China and the United States of America. Moreover, it was an ID campaign in which the PRC could engage discreetly its key ally: the domestic US opposition to US Pres. Donald Trump.

Strategically, the crisis was less about the fairly prosaic progression of the healthcare implications of the coronavirus disease, and more about which government and social group could best exploit fear (to the point of mass hysteria in many countries) to drive new opportunities.

After all, for example, there had been no worldwide social and economic panic when the (H1N1)pdm09 virus infection reached pandemic proportions in 2009-10.[76] That episode alone led to a contagion of between 43.3-million and 89.3-million people in the United States alone, with a reported 274,304 hospitalizations, and 12,469 recorded deaths (estimates ranged from 8,868 to 18,306 deaths) in the US alone. The US Centers for Disease Control (CDC) estimated that between 151,700 and 575,400 people worldwide died from that virus during its first year.[77]

The other notable outbreak of a coronavirus was Severe Acute Respiratory Syndrome (SARS-CoV), which first broke out in Asia in February 2003, spreading to 29 countries, where 8,096 people were infected and 774 of them died; it had been contained by July 2003.

So why did COVID-19 erupt so violently as the cause of a global fear pandemic?

Part of it was due to the changed psychological condition of the social framework. But, on top of that, came the issue of who seeks to ensure that the crisis "did not go to waste". *Cui bono* (who benefits) from the spread of the panic?

Three main groups *sought* to gain — or were *compelled to* seek to gain — from the outcome of the crisis:

> ➤ PRC Pres. Xi Jinping and the Communist Party of China (CPC), although this is not necessarily a solidified *bloc;*

76 See, Pickford, Andrew: "Dealing with Influenza Pandemics", in *Defense & Foreign Affairs* **Strategic Policy**, 8/2009. It appeared on August 14, 2009, in *Defense & Foreign Affairs Special Analysis* as "Perception Management and Dealing with Influenza Pandemics in Western Democracies".

77 "The 2009 H1N1 Pandemic: Summary Highlights, April 2009-April 2010", published by the US Centers for Disease Control and Prevention. Updated as of June 16, 2010.

➤ US Pres. Donald Trump; and
➤ Anti-Trump US globalist-left opposition groupings, including much of the Democratic Party.

The Xi Perspective

FOR THE CPC, THE GLOBAL pandemic of COVID-19
fear came with two key components:

➤ *Firstly*, on the negative or defensive side, the crisis
invoked the necessity for the CPC to stop the damage to the PRC caused by (a) the loss of production
in domestic factories, (b) the loss of foreign direct
investment, (c) the loss of prestige which further
damaged the PRC strategic standing, including
the loss of credibility for its currency and economic statistics, and (d) capital flight from the
PRC.

This led the CPC into various aspects of denial (self-
denial, and denial to a wider audience, depending on
particular circumstances), and to physical countermeasures, such as forcing the continuation, where it
could, of ongoing physical links with the outside trading world, and the appearance of "normalcy" so that
prestige and influence would not deteriorate further.

At the same time, however, PRC officials became increasingly bellicose in their threats to societies which
Beijing determined had begun to waver in their sub-
mission to the PRC or to its Belt & Road Initiative
(BRI) ideology. This behavior revealed the level of
concern with which the CPC leadership viewed the
threat implied by the COVID-19 crisis, coming as it

did on the heels of a PRC economic slowdown which can be traced at least to 2008.[78]

> *Secondly*, on the offensive side, the crisis became an opportunity for the CPC to avoid domestic blame for the PRC's economic collapse, which had been underway for several years even without the COVID-19 crisis; and to possibly drive the direction of the US elections of November 3, 2020, in order to eject incumbent Pres. Donald Trump from the Presidency and his Republican Party from power in the Congress.

It is worth identifying the reality that there were, by early 2020, two main obstacles to the PRC's rise to strategic global pre-eminence: the behavior and policies of the CPC itself; and the continuation in office of US Pres. Donald Trump, who had reversed some three decades of US presidencies which had actually enabled (through benign neglect or active cooperation) the growth of PRC strategic power.

It was unlikely that the CPC would address its challenge by significantly altering its own behavior.[79] The most obvious course of action was to utilize the crisis — to turn it — to ensure that Pres. Trump did not gain

---

78 See, for example: "Global Event: Managing the PRC Implosion", in *Defense & Foreign Affairs Special Analysis*, February 20, 2020, and in *Defense & Foreign Affairs Strategic Policy*, 2/2020. Also: "Beijing, Increasingly Desperate, Continues Assault on Eswatini", in *Defense & Foreign Affairs Special Analysis*, March 3, 2020, and in *Defense & Foreign Affairs Strategic Policy*, 3/2020. And "State of the World: Parlous, Transforming, Yet in Some Ways Stabilizing, Optimistic", in *Defense & Foreign Affairs Special Analysis*, February 4, 2020; also in *Defense & Foreign Affairs Strategic Policy*, 2/2020.

79 See: "China's Communist Party Plans its COVID-19 Recovery", in *Defense & Foreign Affairs Special Analysis*, March 10, 2020, and in *Defense & Foreign Affairs Strategic Policy*, 3/2020.

a second term in office at the November 3, 2020, US elections; nor that his Republican Party should gain dominance in the Congress.

Pres. Xi began quickly to utilize the PRC's front organizations and political links to ensure a number of immediate responses to the crisis.

Of primary concern was to project an image of absolute control by the Government to the crisis, by seeming to isolate the epicenter, Wuhan, but then moving to get the economy geared up again as quickly as possible.

The PRC put immense pressure on a number of its BRI-link countries — particularly Iran, Thailand, Pakistan, South Africa, and Ethiopia — to maintain unbroken air links to ensure that PRC citizens could move freely around the world. For the most part, however, the Xi Government was, despite heavy-handed and bellicose statements by PRC ambassadors, unable to stop many of its major trading partners from quarantining the PRC.

The resultant trade isolation (fewer raw materials in; no goods out) pushed the PRC economy into its worst drop in decades. Even in the third quarter of 2019, official PRC statistics showed a slowed rate of growth to the lowest level since 1992. In fact, the PRC "growth" was already then, in real terms, in negative territory. So, apart from the stimulus funding of the PRC economy, the Xi Government had to project "statistics" in such a way as to show that its containment of the virus had succeeded and that it could, by early March 2020, resume more-or-less normal economic activities.

In this process, too, it had to move perceptions away from the reality that this was a "Chinese problem", and make it seem that it was a global issue in which the PRC was just one of the victims. And, moreover, that the crisis had originated in a US "biological weapons laboratory". This was in response to early speculation in the US media that the virus had somehow slipped from a PRC Government facility, the Wuhan Institute of Virology, a level four biosafety laboratory.

The reality is that — whether the virus had been identified in a laboratory setting or not — the COVID-19 virus and others like it were not good candidates for *normal applications* of biological warfare, given that they are difficult to control, causing indiscriminate damage to all.

The critical objectives for Pres. Xi, then, were to avoid blame for having allowed the virus to take hold; to get the PRC economy working again immediately; to use a targeted information dominance campaign on the handling of the pandemic to specifically punish the US President; and to restore order and loyalty in the BRI chain nations, while maintaining the position that the PRC remained a rising power.

Beijing would attempt to ensure that the residual impression from the crisis would be that it was the US which mismanaged the event; that the PRC was the power which handled it responsibly; and that Trump was gone. Under that outcome, regardless of the inherent weakness in the PRC economy, Beijing would emerge strategically more powerful from the crisis.

The Trump Perspective

FOR PRES. TRUMP AND HIS Government, the COVID-19 crisis clearly presented an opportunity to push the PRC economy into a possibly irretrievable decline, thereby ending the chance of long-term global strategic competition to the US from the CPC.

The question was whether there was a necessity for the US to intervene to accelerate the crisis, or whether the PRC was already in an economic decline which would cause it to end its threat to the US without intervention. Would deliberate US intervention to exacerbate the COVID-19 crisis produce uncontrollable consequences?

Were there precipitate actions which the US took which did, indeed, lead to escalation from a normal healthcare incident to the creation of the real strategic viral pandemic, fear?

Significantly, given that the positive state of the US economy going into 2020 was the best factor working for Mr Trump's re-election, it was, in fact, *not* desirable to help stimulate a PRC economic decline in 2020, the US election year. The global spread of economic decline which was likely to result from the PRC's dilemma was to be welcomed *in some respects* by the US, *but not in 2020.*

The US put the first flight into Wuhan, the epicenter of the COVID-19 contagion, to extract US citizens on January 28, 2020, less than two weeks after the US and the PRC had signed "phase one" of a trade deal to constrain the bilateral trade war which had been building for 18 months. The Trump White House indicated that it intended to move to a second phase in the trade agreement before the November 3, 2020, US elections.

The extraction from Wuhan of other foreign nationals began almost at the same time as the US extractions, but arguably the PRC Government could — and did — construe that this apparent evacuation of foreign nationals was coordinated by the US, and began the panic and the crisis which ensued.

Clearly, however, there was no way that the extraction of foreign nationals from Wuhan could have precipitated the spontaneous explosion of global social fears over a virus which was not as virulent as (H1N1) pdm09. In other words, the resultant fear pandemic was not logically predictable.

What became clear, however, was the progress since 2009 in the impact of social media and the rising (or returning) state of "group-think" or political correctness. This has already merited comment in the reality that, as public perceptions of fear or concern arise over economic or physical safety, so the flight toward identity security (political correctness) escalates almost exponentially.[80]

The US Domestic Opposition Perspective

FEW MEMBERS OF THE US Democratic Party wanted, in 2020, to see the People's Republic of China supplant the US as the dominant world power.

---

80 See, Copley, Gregory R.: *Sovereignty in the 21st Century and the Crisis for Identity, Cultures, Nation-States, and Civilizations.* Alexandria, Virginia, 2018: The Zahedi Center at the International Strategic Studies Association.

Most of the party's leadership agreed with their Republican Party counterparts that the PRC had been engaged in predatory activities hostile to the US, including intelligence and cyber operations, and the theft of US intellectual property (IP).

But, for many in the party, the Washington mantra dominated: the urgent overtakes the important. In other words, the party could do nothing unless it could regain control of the White House and the Senate. Therefore, for many, the primary obstacle was the incumbent in the White House, Pres. Trump. An expedient, arm's-length alliance with the CPC to take advantage of (and perhaps contribute to) a crisis to be rid of Trump was clearly acceptable to some.

Mrs Clinton, when she made her statement in Brussels, was drawing on what she had learned from her activist mentor, Saul Alinsky, who wrote *Rules for Radicals*, in which he noted: "In the arena of action, a threat or a crisis becomes almost a precondition to communication."[81] But Alinsky was hardly the first person to comprehend the opportunity which resides in crisis, even though he instilled it firmly in the operating methodology of Mrs Clinton.

Alinsky's articulation of the theory was consciously utilized to create crises in the Balkans, the Middle East ("the Arab Spring"), and the George Soros-funded "color revolutions". All of these attempts to create crises were based not just on fear, however, but on frustra-

---

81 Alinsky, Saul: *Rules for Radicals: A Practical Primer for Realistic Radicals.* New York, 1971: Random House.

tion, the cracking of façades to allow suddenly rising expectations, and the necessity for some external stimulus or sponsorship of these expectations.

Crises can be, and usually are, a form of proxy warfare, and the "color revolutions" and "Arab Spring" of the early 2010s were very much the products of events in which the care and feeding of the phenomena were in the hands of wealthy state and private sponsors. But crises born of spontaneous combustion and rapid social contagion, such as the global COVID-19 panic, are phenomena which require little "care and feeding" to gain their traction, but considerable skill to channel into directions desired by ID managers.

Mrs Clinton, a former Democratic Party US Presidential candidate and former First Lady, was well aware of the need to exploit any opening against her political rival, Pres. Trump. So were most of the Democratic Party leadership who had already spent three-plus years trying to overturn the November 2016 Presidential elections, to no avail.

The use of the COVID-19 crisis was a logical vehicle to seize.

A decline, or pause, in the vision of a Trump-delivered economic turnaround for US voters would serve well the cause of removing Mr Trump from office. Thus, the COVID-19 crisis was seized upon as evidence of Trump mismanagement.

Pro-Trump television personality Trish Regan, on Fox Business Network television, called the chorus of attacks by Democrats and the "liberal media" on Pres.

Trump a "coronavirus impeachment scam", referring to the failed 2019-20 Democratic Party attempt to impeach and try Pres. Trump — and remove him from office — for "abuse of power". She was not wrong.

Even *The New York Times* picked up and printed as fact claims by PRC-backed websites that the coronavirus was concocted in a US military laboratory, and was not, in fact, a PRC-origin problem. What was significant, however, was that the COVID-19 crisis was likely to peak before the November 3, 2020, elections. What had *not* peaked, however, was the extent of real damage being done to the US economy.

So this would be the residual perceptional issue on which to fight the election.

Conclusions

THE WORLD MAY HAVE REACHED a structural breakpoint with the COVID-19 crisis. It was unlikely that the same degree of reliance on the PRC as a manufacturing hub would remain in the aftermath of it.

The PRC would need more than a short-term financial stimulus to sustain economic and strategic momentum. To remain competitive with the US, it would need to revert to a similar economic model, which would include the post-Mao Zedong liberalization model of Deng Xiaoping (1978-92).

Pres. Xi was unlikely to accept that.

Moreover, even midway through the crisis, the PRC was struggling to sustain its prestige and influence. By March 2020, it had already abandoned the prestige pillars of its naval expansion program, its two proposed nuclear-powered super-carriers (very large aircraft carriers) which had been planned to be on a techno-logical and size level of their US counterparts.

That spelled the end of the planned military equiva-lence which the Communist Party of China and the People's Liberation Army envisaged with the United States. The boast of global hegemony by 2049 for the PRC was, for the moment, set aside.

Did Xi's new maoism merely start the Long March Backward?

That was not Xi's intention, of course: he had a broader march forward in mind with the declaration of the New Thirty Years War with the US. The irony was that Xi had a very real chance that his war to re-move Pres. Donald Trump in 2020 could succeed. However, in that event, would the subsequent decline of pressure on the PRC from Washington still com-pensate for the structural economic weakness of the PRC going forward?

XIII

Alliances and Trust in an Uncertain World

An ally has to be watched, just like an enemy.

— Soviet Minister of War Leon Trotsky

I T WAS INEVITABLE THERE would be a "trust deficit" in how nations interacted in the 21st Century.

The world transformed after the Cold War; the captains and kings had departed the battlefield, and the need for the "big alliances" had, for a time, faded.

An entire volume could be devoted to the study of the dysfunction of each legacy alliance, but let us deal here with only a few examples.

By 2020, not one major global power had the unqualified support of any of its alliance partners, rhetoric aside. Subordination or subservience was based solely on an accounting of the cost-benefit ratio. There were still times when a junior partner in an alliance would make unilateral sacrifices for an alliance leader, but only because the cost of refusal was too high.

Qiao Liang and Wang Xiangsui, writing in 1999 in *Unrestricted Warfare,* said that they believed that the "First Gulf War" (1990-91) ended the age of the big alliances. They may have been partially correct, at least for the then-foreseeable future. And that also applied to the Shanghai Cooperation Organization (SCO), begun in Shanghai on June 15, 2001, on the foundations of the 1996 Shanghai Five Group.

They noted: "[T]he age of fixed-form alliances … had begun with the signing of the military alliance between Germany and Austria-Hungary in 1879. Following the Cold War, the period in which alliances were formed on the basis of ideology faded away, while the approach in which alliances are built on interests rose to primacy."[82]

They believed that the coalition cobbled together by US Pres. George H. W. Bush to attack Iraq led to the appearance of the "overnight" alliance.

But there were — and are — always rationales for "enduring" alliances, based on deeply-rooted common identity, a connection possibly more important even than common interests, or common geographical features. This has applied, for example, to the common sense of identity of German-speaking peoples, or English-speaking peoples, Francophonie, and so on. This does not, however, preclude the rise of differences within those "common identity" alliances.

Whither the "world's most powerful alliance"?

THE UKUSA ACCORDS — the "Five Eyes" intelligence-sharing alliance of the United States, United Kingdom, Canada, Australia, and New Zealand — had become

82 *Unrestricted Warfare.* Op cit.

seen by the early 21st Century as the most influential or powerful strategic *bloc* in the world.

It represented the "Anglosphere", the major English-language grouping of Western states. It had transcended NATO. But "Five Eyes" had atrophied by the early 21st Century, and was no longer providing its members with the strategic cohesion, operational benefits, and shared values which marked its early years.

Gone was the common understanding on overarching questions on the global strategic architecture. The results would be evident if the alliance had been working well, and they were not. At least on deeper levels.

The failure to achieve commonly-agreed outcomes or express common purpose on areas of grand strategic importance was symptomatic of the reality that the alliance had become fixated on process, rather than outcomes. The achievement of a *relative* level of common security clearance levels meant that the flow of intelligence product between partners continued to grow, particularly as electronically-gathered or -processed intelligence began to be automated and fed into the pipeline. But flow represented mass, not useful finished intelligence.

As process dominated, outcome considerations reduced. It moved Five Eyes from a strategic alliance to, more or less, a tactical interaction.

I raised this at the Australia-Canada Economic Leadership Forum, in Melbourne, Australia, on February 13, 2020, in the bilateral Australia-Canada context:

The UKUSA Accords — "Five Eyes" — have commoditized the Australia-Canada intelligence exchange, and this has removed much of the value of the process. Traffic volume does not equate to quality intelligence or quality strategic analysis. What is lacking are exchanges of strategic appreciations between the leaderships of Canada and Australia. There is a need to establish a separate strategic intelligence link between the offices of the Prime Ministers, and senior intelligence community (IC) leaders, which convey analysis of strategic trends of common interest and importance to both countries. This may be expanded to others in the Five Eyes community, but could be started on an intimate basis between Canada and Australia.

I went on to note that while Australia-Canada economic relations were improving more rapidly than expected, and had the potential to grow exponentially, there was a need to re-evaluate strategic links because those strategic links were not being regarded as of primary importance by either government, but particularly by the Government of Canada.

The Canadian Government had not appeared to have yet awakened fully to the fact that its Indo-Pacific strategic considerations were now more profoundly urgent than — and of equal importance to — Canada's trans-Atlantic concerns. The January 8, 2020, loss of a significant number of Canadian citizens and residents aboard the Ukrainian International Airways Boeing 737, Flight 752, shot down by Iranian Air Defense Forces highlighted the reality that Canada's trans-Atlantic and its Indo-Pacific considerations had merged, half way around the globe from Ottawa.

Moreover, the Tehran incident also highlighted the

reality that the Canadian Government had placed the blame for the deaths on the shoulders of the United States — its Five Eyes partner — rather than the Iranian Government which shot down the aircraft in a mistaken response to a misperception of imminent US threat. The fact that the Canadian Government blamed the US for Iranian actions showed the ongoing level of slipping trust between the partners, just as did the US Administration's public condemnation of the United Kingdom's attempt to sustain a balance between its commitment to security solidarity with the US and its need to handle its relationships carefully with the People's Republic of China.

That was over the UK's attempt to keep the PRC's Huawei 5G communications technology outside the secure ring of policy-level communications while not forbidding Huawei from literally all sectors of the UK commercial communications community.

At a more mundane level, it was clear that the intelligence flow within Five Eyes, between Australia and New Zealand, were now less than fully effective, because of ideological differences between the Labour Party Prime Minister of New Zealand, Jacinda Ardern (also Minister for National Security and Intelligence), and the Australian Liberal-National Coalition Government of Prime Minister Scott Morrison. The result was that, for example, Prime Minister Ardern failed to heed the warnings from the Australian Intelligence Community of the prospect of a terrorist attack, which then occurred on March 15, 2019.[83]

It was not insignificant that there continued to exist significant distrust between the leftist/green New Zealand Government and the conservative US Trump Administration. But this cyclical distrust between Labour governments in New Zealand and the US (even some Democratic Party administrations) has consistently impacted the strategic relationship.

Even the Five Eyes relationship which the US had with New Zealand was, by 2020, opened to question by the fact that the current NZ Government had shown itself to be susceptible to pressures from the PRC, to an even greater extent than recent Australian governments, which had been under consistent pressures from Beijing.

Similarly, left-of-center Canadian Prime Minister Justin Trudeau had been reluctant to work with G20 partner Australia as long as conservative Prime Minister Scott Morrison was in office. This was despite the traditional Commonwealth military/wartime and cultural links, and the reality that Australian-Canadian trade and investment links had escalated consistently in recent years. These links were maintained by private sector initiatives and the traditional links between the two countries' bureaucracies. But the hallmark of the dysfunction within Five Eyes has been the Canadian failure to understand or trust the US, a phenomenon which reached new heights with the coincidence of the

83 See: "New Zealand Terrorist Attack Raises Serious Questions; Triggers Further Rift with Turkey", in *Defense & Foreign Affairs Special Analysis*, March 25, 2019.

Trudeau and Trump administrations.

In short, the UKUSA Accords had settled down into a commoditized processing of routine intelligence, even though the existence of the Accords implied an unprecedented level of trust and common fundamental interests among the five "Anglosphere" states and their sharing of a common language and British cultural base. And, indeed, there exists within the Alliance varying degrees of interdependency, usually expressed bilaterally between members and the US.

As a result, to varying degrees, the strategic commonality and interaction among members had atrophied. There were several milestones and catalysts for the polarizing of interests. One was the fact that three of the members shared a north Atlantic (NATO) orientation: the UK, Canada, and the US. The other was the UK's gradual slide into the European Community and then the European Union (and now the UK's exit from the EU). And the third was the failure, or tardiness, of the NATO component of Five Eyes to prioritize the challenge to them from the PRC.

Indeed, there was still a reluctance by Canada to see the PRC as a potential threat to its interests, although naked hostility by Beijing toward Canada at the end of May 2020 partly cured that. The Trudeau Government had, however, been impacted by the pro-Mao views of the Prime Minister's father, former Prime Minister (1968-84) Pierre Trudeau. Even at the Australia-Canada Economic Leadership Forum on February 13-14, 2020, there were Canadian references to the participation of a Canadian with Mao Zedong on the Long March (1934-35).

Australia and Canada share, as they have always done, a common interest in managing polar strategic environments. This would be of growing interest as, in particular, the People's Republic of China and the Russian Federation expanded their strategic needs to dominate the polar maritime and resource environments. Canberra and Ottawa share a need, then, for specific intelligence sharing and operational compatibility in dealing with these challenges to their sovereignty and spheres of influence issues.

Moreover, there was a need to share scientific intelligence and analysis on the prospects for changes in operating conditions in the polar regions. A watching brief needed to monitor the possibility, however remote and however this may differ from public political perceptions, that the current opening of Arctic sea routes, including the North-West Passage, may not necessarily enjoy a permanent status.

Australia and Canada have common interests and common values which needed to be extended to greater revived cooperation in defense matters. This consideration would also be extended to include the United Kingdom, which was, in 2020, reviving its Commonwealth linkages in the defense arena, and particularly related to the Indo-Pacific region.

Common and routine dialogues between Canada and Australia in the defense arena, from military appreciations of the strategic context to cooperation and special consideration to mutual defense procurement cooperation, needed to be substantially upgraded. This would logically occur on governmental and private sector levels, learning from the Australia-Canada Economic Leadership Forum.

The haphazard way in which the 2019 sale of retired Royal Australian Air Force F-18A/B fighters to the Royal Canadian Air Force was managed should have served as a wake-up call to the fact that Australia-Canada defense cooperation could be more effective than it had been. Certainly, the mutual acquisition by Australia and Canada of British *Type 26* frigates signaled a growing liaison, not just between those two countries, but with the UK.

There were, indeed, extensive Australia-Canada defense exchanges, but nothing which seemed to impact the Canadian refusal to accept a greater focus on Indo-Pacific issues, despite the reality that Canada's future depends to a growing degree on the Indo-Pacific.

But by 2020, it had become clear that the "world's most important strategic alliance" had become less than strategic in its liaison and cooperation. Ramping up the volume and commoditizing the exchange of intelligence had ceased to be the reflection of strategic policy commonality. The cautious creation of "Five Eyes Mk. II" would need to add a strategic layer of communications between members, and could probably only begin on a bilateral basis.

It may be that my proposal of a Canberra-Ottawa link could be preceded by new bilateral links between (separately) Canberra and Whitehall, and Ottawa and Whitehall. Many Canadians and Australians embraced the concept of bringing the UK into the emerging Comprehensive and Progressive Agreement for Trans-Pacific Partnership (CPTPP). The CPTPP does not include the US — the US Trump Administration withdrew the US from it in 2017 — which would begin a path toward greater UK, Canada, Australia, and New Zealand strategic-level cooperation.

In the meantime, Five Eyes had slipped into the realm of tactical process. Its members, if they wished to sustain the Alliance as something of real strategic value, would need to develop an overlay of common thinking, if that was still possible.

That was the essence on which a Western alliance remained feasible, given the essential fragmentation of purpose among most NATO members. But even the ancient principle of *casus fœderis* — when one ally must come to the aid of another in the event that it is attacked — had become vitiated by the late 20th Century within NATO as well as within, for example, the ANZUS (Australia-New Zealand-US) alliance.

So the firm resolve of most alliances by 2020 had slipped into the realm of "maybe" one party would come to the aid of another in a meaningful conflict. But the reality, in the world of amorphous warfare and undeclared but total war, was that the shaping of alliances themselves needed to become more nuanced.

Alliances in the post-2020 world needed, more than ever, the underpinning of common ideals.

XIV

Global Movement in a World at War

Population warfare meets the new age

CRISES ALWAYS SPUR PEOPLE TO MOVEMENT. But economic crises tend to be among the more gradual in incentivizing a tidal swell of population movement

Unless the economic descent is rapid and catastrophic, akin, in many ways, to the driving whip of invasion, civil war, or natural disaster.

We are also entering a new era of what can only be called Population Warfare: the *manipulation* of the movement or shaping of entire communities to create strategic outcomes. I am calling it "a new era" to distinguish it from the variety of ways in which population warfare has been used throughout history.

Population movement, and therefore population warfare, is now more susceptible to suggestion on a large and organized scale than ever before. The Internet and social media, as well as globalized broadcasting, compound the ability to achieve mass suggestion and create the drivers of viral fear.

The difference in population impact at the beginning of two essentially similar global health phenomena — the 2009-10 (H1N1)pdm09 virus and the 2019-20 COVID-19 virus — showed how much the impact of mass, instant communication had transformed in just one decade of the 21st Century.

That the H1N1 epidemic of 2009-10 was extremely serious as a global-scale epidemic was not in doubt, as we discussed in Chapter XII ("Fear"). Yet there was no global panic; financial markets did not convulse; neither did the great economies of the world tremble nor did lesser societies collapse. To some extent, of course, the economies of the world were still numb from absorbing the financial crisis of 2007-08, described as the worst financial disaster since the Great Depression of the 1930s.

That the COVID-19 virus, a decade later, seemed to have a higher mortality rate than the H1N1 variant of 2009-10 was absolutely unknown — and unable to be predicted — when the later virus first came to widespread attention in early 2020. And yet the second disaster, widely expected to be of a lower contagion level than the first, created *immediate* global panic and such a draconian response that the global economy went directly into convulsions.

One major difference was the reality that contagion rates of fear through electronic communication are (and specifically *were* on this occasion) more virulent than through direct human communication. The other great variable was that the COVID-19 crisis began in Central China at a time (discussed below) that the Chinese population was traveling abroad in unprecedented numbers and foreigners were traveling in to the virus epicenter in greater numbers than ever before. This physical link, facilitated by the exponential growth in airline connections, clearly was a factor in the physical linkage.

But the real pandemic, and the real population driver, of the COVID-19 crisis of 2020 was the *fear* pandemic. The question became, assuming it was a crisis of accidental origin, how it could be steered by the conscious action of governments, who would, or could act in both a defensive and offensive capacity using the large-scale population momentum.

There was no question but that the 2020 event would put a temporary hold on the mass physical movement of populations. However, the economic wasteland of the post-2020 period, globally, was another matter altogether. Even without the physical movement of populations in the momentous year of 2020, the *motivation* of large population *blocs* was at stake.

In many areas, the question became: would they lie dormant or would they revolt? In others, it became: how could their voting in elections be influenced?

The outcomes would be profoundly strategic in these and other cases.

Populations rarely migrate *en masse*, and of their own accord, in times of plenty, security, and happiness. But, facing the specters of starvation and despair, people first look back nostalgically at the lives their forebears had built. Then, in the present, see that their history of survival has evaporated. And gradually and reluctantly look to the future and to a place where survival may be assured.

Security crises, on the other hand, spur *immediate* response as people flee imminent danger. In those circumstances, however, migration is often difficult, impeded by conflict and danger, as during the wars in Yugoslavia as it broke apart after 1990. Sometimes the crisis drives forward on a broad front, pushing civilian populations before it. As in the Syrian civil war of the 2010s.

And those displaced populations, unable to return to their homes, find uneasy refuge where they can. Victims of the Syrian war in the 2010s, and fighting in Iraq and Afghanistan, and fleeing internal issues in Eritrea, then found themselves in limbo — mostly in Turkey — and were pushed by fortune or by political design on to further destinations. Significantly, those refugees in Jordan and Lebanon found themselves less pressured to move on.

It is important to see where populations are merely the collateral damage of wars undertaken for other purposes, and where the goal of a government may be to specifically use a population group as a tool of warfare, or as a specific target of warfare. And whether population warfare has been engineered for any of a range of strategic outcomes.

Stefan Possony's treatise on *umvolkung*, or ethnomorphosis, discussed in Chapter III, looked at the specific strategies of the Communist Party of the Soviet Union (CPSU) and the Communist Party of China (CPC) in the 20th Century, and these strategies particularly formed aspects of population warfare. So, too, do the conscious policies of genocide undertaken by the USSR, the PRC, Germany, Croatia, Cambodia, and the Ethiopian *Dergue* in the 20th Century.

We saw the conscious mobilization of the Western media in the 1990s to galvanize hostility toward the Serbian people during the war which broke up Yugoslavia. That it was a false narrative which motivated political action against Serbia by most Western governments and societies in the 1990s was to become lost in the retrospective historical analysis. But it was merely a refocusing of the Croatian and Islamist genocidal actions which had flourished through deliberate government policies against Serbs (largely by the briefly-independent *Ustaše* Croatian state of 1941-44).

But in the 1990s, the population warfare strategies, heavily engaging dehumanizing pseudospeciation of the Serbs, had the viral force multiplier of the print and electronic media. The strategic impact, arguably, would have been even more rapid and pervasive two or three decades later as the Internet and social media became the main instrument of mass population guidance.

We tend to view *umvolkung* and genocide as merely abhorrent and aberrant crimes against humanity, forgetting that they are often deliberate and effective tools for the gaining and consolidation of power over a domestic or conquered society.

It was only in the 20th Century, however, that we created names for these phenomena, even before we fully understood — and it is probable that we still do not understand even now — their deliberate use as a tool of warfare and power.

The 21st Century had already seen the conscious and strategic use of population warfare techniques by Turkey and India, within the first two decades of the century, and by Croatia in the 1940s and 1990s.

Not all great population phenomena are the result, of course, of human engineering. Natural disasters, too, result in often involuntary, or reluctant, rapid movements of peoples, but these tend to be localized and short-term, and more-or-less manageable because of that.

Health pandemics cause panic, and the more widespread they and the panic are, the more frenzied the search for safety, but that — because of the intensity of pandemics — usually means a search for "safety in place".

What the world witnessed in 2020 was a global health phenomenon which triggered an exponentially larger fear pandemic, followed rapidly by an economic crisis, and then a security crisis. It was the exaggeration of the economic crisis in the wake of the 2020 health epidemic which would produce dramatic political and security motivations for people to uproot themselves in search of survival.

We do not know the drivers behind the piecemeal,

but nonetheless, mass migrations which twice spurred the Celtic peoples of the Central Asian steppes, starting some 5,000 years ago, to plod their way slowly across Eurasia until they reached the islands scattered West of Europe, and could go no farther. It was a process which evolved a number of Celtic cultures, which would eventually become the Britons (Brythonic Celts) and Gaelic Celts, and so on.

The impact of their collective journey was to be profound upon all of Asia Minor, Europe, and the British Isles, and ultimately the world.

People in movement across cultural, geographic, and linguistic divides transform the characteristics, productivity, and national security of the countries in which they settle, at least for a period.

Societies of common beliefs, language, and mutual trust take time to form, and, until that state is reached, optimal performance in national affairs and strategic warfighting is difficult to achieve.

Trans-national population movement in the first quarter of the 21st Century and the later decades of the 20th had a profoundly destabilizing impact on many nation-states. It affected the areas of origin; the areas of transit; and the areas of destination. But the phenomenon seemed set to escalate in the second quarter of the century because of the economic downturn of the People's Republic of China and the downstream consequences of that.

Not only would this — and the food and water issues — drive emigration from the Chinese mainland into the wider world, it would dislocate fragile economies which had become existentially dependent on the PRC.

At particular risk were the populations of sub-Saharan Africa.

The pivotal impact of the 2020 economic crisis in the PRC, caused by the coronavirus (COVID-19) epidemic, meant that some 80 percent of funding for Beijing's Belt & Road Initiative (BRI) projects had been quietly dropped from the budget. The social impact of this funding cut in Africa would be demonstrated in a further rise in population flight from sub-Saharan Africa to Europe, regardless of how much the European economic environment itself had declined.

As well in Africa, already suffering from severe economic dislocation, the COVID-19-related crisis saw a localized hostile reaction toward Chinese people who had migrated to Africa. Similar xenophobic reactions were already in play in parts of Africa — particularly South Africa — against other Africans who had migrated within the Continent in search of work.

It is necessary to differentiate between spontaneous population movement and conflict-engendered situations (whether manmade or natural), and deliberately-engineered population warfare.

Offensive and Defensive Population Warfare: Conscious population warfare, like formal military operations, takes account of the strategic terrain. And that terrain is as much fixed geography as it is transitory and biological (such as human, agricultural, and water). That means that it must be prepared for opportunistic and reflexive response to social dynamics.

There was no doubt, for example, that Turkish Pres. Reçep Tayyip Erdoğan was already highly conscious of the political leverage he inherited over Germany when he took office — then as Prime Minister — in 2003 as a result of the Turkish migrant presence in Germany and other European states. It gave Erdoğan a voice and a source of street power in the heart of the European Union, something he consciously exploited over the coming two decades.

The question is at what time did the Turkish Prime Minister (later President) seek to translate that inherited and static gift into a weaponized, dynamic strategic capability?

He had expressed an admiration for the resurrection of the caliphate which had existed in the Ottoman Empire until 1924. In the 18th Century, the Ottoman Sultans had themselves resurrected the ancient Muslim notion of the caliphate in order to unite its far flung and weakening empire. Turkey's secular leader, Mustafa Kemal Atatürk, however, abolished the caliphate in 1924. But there is little doubt that Erdoğan saw the potential in creating in himself a secular as well as religious power base which would extend beyond modern Turkey's borders.

Erdoğan, then, already felt that he could, and should, exercise control over Muslims in former Ottoman lands. He certainly used this position to help ensure the creation in Iraq and Syria of the militant Sunni

Muslim *jihadist* movement, *asad-Dawlah al-Islam-iyah fi al-'Iraq wash-Sham* (DI'ISH), otherwise known as the Islamic State in Iraq and al-Sham[84] (ISIS).

That, of course, was proxy warfare, but was it also population warfare? Only in that DI'ISH was a key tool in Turkey's proxy war against Syria, in particular, and the US. And this played a key rôle in helping transform the Syrian population into a roiling mass, making the country uncontrollable during the Syrian Civil War (from March 2011). This drove a massive Syrian refugee exodus to Jordan, and back into Turkey itself, from whence the hapless exiles were consistently pushed in deliberate operations into neighboring Greece and into the heart of the European Union.

The Turkish Government, with the active management of the Turkish National Intelligence Organization (*Milli İstihbarat Teşkilatı:* MİT), between January 2015 and March 2016 began facilitating the illegal movement of its refugee "resource" or weapon into the European Union, overwhelming the EU's border controls and creating a new population reality in the heart of Western Europe. It profoundly impacted immediate economic frameworks, and began — or accelerated — the change of the nature and beliefs of many European states, particularly Germany.

That Erdoğan was able to stop at will the mass movement of peoples was evident when he did so, upon cash payments by the European Union to Turkey. He main-

---

84 *Bilaad as-Sham* (literally "land on the left-hand" relative to someone in the Hejaz facing east) was a Rashidun, Umayyad, and later Abbasid Caliphate province in what is now the Levant. It essentially included Syria, and other territories.

tained two key strategic objectives: to punish the EU for, by default, rejecting Turkey as a member of the Union, and to weaken neighbor and rival Greece. Moreover, MİT also added Afghani, Iraqi, and other refugees into the population bulk it pushed into the EU.

It was a form of warfare — short of prompting a kinetic, or formal military response by neighboring states — which would have enduring consequences. Turkey's population warfare since 2003 was entirely offensive in nature, against multiple targets in Eurasia and the broader Middle East and Africa.

Meanwhile, the People's Republic of China consistently in the 21st Century, and particularly since the rise of Pres. Xi Jinping in 2012, was undertaking population warfare in offensive and defensive mass operations. Among other things, it flooded the world with Chinese people on a variety of witting and unwitting missions.

In the defensive aspect of its strategy, the Communist Party of China deployed its citizens abroad to help alleviate some of the burden on domestic food and water supply. The PRC did not lack foreign exchange, but it did have a domestic infrastructure which was straining to meet demand. In 2017, tourists from the PRC traveled overseas on 131-million occasions. They not only relieved the burden on domestic supply, they were able to sense that they were now a privileged people, dampening discontent with the Government.

In 2016, PRC figures show that its tourists spent $261.1-billion while traveling abroad. This continued to build the reliance of foreign states on the PRC. In a normal free-market state, foreign travel is the business of the individual. For the PRC, it was a matter of serving State or Party needs. And it did so.

By 2018, the number of PRC students studying abroad had reached 662,100, and in 2019 the number of PRC students in the US alone had reached a registered number of 369,548. Most of these students had the legitimate goal of gaining a prestigious international education, along with important language skills, all bringing personal career opportunities. But the Ministry of State Security, the primary intelligence agency, along with the Military Intelligence Department, and other agencies, blended this traffic with a high component of intelligence collectors.

It was no surprise that the PRC's leading position in the development and deployment of hypersonic weapons systems by 2020 coincided with the reality that the biggest cluster of Chinese students in Australia was around the University of Queensland, home to the UQ Center for Hypersonics, the world-leading university research facility on the subject. The deployment of students, business executives, and specialist researchers to facilities around the world disguised a massive scientific intelligence-gathering operation.

But it was in Africa where for the decade or so leading up to 2020 the PRC deployed millions of its citizens to work on a range of projects. There were at least more than 1.1-million Chinese immigrants in Africa in 2012, compared with less than 160,000 in 1996. By

2011, there were about 2.5-million Chinese living in Europe. And by 2020, it was estimated that there were well more than two-million living in Africa, with some commentators in the PRC postulating the desirability of moving 300-million Chinese people to Africa to alleviate the population burden at home.

That was never realistically expected to happen, and, in fact, Chinese migration to Africa appeared to peak in 2019, and the 2020 economic crisis impact in both Africa and the PRC seemed set to see a reduction in the deployment of Chinese citizens to the Continent. But the mass movement of Chinese to Africa had already served a significant purpose: within a decade, China literally owned the Continent; it had become the suzerain power over Africa, extending into every African economy. Beijing achieved what no single European entity, or the United States, had been able to achieve in the preceding century. And in so doing, it helped dominate the trade in critical minerals — not just base minerals to feed the PRC's industrial needs — such as rare earths and precious metals.

Beijing's seizure of Africa was a strategic coup of immense proportions, and included the development of a significant logistical infrastructure. All without firing a shot. Whether it would be able to sustain that dominance through the 2020s and beyond was open to question. The 2020 COVID-19 crisis had further ruined the economies of Africa; or at least had accelerated their decline. Few remained stable.

The PRC's biggest African client-state, South Africa,

was, by 2020 on the verge of collapse.

There was no doubt that under Pres. Xi Jinping, the Communist Party of China intended to become the dominant global influence, emulating Britain's pervasive dominance in the 19th Century, by bringing the Chinese official language (Mandarin) into common global useage. Again, this aspect of its population strategy may have been overly ambitious, but the level of its success by 2020 — at a time when the PRC's economy was fragile and resiling — was significant for an effort begun only a decade or less before.

Russia, too, in the post-Soviet era has attempted to use population dominance to achieve geopolitical gains, or to re-capture geography once under Imperial Russia and the Soviet empire. The polarization of Ukraine — essentially the area of the genesis of Russia itself — in the early 21st Century ensured that Moscow would have to use the substantial minority in the country which identified as "ethnic Russian".

In the 2001 Ukrainian census, 8,334,100 identified as ethnic Russians (17.3 percent of the population of Ukraine). Little wonder that Moscow used its population dominance in the East of Ukraine to help reclaim the Crimean Peninsula from Ukraine in March 2014. Crimea, in fact, represented a key geopolitical asset for Russia, enabling it to have a southward warm water projection which could take it into the Mediterranean and the Levant.

Why would it *not* use population as a means of achieving critical strategic mass when such a pivotal element of national strength was at stake? It might be difficult to say whether the Russian population strategy on this occasion represented offensive or defensive operations, or a combination of both.

Much research needs to be done in understanding how demographics and sociology can be employed — and often are employed — in population warfare, as well as in domestic population strategy and management. And the point of these few examples is not to deliver an exhaustive overview, but to highlight the need to look at population movements through the lens of structured policy and warfare.

Moreover, population strategic movement (sometimes short of hostile action) is implicitly tied to psychological warfare in protecting or defending such actions, or as part of an offensive information dominance campaign which would include linguistic and cultural dominance.

It is easy to see the failure of the Myanmar Government to preserve its international political freedom of action when it undertook the expulsion of some 700,000 Muslim Rohingya people, *en bloc*, from Rakhine State in the country's north in 2017-18. The Rohingya were essentially ethnically and religiously linked to neighboring Bangladesh, which was where they were pushed by the Myanmar Army, in order to preserve the Buddhist nature of Myanmar.

There was little doubt, however, that the Myanmar Government prevailed in preserving the state's sovereignty as it saw fit, but suffered a significant international defeat by losing the information war on the episode. What was significant was that the trigger for the Government's suppression and expulsion of the Rohingya began, in fact, with an attempt at population warfare by Turkey to turn the Rohingya Muslims into an ally against the Buddhist majority. And that Turkish strategy failed completely.

Similarly, there were cohesive efforts by the PRC and others to coordinate, inspire, and use "caravans" of illegal migrants from Central America to attempt to push through US southern borders in 2018 and 2019. These were part of a very deliberate pattern of population warfare strategies. If nothing else, they served to polarize US internal politics and help sustain the PRC's objective of isolating and defeating incumbent US Pres. Donald Trump in the November 2020 presidential election.

These examples were merely current approaches to ancient practices.

The colonization of the Americas and Australasia by European powers in the 18th and 19th centuries were of the same mold, even if they had ostensibly different motivations. The use by Hitler of the existence of the German populations (German Bohemians or Sudeten Germans) in Czechoslovakia to justify the invasion of that country in 1938 was manifestly a conscious population strategy. It was part of Hitler's *Ostsiedlung* ("Settling of the East") strategy.

The United States, conversely, deliberately flooded mainland Americans into Hawaii in order to be able to dominate a vote on the Hawaiian Islands in 1898 to annex them to the US. That gerrymandering of the vote in Hawaii still resonates with the ethnic and native population of the islands, but it provided a critical geopolitical element to enable, ultimately, the US to dominate the Pacific.

Hawaii, by the 21st Century, became a profound key in the US strategic war with the PRC, just as it was in its 1941-45 war with Japan.

It is easy to forget that "government" is *entirely* about the management and needs of populations. Population warfare — the use of populations in many forms to achieve existential national and sovereign needs — is therefore a legitimate area of study. *How* population warfare is conducted, and its objectives, are also legitimate areas for the discussion of ethical and perceptional behavior.

But we cannot pursue any legitimate discussion of total war — particularly in the 21st Century — unless we accept population warfare as a critical component of conflict.

Among other things, it raises questions about its impact on modern concepts of democratic governance and on the interpretation of "democracy" itself.

"Many forms of Government have been tried, and will be tried in this world of sin and woe. No one pretends that democracy is perfect or all-wise. Indeed it has been said that democracy is the worst form of Government except for all those other forms that have been tried from time to time."

— Winston S. Churchill, November 11, 1947

THE NEW TOTAL WAR

XV

The Transformation of Democracy

D EMOCRACY HAS ALWAYS BEEN MANIFESTED in human societies. It existed as the default condition of society long before the Hellenes gave a name to it.

It was the implicit acceptance and voluntary delegation of rôles in a society by and to all of its members.

Even the powers of leaders — from street crowd orators to tyrants and elected office-holders — is ultimately on loan from every individual willing to grant and accept that power. Constraining it into formulæ, modernizing it into the Scientific Age, and adapting Rousseau's "social contract"[85] into measured participatory governance represented merely the modern fashion of democracy.

The events of 2020, particularly the "fear pandemic" which accompanied the global coronavirus outbreak, allowed "modern democracy" to pass through an evolutionary progression toward the further assignment of individual rights to the collective mechanisms of formal and informal governance.

85 Rousseau, *The Social Contract*. op cit.

Most societies, in other words, began to take on an appearance of "voluntary tyranny", and mostly apparently benign and purposeful autocracy.

But that alone spelled the end of the modern — that is, 18th to 20th centuries' — concepts of associating "democracy" with "freedom".

Given that all other forms of social organization have changed during this period — the "Scientific Period" in the Age of Enlightenment, roughly the 16th through 18th centuries until the early 21st Century — why should we expect that our iteration of "democracy" would remain unchanged? Indeed, it had *not* remained unchanged, but like all human-constructed concepts it is subject to human-like lifespans.

Human fear of change includes a great fear of any sudden rupture in our pattern of living and socializing. We have, however, undergone a profound change in our social, governance, and organizational patterns and technologies since the end of World War II. Even in the century or so before that, we had been altering our social patterns profoundly.

Wealth and technology transformed hierarchical societies into flat organizational patterns from about 1990 onwards. The 21st Century world, then, had become as profoundly changed as could be imagined since, say, even the mid-19th Century when we were already well-embarked upon an era of scientific thought. And yet we still fear change; indeed, still view our social structures through antique lenses.

The reality, however, as the 2020 pandemic showed

*was not so much that we feared change (which we do),
but that fear changes us. And it did.*

A collapse or re-orientation of wealth and success in
the 21st Century should be expected to provide a sudden disruption in the linear and seemingly gradual
evolution of "democracy" since the 17th Century.
Does this spell an end to this particular era of democracy? Or does it merely drive it back into more
nuanced and regionally-applied forms of some kind of
"social contract" — spoken or unspoken — which
adapts to different cultures?

There is an irony in the realization that, through the
passage of time, *some monarchies begin life as tyrannies,
and almost all gradually move in the direction of maxi-
mizing democracy and freedom.* And most societies
which begin as truly democratic republics gradually
move in the direction of *minimizing democracy and
freedom.*

The current national monarchical states of Europe,
Asia, the Commonwealth, and Africa, have moved
along the lines I describe. The avowedly democratic republics of the United States, India, Nigeria, Turkey,
and so on, had also moved by the early 21st Century
along the evolutionary path I suggest: *away* from freedom.

It is evident through history that societies facing crisis are prepared to abdicate their freedoms and assign
their rights to leadership. They accept, in other words,
voluntary tyrannies in order to survive, abandoning
flat social structures for vertical ones. And that is what

we saw occurring in 2020. The question remained as to whether there would be a mechanism which would fully unwind that process.

We already saw that the threats during World War II caused Western societies to transform themselves partly into autocracies — tyrannies in the historical best sense of the concept[86] — to cope with the crisis. They became, in a sense, extremely hierarchical and autocratic to meet the demands for efficient decisiveness at a time of imminent danger.

The end of World War II saw states which were traditionally "democratic" voluntarily discard many of the trappings of tyranny and autocracy which had been necessary for war. But none of them abandoned all of those trappings. And each successive crisis saw an accretion of the powers of those in office and in the bureaucracies of state, and a relative acceptance of this reality by those who believed that modern society demanded more voluntary relinquishment of individual rights.

---

86 *Encyclopædia Britannica* in 2020 noted: "Tyranny, in the Greco-Roman world, an autocratic form of rule in which one individual exercised power without any legal restraint. In antiquity the word tyrant was not necessarily pejorative and signified the holder of absolute political power. In its modern usage the word tyranny is usually pejorative and connotes the illegitimate possession or use of such power. For the ancient Greeks, a tyrant was not necessarily a bad ruler; in its original form (*tyrannos*) the word was used to describe a person who held absolute and personal power within a state, as distinct from a monarch, whose rule was bound by constitution and law. Some tyrants were usurpers who came to power by their own efforts; others were elected to rule; and still others were imposed by intervention from outside." *This author notes:* Use of the term "tyranny" in the 21st Century had come to embrace autocracy, in which absolute control lies in the hands of a single person or with the grasp of a tightly-held group. The reality is that the ability of any modern society to apply autocratic governance across entire societies is, in practicable terms, difficult for any protracted period, given the reality that the almost infinite variables in societies — expanding as they become larger and more diverse — precludes management of ubiquitous governance.

But that process has historically been seen as cyclical, and associated with the life-cycle of empires and civilizations. We forget at our peril that these cycles are contracted or expanded by our behavior.

Still, the 21st Century, particularly punctuated by the crises of 2020, did see a substantial spike in the powers of government, almost universally. This would determine both the economic and the military responses which would be applied moving forward to the middle of the 21st Century.

The growing centralization of powers — which is, by definition, the process of movement toward autocracy (or tyranny), and away from "democracy" — would be seen for some years as necessary to cope with the additional and ongoing crisis of the evolution of economics in an age of decline. By that we mean the decline in population sizes, and therefore market sizes, which require different mechanisms than societies which are constantly expanding in market size.

XVI

Change

and the People's Republic of China

VEN THE WORD "CHANGE" implies suddenness: a moment in time when something which was is now gone, and something new takes its place. A watershed.

But rarely is change unforeseeable.

So even though events may take us by surprise, there are rarely "black swan events"; things which were unknowable. There is only the reality that we did not look, did not understand; could not comprehend.

The responsible alternate phrase for a "black swan event" is "intelligence failure".

By 2020, as the world entered a dramatic era of change, we were already seeing things which, five years earlier, were considered unthinkable but which were now coming into public acceptance. In every instance, we were told that change was coming, but we chose not to think on it, or what it implied.

In the US, a decade before that, it would have been unthinkable, treasonous, to discuss possible secession of a state of the union of the "United" States of America. Now it had become openly discussed; even advocated. In the West, a decade earlier, the concept of the usurpation of Western cultural and political superiority — the "end of history", as Francis Fukuyama so incorrectly called the "triumph" of Western "democratic" philosophy[87] — was also unthinkable. By 2020, the death of the brief, modern era of democracy was widely coming into acceptance, along with the embrace by urban utopian globalists of the death of classical liberalism in favor of rigid, doctrinaire, illiberal "liberalism". Again, the co-option and weaponization of words saw "liberalism" come to mean exactly the opposite of its literal concept.

Where does this take us? Even if we accept that the old order changeth, what next?

Would "China" — the People's Republic of China (PRC), or, more accurately, the Communist Party of China (CPC) — save the comfortable lifestyle of Western urban societies? That was an almost global belief by the end of the first decade of the 21st Century: that cheap PRC-made goods would continue to be sought by the West, and the PRC would make the rest of the world rich by buying its raw materials, energy, food, and luxury manufactures.

But why should it? Even if it could?

What does the CPC owe to Western societies? Why *would* the CPC save Western societies or their economies for any reason other than to serve the Party? As we

---

87 Fukuyama, Francis: *The End of History and the Last Man.* New York, 1992: Free Press.

saw, by 2020, the CPC was in a battle for its own survival; it was in no mood for global altruism.

The CPC, as did the (now-defunct) Communist Party of the Soviet Union, regarded its own people as tools to sustain the power of the Party leadership. So why would the CPC regard foreigners to be worthy of higher status than even the Chinese people from whom it demands no dissent?

What we were seeing in the early 21st Century was a tortuous attempt to rationalize the view among elements of societies and governments in Western Europe, and even Canada, Australia, and New Zealand, that they could "replace" their strategic relationship with the US with a relationship with the PRC. In Africa, already, many people had recognized that they have traded their post-colonial "freedom" — which entailed ongoing relationships with their former European colonial partners or with the US — for *de facto* subordination to the suzerainty of "China": in fact the CPC.

Can we forget that we are talking of the same Communist Party of China which oversaw the murder, in one form or another, of at least 60-million of its own people during internal purges from the "Great Leap Forward" to the "Cultural Revolution"? The same CPC which destroyed the lives of so many Chinese people who resisted Pavlovian and other psychological conditioning to bow to the Party. And which today pushes many elements of its society into sequestration for "re-education" or liquidation.

Yet we accept the words of the CPC that it is somehow due some massive redress for the shame inflicted on it in the 19th and 20th centuries by outside powers, none of which dared — even with the shameful "rape of Nanking" — kill anything like as many Chinese as did the CPC.

We forget that the CPC allowed the Nationalist (*Kuomintang*) Government of Chiang Kai-shek to exhaust itself in defeating the Japanese invaders in World War II so that the CPC could then win a "civil war", in which the CPC's *stated objective* was to actually *end* China's sense of its history and identity. After about 2012, the CPC reversed itself and now pays tribute to much of Chinese history and identity. But at what cost?

In the cases of Australia, New Zealand, continental Europe, and much of Africa, there has been *a reluctance to assume the true meaning of sovereignty,* which implies not only freedom to make one's own choices, but the *responsibility to safeguard one's choices and freedom.* These regions assumed that they *must* subordinate themselves to a new overlord, now that their old ones seemed to have disappeared, declined or have appeared to waver. The new overlord for many is the sole new claimant to "global hegemony": the CPC, loosely disguised as "China".

Saudi Arabia and the United Arab Emirates in 2019 appeared to have feared that the US would no longer protect them against Iran, and briefly sought Beijing's and Moscow's protection, foregoing the chance to assert sovereignty. They quickly realized that neither

Beijing nor Moscow could save them.

Great traditional or historical powers, such as Egypt, Iran, and Ethiopia, and even India (which is only recently an holistic entity), have re-set their priorities around the great identity and prestige of their history. Yes, they may accept the need for alliance with the PRC or Russia (or the US), but they see themselves as finally being able to re-assert their own identity. That today's Turkey is also attempting to re-assert its Ottoman and pan-Turkic identity, dominating a pan-Islamic order, is equally unsurprising, but was unlikely to succeed, for lack of a realistic framework of economic and social underpinnings.

So change was well upon us by the start of the third decade of the 21st Century.

US Pres. Donald Trump had effectively responded to the CPC's September 2018 declaration of a "New Thirty Years War" against the US. He said in late August 2019 that he could, and might, stop all US businesses from engaging in the PRC economy. Beijing may have briefly believed that it could use this to ensure the downfall of Pres. Trump in the US 2020 Presidential elections. But it became equally possible that the PRC could find itself in grave economic peril by that time. If the US was preparing to confront the PRC, then now may be its best opportunity if it was to avoid a later military confrontation.

Who could blame the CPC for assuming it could move to the strategic ascendancy without resistance?

US Presidents George H. W. Bush, Bill Clinton,

George W. Bush, and Barack Obama deluded themselves that they could ignore the PRC and that it would, in its rise, willingly subordinate itself to the US-dominated "rules-based order". But why would it? Instead, the CPC planned its rise on a linear plane, forgetting that nothing in history is inevitable. And then, US Pres. Trump prepared for strategic and economic confrontation to sustain the US and Western dominance, even if Western publics were unready. Even if the CPC could not itself fully grasp the *volte face* in US strategy.

Thus, massive change began to occur. It involved considerable pain. It was unavoidable. It was a time, once again, for nations to see themselves as nations, and to take sides. Given the dramatic hollowing out of the PRC economy (affecting global growth for a decade), it was not an automatic assumption that change favored the CPC.

The CPC had, by May 2020, mostly handled its strategic campaign against the US and its principal allies (particularly Australia and Japan) with exceptional skill. It had profound momentum on its side, and could sense the possible defeat of US Pres. Trump in the November 3, 2020, elections, eliminating the major threat to the CPC's survival.

But what had the CPC done to stave off internal economic collapse in the PRC? At the end of the day, the CPC's main enemy was itself. And the US' main enemy was also itself, helped by the CPC.

Thus we became children of the Chinese curse: we live in interesting times.

XVII

Why 2020 Matters

*The 2020 Fear Pandemic breakpoint moved the world from
"strategic competition" to semi-formal hostilities*

THE RUSH TO AN OVERT wartime footing began consciously and urgently in the first quarter of 2020 between the major players: the United States of America and its allies and the People's Republic of China.

The PRC, however, had already begun strategic, offensive amorphous warfare operations. It knew that it would need to face the US and its allies at some stage, and had codified its planning into strategic and military doctrine by 1999. By 2012 or so, it had distilled this effort into concrete planning, sufficient for PRC Pres. Xi Jinping to actually formalize, to his own team, his declaration of war against the US in September 2018.

Whether or not he planned that the crisis should come to a head in 2020, or whether the COVID-19 trigger was planned or merely exploited by Beijing, is irrelevant. The PRC was already at war — of necessity because of its imploding economy — and it was merely a matter of time before the US and its allies overcame the mood of dependency on the PRC as a supplier nation, and responded to the threat.

So it was not just about the "battle" to cope with the COVID-19 (coronavirus) epidemic, or the global fear pandemic which it engendered. Rather, those contagions merely (and finally) broke the cycle of globalist aspirations and the belief in the indissoluble nature of interdependence.

It allowed what was already emerging as a fundamental move toward a new, bipolar global competition to come into the open. All the while, in the build-up to 2020, Beijing was working consistently to peel away Washington's allies. Indeed, the 2020 crisis was to cripple some Western economies so that a number of Washington's allies were, in fact, temporarily crippled and distracted.

By the end of March 2020, the global framework had changed sufficiently to become — behind the headlines about COVID-19 — about which system and ideology would triumph in the decades after the watershed. That meant a race by each of the major antagonists to determine how quickly national productivity could be resumed.

Even so, the failure of most major societies, including the PRC, to prepare for health pandemics, natural disasters, and associated contagions of fear was a significant condemnation of the transformed realities of the "globalist"-dominated political structures. The world was returning to earlier lessons of national self-reliance.

In order to gain the post-epidemic political high

ground, the PRC was first to "declare victory" in managing the COVID-19 epidemic and to send its population back to work. This defied the evidence which showed continuing levels of contagion in the PRC. However, it was clear that the epidemic, having its origins in Wuhan in the PRC, would likely peak first and begin to recover first.

Still, it was the degree of top-down control which PRC Pres. Xi Jinping enjoyed — in contrast to Western heads of government — which enabled the PRC to "declare victory", and to resume his offensive against the West in a now fairly blatant fashion. But then, revived levels of contagion meant that his rush to claim victory was premature and would more probably come to haunt him.

The overall nature of the re-structured strategic balance would be less affected by a few weeks (or even months) in the battle to re-start economic activity than by underlying fundamentals in systems. Meanwhile, as the information dominance (ID) wars between the PRC and the US and its allies ramped up, both sides were careful to ensure that the risk of actual physical challenge was minimized.

What were some of the important immediate outcomes and questions raised by the 2020 Fear Pandemic?

> 1. The global economy and the economies of most states had been dramatically weakened, and they would remain relatively weakened and transformed for some years; in many cases for decades.

This meant that economic deprivation would reach more pervasively down into the mass of society, reversing the trend of the past seven decades. It would exacerbate the polarization of societies, but seemed likely to push the trend toward forms of nationalism more than it would reinforce the ideology of globalism;

➤ 2. The power of central governments was dramatically increased, and the rights and freedoms of individuals more constrained. By late March 2020, the situation in most Western societies had approached a quasi-martial law environment, with little social resistance;

➤ 3. Funding for R&D, national security, and consumer spending was set to decline, further exacerbated by the reduction in core size/wealth of most populations in advanced economies. The question was whether the limitation in wealth would exacerbate or constrain inflammatory populism and social action;

➤ 4. The rôle of global bodies was weakened, as was the rôle of alliances. This was to lead to a re-thinking of alliance structures and how to manage them. It was, even if only for reasons of fiscal constraints, to lead to an increasing momentum toward the bilateralization of trade, even to the point, once again of thinking in terms of structured barter or counter-trade dealings;

➤ 5. The reach of formal military structures began to be inhibited by funding. This opened seams in the global power framework. It allowed space for more independent, regional actions;

➤ 6. While the Communist Party of China (CPC) probably had the strength to enforce control over the People's Republic of China (PRC), was it becoming doubtful that the European Union (EU) would have sufficient cohesion to enforce control over its member states? If the EU could not "hold it together", would this give impetus to Turkey to expand its neo-Ottomanist drive in the Eastern Mediterranean and Balkans? Did the United Kingdom escape from the EU just in time to preserve its economic base? Did the EU's poor handling of the crisis end forever the chance of bringing Serbia into the Union? And what would this new dynamic do for the encouragement of separate geopolitical alignments, such as the creation of the Three Seas Initiative[88] as a potentially viable successor to part of the EU? Could Three Seas gain traction if Serbia continued to be excluded, given its regional hub importance for the north-south infrastructural needs of the Alliance?;

➤ 7. What skills would be necessary in the post-2020 environment? Would the global economy sober enough to embrace the restoration of practical skills training instead of ideological education

---

88 Three Seas Initiative is a forum of 12 states in the European Union's Central and Eastern European sector, facing Russia. It implies links from the Baltic Sea to the Black Sea, to the Mediterranean Sea. It met for the first time in 2016 in Dubrovnik, Croatia. Member states include Austria, Bulgaria, Croatia, Czech Republic, Estonia, Hungary, Latvia, Lithuania, Poland, Romania, Slovakia, and Slovenia.

which had little market, while an impetus toward revived domestic manufacturing (rather than foreign-sourced manufacturing) began to see significant demand for trained skilled workers?;

➤ 8. There was a widespread belief that the crisis had caused a collapse in petroleum and gas prices to the point where the US domestic shale industry would be forced from the marketplace, re-opening the US to the need for imported energy. But this was likely both untrue and irrelevant, and the US would remain considerably less vulnerable to energy exposure than the PRC;

➤ 9. The PRC would continue to see extreme vulnerability to food and water shortages, which could only be ameliorated by (a) dependence on imported food and agricultural products, much of which would need to come from the United States (given that other suppliers could not meet the demand), and (b) reduction in the lifestyles and numbers of the PRC population, a factor which would have significant social-political ramifications;

➤ 10. The longer the constraints on societies imposed by the crisis, the more profound were the post-crisis attitude changes likely to be. In other words, if the crisis lingered in various forms through 2020, it was likely that the year would be seen by society and historians as a break-point equivalent to the world wars of the 20th Century;

➤ 11. Nowhere in the world had we seen the development of economic theories or approaches to managing societies in decline in terms of economics as well as in terms of the downward transformation of market size and demand. Studies of recent-term lessons from Japan, Russia, and Germany would be helpful, even though these examples all still predicated their economic thinking — despite market size decline — on *growth* in economic opportunity. But they did so with notable shortcomings;

➤ 12. Africa, which had moved from a Continent gradually modernizing within the framework of a Western model to one dependent almost solely on the PRC, was likely to be left in an almost ruinous situation by late 2020 and beyond. African societies would themselves be forced to evolve new economic models. There was a likelihood that the US would strongly move, in the post-crisis period, to strengthening its dominance in the Americas (where the PRC, in particular, had built a strong presence), and also in Central Asia, as a means of providing an alternate path in the Eurasian Silk Road complex. But that was not guaranteed.

The COVID-19 pandemic did little to seriously impact the historical demographic cycles in global population numbers. The trend toward population decline was already set in place in the second half of the 20th Century and was only now becoming evident. Similarly, the disruption to the global economy also began before the COVID-19 crisis, largely as a result of the global demographic transformation, but the 2020 crisis became an iconic break-point.

The post-COVID-19 world would thus be markedly different, structurally, than the world which preceded it. But most significantly, the perception of that "new" world would have changed, ensuring that a linear extrapolation of older remedies or progressions of earlier thinking would no longer be acceptable.

It is important to again stress that the two underlying strategic trends impacting the US-PRC competition had begun well before the 2020 pandemic scares. The PRC economy had been essentially in decline for several years, disguised by ongoing state-sponsored investments in infrastructure projects, which boosted the appearance of growth in the gross domestic product (GDP). Moreover, the PRC's water shortage and quality problems had reached almost panic levels over that same timeframe.

In a talk in Perth, Western Australia, on October 23, 2019, I noted:

> [The PRC] has almost 20 percent (18.4 percent) of the world's population, and yet only seven percent of its water, and of that water some 25 percent, at least [as the PRC Government acknowledges], is polluted, along with much of its agricultural water table [to a far greater degree than the PRC Government acknowledges]. And the problem is getting worse. The great water source, the aquifers flowing from the melting snows of the Tien Shan Mountain range in Central Asia, is reducing for the moment.
>
> The result of this, and the fact that Chinese agricul-

ture has not modernized to any great degree, is that the People's Republic of China is perhaps more strategically dependent on imported food than any great power since Rome. And Rome, arguably, collapsed, finally, for that very reason: its foreign sources of food became less dependable. The PRC Bureau of Statistics in the 1980s recorded that there were some 50,000 rivers in mainland China. But by 2017, there were only some 23,000. Beijing, serviced by the so-called "Three Gorges Dam", recorded in 2017 that 39.9 percent of its water was so polluted as to be unusable. Tianjan, a principal port city of the north (and with a population of 15-million), had only 4.9 percent of its water in a potable state.

The growing urbanization of the constituent populations of the PRC has made the food and water crises more and more urgent. Urban populations use far more water than rural societies. They also demand more water-intensive food, such as pork and beef, especially as the city-dwellers become more prosperous. And the PRC's urbanization rate continued apace: by the end of 2017, some 58.52 percent of its population was urbanized, compared with only 17.92 percent in 1978.

You can see where this is going. And we have not even touched on the impact of air quality on health in the PRC, or the fact that urban-related diseases, such as diabetes, were rising at a higher rate than in other industrial economies; or the fact that a rapidly-ageing population was transforming the economic viability of the state.[89]

89 This talk also formed the basis of a report entitled "Sovereignty in the Age of

And by late 2019, it became clear that the PRC was unable to continue pursuit of military equivalence with the US. Minnie Chan, writing in *The South China Morning Post* on November 28, 2019, noted that the PRC Government had canceled plans for the People's Liberation Army-Navy (PLAN) to build two nuclear-powered very large aircraft carriers to compare with the capability of US super-carriers. The PLAN already had two, smaller, conventionally-powered carriers afloat with two more abuilding. The reasons for the cancelations of the prestige super-carrier program were cited as "technical challenges and high costs".

The PRC had significant technologies which briefly leapfrogged the US, particularly in the areas of hypersonic weapons and space, but belatedly a more resilient US economy was beginning to redress the years of neglect by all US presidents between Pres. Ronald Reagan (1981-89) and Pres. Donald Trump (2017-). The US was slowly beginning to compensate for the sense of smugness and hubris which pervaded its global thinking after the end of the Cold War in 1990.

But the US had, along with most European powers, subcontracted most of its manufacturing to the PRC in the post-Cold War era, and the COVID-19 epidemic — and the US-PRC "trade war" which immediately preceded it (and which was set to resume significantly in late 2020) — saw the extent of global dependence on mainland China factories. Beijing was counting on this

Beijing: Can the PRC 'Save' Australia? Or Any Nation?", in *Defense & Foreign Affairs* **Strategic Policy**, 11-12/2019.

dependence to re-start its economic push in the second quarter of 2020.

But would that manufacturing/export revival be sufficient to re-start the PRC economy, which was essentially already hollowed out?

And was the US (and Western) dependence on the PRC manufacturing sector likely to be the same as pre-COVID-19? Unlikely, given the reality that global demand would have declined substantially for at least the remainder of 2020 because of the economic impact of the crisis, and because a number of efforts to restore domestic manufacturing of key products had already begun in the US, Canada, Australia, the UK, etc.

Moreover, the weakness of the PRC position, economically, was borne out by the understanding that it had made dramatic cuts in the first quarter of 2020 to its investment in its Belt & Road Initiative (BRI) global supply chain. BRI had, in its origins, been conceived merely as a material and transactional form of maoist globalist ideology; a way to bind foreign states to the PRC as "tributary" states and to provide the PRC with its resource needs and markets. But most of the BRI contracts and loans to foreign states had not been calculated on a realistic market basis.

It was merely "financial maoism".

Reports from Beijing indicated that funding for BRI projects had dropped in early 2020 by some 80 percent over the same period a year earlier. But some of these cuts were already well underway by the time the COVID-19 crisis struck.

Hong Kong-based *The South China Morning Post*, reported on October 10, 2019, that investment in BRI had begun to drop in 2018. It noted: "The value of new projects across 61 countries fell 13 percent to US$126-billion in 2018 [compared with the previous year], with the figure falling further in 2019." In fact, it said that investment had fallen a further 6.7 percent in the seven months leading up to August 2019, and existing contracts were reduced by 4.2 percent in the first eight months of 2019.

The *Post* article continued: "[I]n the first half of 2019, China's investment and construction activity around the world plunged by over 50 percent compared to the first half of 2018, while new projects under the belt and road plan dropped sharply, according to a report published in July by Derek Scissors, resident scholar at the China Global Investment Tracker from the American Enterprise Institute." Scissors said Chinese SOEs were still moving car and steel capacity overseas and building new motorways and cement plants in developing economies, but that was now "on a smaller scale" compared to the 2016 peak.

The cutbacks were not only caused by Beijing.

By late 2019 and early 2020, a significant number of major programs in the BRI which had received commitments from foreign countries were canceled or scaled-back. These were particularly evident in Pakistan (which has a major strategic need to depend on Beijing), Malaysia, Myanmar, Bangladesh, and Sierra Leone. The arrival of the new Government in Ethiopia in April 2018 had already seen that country sour on involvement with new BRI projects.

To a degree, all this decline in the PRC's economic reach was likely to see the PRC attempt to regain global market share by dumping of goods onto the global marketplace in a bid to ensure that nationalistically-oriented commitments in the US, Europe, Australia, and the like did not attempt to rebuild their own manufacturing sectors. So the response by client states to PRC attempts to recapture markets and prevent the rise of national or sovereign independence would be a measure as to how much Western leaders learned from the crisis period of early 2020.

For this reason, strategically, it was critical for the Communist Party of China to ensure that Donald Trump was not re-elected to the US Presidency on November 3, 2020, and that the Democratic Party in the US would strengthen its position in the US Congress.

As a result, the CPC's information dominance warfare against the US was geared specifically toward the downfall of Pres. Trump, and in this it sought to enlist the support of the anti-Trump sections of the US polity. There were clearly some elements of the US political community which were prepared to align with Beijing — albeit not overtly — in order to ensure the removal of Donald Trump and the ascendance of Democratic Party presumed candidate Joe Biden.

So the US 2020 elections would become the next major break-point in the now overt US-PRC war.

GREGORY R. COPLEY

XVIII

What Fear Hath Wrought

And Where Does It Lead?

S O OUR WAY OF LIFE became our way of war. Or did it? Perhaps briefly. Perhaps into the infinite future. The tide moving toward a fully-embraced 21st Century-style total war had clearly and solidly begun by 2012.

The inflection point of the 2020 health and economic crisis merely made it irreversible.

The question as we prepared for the final 80 percent of the 21st Century was how we would restructure to address new realities.

Much of the world moved closer toward centralized, command economies or autocracy to create efficiencies of population control. Some of the supranational constructs — the United Nations, the EU, the Commonwealth of Independent States, and the Shanghai Cooperation Organization, for example — were weakened as the return to hierarchies became focused on the nation-state model.

Some states which had been artificially created as a result of colonial boundaries after World War II were showing signs of reverting to older, more natural linguistic, cultural, and tribal lines.

There were tensions as some federal structures either attempted to compound centralization or to loosen back to confederal linkages.

The pivotal inflection of 2020, however, accelerated the movement cycle back in favor of hierarchically-structured nation-states. This was neither necessarily good nor bad; it was a natural response to conditions.

Meanwhile, Beijing had already made it clear in 1999 that when it went to war with the US it would be a new kind of war.[90] People's Republic of China (PRC) Pres. Xi Jinping then announced in September 2018 his "new 30 Years War" with the US.[91]

But there seemed to be no "Pearl Harbor" moment, so the rest of the world disregarded the declaration of war. That was a mistake.

It became clear that the 2020 COVID-19-inspired "global fear pandemic" laid out the battlefield terrain and saw the opening shots emerge from the PRC in a variety of strategic formats. To be sure, COVID-19 was not itself the "Pearl Harbor moment"; it was the subsequent *fear pandemic* which drove down the global economy.

---

90 *Unrestricted Warfare.* op cit.
91 See Bodansky, Yossef: "Beijing's 'New thirty Years War'", in *Defense & Foreign Affairs Strategic Policy*, 10/2018. And also: "Is "The New Thirty Years War" Already Escalating?", *Defense & Foreign Affairs Strategic Policy*, 11-12/2018. See also, Copley, Gregory R.: "The Time of Strategic Choice", in *Defense & Foreign Affairs Strategic Policy*, 10/2018.

Beijing could not wait any longer to begin strategic operations — the new form of "total war" — if it was to survive as a global power and to assume primacy even within his symbolic 30-year timeframe. Shakespeare (*Julius Cæsar*, act four, scene three) noted:

"There is a tide in the affairs of men, Which taken at the flood, leads on to fortune. Omitted, all the voyage of their life is bound in shallows and in miseries. On such a full sea are we now afloat. And we must take the current when it serves, or lose our ventures."

From Beijing's standpoint, given that the PRC economy was already in massive decline, it was critical that the economies of its strategic rivals should also be forced into decline. That may or may not have been a planned aspect of the PRC's COVID-19 response strategy, but it certainly was quickly adopted by Beijing.

In other words, if the PRC could not reverse its economic decline, its strategic competitiveness moving forward was critically dependent upon seeing its rivals decline commensurately, or even become crippled. It was not a race to the top; it was a race to avoid being first to the bottom.

And from Beijing's standpoint, too, this was to be a war engaging broad-form population warfare strategies, as well as "legal warfare" and "media warfare", all particularly harnessed to electronic communications, in turn linked to a range of strategic and tactical psychological and psychopolitical operations.[92] That was clear from the benchmark PRC 1999 study, *Unre-*

---

92 See Glossary for further discussion on these doctrines.

stricted Warfare, which has now emerged literally as the textbook of the new "total war" against the US and the West. And it was constantly revised after 1999.

It was also all connected, as far as Beijing was concerned, to economic and social warfare, including population warfare, on a variety of levels. And only tangentially — in the short-term — was military force projection a component. Military confrontation involved risk if, for example, the US was to be directly engaged with force. So it was a strategy by which the PRC required the weakening and splitting of what otherwise would be an overwhelming adversary alliance.

> ➤ One fundamental tenet of the engagement by Beijing was to split the US away from its traditional allies, exploiting schisms which had been festering and expanding since the end of the Cold War.

> ➤ Another, parallel tenet was to then split the internal populations *within* the US and its allies by exacerbating and supporting existing societal schisms.

By such means are solid and cohesive adversaries broken down to be challenged piecemeal, and then each of the separate adversaries weakened internally and prevented from achieving unfettered and decisive action even at a national level. If an adversary society is fighting within itself or preoccupied with domestic issues it cannot pose a threat.

"Splittist" has long been a particularly vitriolic epithet used by Chinese communists to denigrate those who split away from the Communist Party of China (CPC), or attempted to split the country away from the CPC. Now, splitting strategies are employed against the enemies of the CPC.

Beijing's approach was learned at a strategic level from the Western strategy of the Cold War, which was to exacerbate to the point of fracture the People's Republic of China links with the Union of Soviet Socialist Republics (the USSR). To drive a wedge into the natural Sino-Soviet rift.

Beijing understood this and allowed itself to be part of that Sino-Soviet splitting operation when CPC Chairman Mao Zedong met with US Pres. Richard Nixon on February 21, 1972. At that time, the Soviet-PRC alliance was one of convenience, but it was never an easy match. Indeed, the Russian Federation *modus vivendi* with the PRC by 2020 — it would be difficult to call it an alliance — was fraught with as much mutual suspicion as the Sino-Soviet link of the Cold War.[93]

Beijing, even before 2020, had begun to apply that splitting technique against the West itself.

But, as central as that process became to PRC strategy — or, more accurately, to the strategy of the CPC,

---

93 See: "Chinese Checkmate", in *Defense & Foreign Affairs Digest*, 3/1973. This report, written by Dr Stefan Possony and this author during a time in the Cold War when the West equated the USSR and the PRC as a monolithic communist *bloc*, noted: "The political and actual conflict which exists between the Soviet Union and the People's Republic of China can now be construed as one of the most serious facing man ... second only to the rift which continues between the Soviet Union and the United States of America/NATO, and now may well exceed it in possible flammability. The Sino-Soviet dispute is not basically an ideological one, and is scarcely the border disagreement to which so much verbiage is spilled. There remains a struggle for vast tracts of territory and still greater power." The report continued: "It would seem that the conflict will be a somewhat permanent one."

which aimed as much at subduing the Chinese people as foreign societies — it was only one component which would enable the PRC, economically in decline[94] and militarily no match for even the US let alone the formerly close Western set of alliances, to have a chance at strategic success.

Moreover, it should not be assumed that it is the CPC alone which has moved onto a "war footing" and which saw the new conflict as an amorphous "total war": a total war which has taken on absolutely new dimensions from the shape of "total war" in the 20th Century. US Pres. Donald Trump began moving the US from a passive acceptance of PRC strategic expansionism — which had been underway for two decades at least — in 2017, and then moved into defensive strategic economic policies by late 2019.

Trump knew the PRC was at war with the US even before his Administration took office in January 2017. Japanese Prime Minister Shinzo Abe was also, by that time, already aware of the war, and was preparing Japan for it.

The COVID-19-related upheaval meant that, by early 2020, the prime ministers of Australia[95] and the

94 See, for example, Copley, Gregory R.: "State of the World: Parlous, Transforming, Yet in Some Ways Stabilizing, Optimistic", in *Defense & Foreign Affairs* **Strategic Policy**, 1/2020. That edition noted: "The year 2020 could emerge as the start of the era of relative global chaos or major upheaval. It is the era we have been anticipating, as the impact of core population decline meets economic dislocation, and security and structural uncertainty." And "[T]he PRC was already on economic life-support by the time the coronavirus pandemic began to become known by the end of January 2020. It was clear that the CPC was already well aware of the reality that the coronavirus had begun its broad contagion — with the consequent impact on the PRC economy — when it signed the 'trade deal' with Pres. Trump."
95 See, Copley, Gregory R.: "Sovereignty in the Age of Beijing: Can the PRC 'Save'

United Kingdom were also gradually coming aboard with the reality that they had been forced onto a war footing. What is significant is the degree to which public opinion in Africa generally, and in Australia, South-East Asia, the US, parts of Europe, and so on, moved against the PRC as a result of the way in which Beijing postured itself during the 2020 crisis.

The CPC — or at least Pres. Xi Jinping — seemed not to care. The velvet glove had, by 2020, been removed to some extent. It began to take advantage of the cover of the crisis to step up actions against rebellious elements in its autonomous Hong Kong region, for example, and to move its sole operational aircraft carrier, the *Liaoning*, into the South China Sea to highlight the perception that its armed forces had not been constrained by the COVID-19 crisis in the same way that the US and French navies had.

But nowhere, however, was the extent of the war — the *type* of the war — openly discussed or understood. It *was* a global total war; one in which all elements of society, indeed of *all* societies, are conscripted.

This was not a "black swan event" — there is no such thing — but it is finally a clarification of the dynamic framework which was emerging for the 21st Century. It is also worth noting that although the Xi strategy may have been ambitious and innovative, it did not necessarily involve any real understanding of the US or the world by Pres. Xi, and more than most of the world

Australia? Or Any Nation?". In *Defense & Foreign Affairs* **Strategic Policy,** 11-12/2019. Based on the author's Geopolitical Address to the Australia-Israel Chamber of Commerce, in Perth, Western Australia, on October 23, 2019.

understood Xi's personal fusion of "China".

Arguably, Xi's view of China and its destiny was, at least by 2020, akin to the mythical view which Hitler had of and for Germany.

But now — 2020 — Xi had committed the PRC to a strategic course of action.

That was the physical component.

So the planning could then begin, by other states, as to how to deal with that PRC action.

1. How Societies Revive

ECONOMIC, SOCIAL, AND strategic recovery in any society beset by major crisis requires clean-sheet approaches and decisive steps to sweep away impediments to revival.

This is impossible — and usually undesirable — in normal conditions, and even in a crisis it is difficult unless societies and government agree that extraordinary steps are permitted. What should be understood is the basic concept, angrily refuted by statists, that it is not the job of governments to control societies; it is the job of societies to control government.

But, in the present climate of widespread fear for the future, the fact that societies also fear change means that:

> ➤ (a) The appearance of normalcy and continuity of institutions must be maintained as far as possible, and the utilization *and revival* of familiar iconic symbols, instruments, language, and faces is desirable; and

➤ (b) The reality that massive change and threat has already been visited upon society means that substantive, planned, further underlying change is now more possible. In other words, change has already occurred: use it to "Re-mould it nearer to the Heart's Desire!", as Omar Khayyám suggested. But what that desire is, or should be, then becomes the primary question.

In the 2020 context, these factors were true as much for the PRC as for the US, UK, European Union (EU), or any other country. The difference in the application of the necessity to clearly specify what outcome is desired, however, lies in the goals and paths which each government wishes for its society.

Every major conflict tends to allow a government to increase its dominance over a society in order to combat an existential threat. How much that dominance is subsequently relaxed following the threat shows the difference between command economies — essentially socialist, fascist autocracies by definition — and classical democracies.

What has been significant in the early response to the fear pandemic which was triggered by the COVID-19 crisis is that many Western nation-states actually began adopting permanent changes which would move their societies closer to the command status normally associated with communist or socialist-fascist autocracies. In this regard, my colleague, Prof. Yuri Maltsev, is wont to cite Friedrich Nietzsche: "Whoever fights monsters should see to it that in the process he does not become a monster. And if you gaze long enough into an abyss, the abyss will gaze back into you."

Apart from the move toward greater control over economies, the move toward cashless societies, toward the implementation of technology-enabled control of individuals (enabling total surveillance and obedience, for example) by definition changes the nature of the societies.

But does greater control over an economy and the minimizing of social freedom lead to the kind of *longer-term* strategic recovery which was ostensibly the declared goal of combating the immediate threat? In other words, like suicide, is it a long-term solution to a short-term problem? Is it a successful operation which kills the patient?

Crisis provides the opportunity for many actions.

Things can be achieved in chaos which could never be accomplished in calm. Positive and negative things. The view of statists, usually, is that the answer to a crisis is more government. That, of course, is antithetical to the free movement and thought of the individual, and therefore alien to entrepreneurship and productivity.

The primary lessons, then, from the 2020 crisis, which caused virtually all major nations to add unsustainably to their debt burdens, should include moves to:

> **(i) Simplify and open** society rather than legislate and control.

Remove inhibitions to economic and social stimulation which do not require state funding.

In other words, reduce the emphasis on activities which require taxpayer funds (which add to national debt). These neither stimulate revenue production by their action, nor enable productivity regeneration to occur. Entrepreneurship generates employment, taxation, and addresses the needs of national self-sufficiency;

➤ **(ii) Eliminate or reduce** the penalties, efforts, and cost of both starting economic enterprises or closing them.

This means allowing corporate bankruptcies to occur. Better to endure short-term losses than to lose long-term economic momentum. Governments are now searching, in any event, for ways to write off, refute, or inflate out of their debt obligations. Why not the productive sector?

Is it not hypocritical to stop the marketplace from moving forward after the failure or collapse of commercial enterprises when governments routinely do so with impunity, often by printing more unsupported money? And many of the commercial enterprises have failed, in any event, due to the actions of governments in suppressing normal market activity. Efficient bankruptcy is the key to economic momentum;

➤ **(iii) Stimulate self-sufficiency** through national and local-level policies which favor the local production of necessities and tools of strategic advantage, **and deny that advantage to the adversary**.

This does indeed require the application — selectively, carefully, and temporarily — of bans on certain imported products in order to guarantee sovereign viability, and it does involve selective use of tariffs. It also involves the denial of some exports to an adversary. *In the case of the containment of the PRC, the US and other food exporting adversary states would deny supply of food to the PRC, given that food and water shortage is Beijing's critical strategic vulnerability.*

Clearly, the "globalism" philosophy, which grew progressively since the end of the Cold War, had swung the strategic pendulum in favor of great powers which sought to dominate markets for their own purposes.

It was the globalist interpretation of "free trade" which, in fact, made many economies totally dependent on a foreign power.

This has particularly, in the 21st Century, benefited the PRC, which was able to use "free trade" to build strategic control of other societies. Beijing is not unique, historically, in utilizing the battle-cry of "free trade", which is ultimately not free to the party which allows itself to become strategically dependent. Britain and the United States have themselves done this in the past.

2. Repurposing Alliances

TREATIES AND ALLIANCES are meant to address immediate threats and opportunities. They do not last forever. Nor should they.

Lord Palmerston said, in the 19th Century: "Nations have no permanent friends or allies, they only have permanent interests." Alliances and treaties are meant to serve specific objectives, and time often vitiates these objectives.

But what was clear was that the People's Republic of China in 2020 lacked a viable alliance network. It treated states such as the DPRK (North Korea) as mere tributary states, and other trading partners as though they *should* be tributary states. Thus their compliance with Beijing must be forced.

The US, for most of the seven decades following World War II, also treated its allies to greater or lesser degrees as tributary states, and, as a result, its alliance structures became greatly reduced by resentments of junior alliance partners. Those partners may return to alliance with the US only through fear of the PRC and, to some extent, Russia.

What occurred in the first decades of the 21st Century, among other things, was that:

> (a) The original purpose for the North Atlantic Alliance (NATO) withered away, and yet the alliance had developed bureaucratically into one of the most effective strategic tools possible;

> (b) The European Union (EU) created a layer of governance and control of Western and Central Europe which inhibited the growth, freedom, and security of most of the members of that union; and

➤ (c) The United Nations moved from being a forum to mitigate differences into one which exacerbated them. The UN had long been weaponized.

Bearing in mind the reality that the EU in many ways
geopolitically overlaps the NATO membership (ex-
cluding Canada and the US, which are in NATO but
not the EU), it was clear that NATO now had a new rôle
in protecting the physical borders of Europe. Significantly, it has not really been deployed to meet this new
rôle.

And that rôle was not specifically against an immediate threat of military intrusion by Russia, but very
specifically in resisting a multi-faceted strategic physical intrusion by Turkey, or facilitated by Turkey, ostensibly a NATO member.

How much, for example, had Europe been strategically inhibited by its inability to resist Turkish-spon-
sored or Turkish-supported population warfare which
weakened the economies and social frameworks of European states for the decade leading up to 2020. Turkey
then attempted to substantially expand and drive this
population-political warfare Westwards after the start
of the 2020 crisis. Moreover, this has not been constrained merely by the onpassage of refugees from the
Syrian civil war, but by "commoditizing" refugees fleeing economic and security challenges in Afghanistan,
Pakistan, Eritrea, and sub-Saharan Africa.

What emerged was that NATO remained a viable
and efficient military alliance for the protection of
Western interests, whereas the EU had not. NATO, in

an attempt to repurpose itself with the collapse of the original threat, the Warsaw Treaty *bloc*, had earlier sought an "out-of-area" mission, and was thus employed in the war in Afghanistan, for example in the first two decades of the 21st Century. But there was no real thought given to a broader redefinition of the Alliance, to include Indo-Pacific partners.

It had the potential to be broadened and renamed to include the ANZUS (Australia-New Zealand-US) Alliance, the US-Japan Security Alliance, and so on, to take on a new purpose akin to the World War II alliance against the nazi-fascist-Japanese *bloc*. Similarly, the UKUSA Accords — the Five-Eyes intelligence exchange between the US, UK, Canada, Australia, and New Zealand — had the capacity to be repurposed with strategic objectives.

Clearly, alliances and treaties all need sunset clauses: dates by which they are either retired or repurposed. The various arms limitation treaties have all either expired through mutual disinterest, or they have been consistently and dynamically given ongoing lives. Or they have become tools by one party to inhibit another.

The successive treaties to limit the construction of capital ships by major navies in the first half of the 20th Century was a classical case of how treaties were overtaken either by technological change or by the change in strategic objectives of the major powers. That included the Washington Naval Treaty of 1922; the London Naval Treaty of 1930; the Second London Naval Treaty of 1936 (by which time the process had become more or less meaningless).

Treaties and alliances are meant to give the signatories breathing space. Nothing more. All that is constant is "permanent interests". And then we need to renegotiate the meaning of "permanent".

Again, as we discussed in Point 1, above [How Societies Revive], the COVID-19 interregnum was the ideal time to revisit national goals, and to redefine the means of achieving them in a world in which the strategic context — the terrain — had clarified in new ways.

We will discuss in Point 4, below, the need to look at alliances within the framework of trade and survival patterns. But it should be noted that the strategic dichotomy which occurred by 2020 — the crystalization of the new bipolar power structure — owed its virility to the West abandoning one of its great World War II allies, the Republic of China (ROC).

One of the biggest self-inflicted defeats of the West was to remove from the United Nations (UN) one of its founding members, the ROC, and to give its seat in the General Assembly and Security Council to the People's Republic of China. The West allowed itself to conflate the Communist Party of China with China itself. The CPC was hardly responsible for the defeat of Japan; neither did it — as ROC leader Chiang Kai-shek did — contribute to the founding of the UN.

The PRC went on to inexorably erode the freedom of action which remained to Taiwan through the consistent manipulation of UN bodies, such as the World

Health Organization, the International Civil Aviation Organization (ICAO), and so on. The damage to Taiwan's flexibility by using ICAO to re-allocate air transport corridors into Taiwanese airspace, for example, helped reduce the ROC's sovereign space.

Beijing understood that its eventual break-out into the Central Pacific was absolutely governed by its ability to break the "First Island Chain" off the East Eurasian landmass. And Taiwan was central to this, and to the US' and its allies' ability to ensure freedom of navigation through the Indo-Pacific.

3. Repurposing Economies

IT IS TIME TO RE-DESIGNATE the economic framework which existed up until 2020 as the "old economy".

And that includes the economic prisms through which we viewed science and technology up to that point. Moreover, it has moved far beyond the confines of "nationalism *versus* globalism", and the abandonment of broader supply-chain thinking. Old, rigid ideological thinking gives way to creativity. So the "new economy" includes some legacies, such as:

> ➤ (a) Global and national economies are constrained by unprecedented levels of debt and debt service;

> ➤ (b) Declining market size due to economic constraints and to the actual decline in population numbers, particularly within key socio-economic market groups;

> ➤ (c) Polarization, because of economic, political

and security factors, of trading networks, leading to greater bilateralization of trade and the need to re-monetize some trade as barter or counter-trade, or define it by creative currency "baskets";

➤ (d) Reduced availability of funding, for a period, for research and development, some commercial infrastructure, and for pure science. On the other hand, viable stimulus to re-engage unemployed workers would likely include some public sector infrastructure packages;

➤ (e) Greater ease by armed forces in achieving re-cruiting targets as commercial jobs fail to take up all available workforce;

➤ (f) Growing distrust of governmental attempts to control the economy by restricting the use of cash as paper currencies lose the "full faith and credit" of governments. This will see a stimulus for the use of alternate forms of "currency", including cryptocurrencies. All of this will lead to a polarization of societies away from governments (ie: lead to greater distrust in government), which can only be contained for a limited period and which will absolutely lead to a further decline in economic productivity, as the PRC has been discovering for the past eight years. This further compounds the challenge of global strategic competitiveness. One antidote to this will be the nationalization of some of the key components of infrastructure to deliver products, people, and energy.

What, then, is to be done?

The stimulation of national economies is very much linked to seeing economies as just that: national. Or at least protected within specific geopolitical regions. That was abhorrent to many globalist free traders, but new realities will shape secure trading patterns.

The first decades of the 21st Century (indeed, the period since the end of the Cold War) saw most countries out-source much of their manufacturing to the PRC. The crash of 2020 saw, then, most countries exposed to an existential dependency on the PRC for vital supplies across all sectors of society.

This resulted in the biggest single erosion of the sovereignty and independence of most nation-states in the world in, perhaps, a century.

The PRC, in order to capitalize on the damage inflicted by the 2020 crisis on most national economies, quickly moved to return to full PRC manufacturing capability to ensure that, as the coronavirus containments were lifted on most economies, the PRC could then dump manufactured goods onto the world market, as well as attempt to boost domestic activity.

This was designed to ensure that national manufacturing in other countries would be disincentivized from being re-established in order to end dependency on the PRC. But the PRC manufacturing base had already begun to outprice itself during the past five years at least (to 2020), and Beijing had to do something to regain its position as the "sole source" for manufacturing.

This meant that the PRC had a vested interest, too, in ensuring that those rising economies which had been beginning to take over the global manufacturing rôles from the PRC were themselves set back. That included the manufacturing sectors of Thailand, Vietnam, and so on.

Hence the need for those nation-states wishing to re-assert a measure of sovereign independence to consider restrictions and tariffs on imported goods as a means to protect the re-start of local industries. The question, then, was how to do this in a way which did not allow also the re-building of work-force complacency and revived union opportunism, knowing that domestic markets were protected.

A variety of actions, then, would need to be considered by those "advanced" societies which had thought themselves somehow in the post-industrial phase, but now found it necessary to revive domestic manufacturing. These could include:

> Eliminating constraints on small to medium businesses by (i) minimizing the burden of tax reporting bureaucracy; (ii) creating a simplified tax structure for small to medium business; and (iii) creating freedoms from heavy unionization for small to medium businesses.

> Repurposing education away from the "pseudo-post-industrial" model which focused on university degrees of questionable value either to liberal, contextual thinking, or to education in spheres of practical value to manufacturing. This would

mean reversing the demeaning and paternalistic view of academia toward "blue collar" workforces, and instead providing technical school educations, and structured trade apprenticeships.

➤ This could and should enable many people to enter the workforce at a younger age, thus stimulating the economy by removing them from society-supported dependency. Moreover, it could also include apprenticeship-like skills acquisition in the armed services.

➤ Eliminating the punitive elements of bankruptcy laws, and lower the barrier to the creation of new corporations to stimulate the creation of entrepreneurial enterprises. Even the US has, in recent years, made aspects of its bankruptcy laws more punitive, but the US still provides the best model in this regard. Australia, for example, has corporate start-up and wind-up practices which are draconian and Dickensian. The more that the state is removed from the process, the more that enterprise and productivity will be stimulated.

➤ Eliminating or reducing the size of centralized governmental structures. Government employment is a burden for any economy. Some of it is vital to ensuring a viable state; most of it is not. Reducing governmental bureaucracies by enforcing a wave of mandatory retirements and a selective freeze on hiring is a far better use of state funds than financing an unproductive economy.

➤ Eliminating legislative constraints on agricultural

efficiency and encouraging programs which help restore soil balance. Ensuring adequate farmer control over water sources, and also reversing the negative impact of the use of chemical fertilizers over the past century.

4. Repurposing Trading Blocs

TRADE IS AN ESSENTIAL TOOL of society. It is assumed that free trade is the vital aspect of a prospering society. But the reality is that only trade *in essentials* is an existential underpinning of sovereignty.

The control of trade and trading patterns is also, therefore, a decisive tool in national security strategy. World Wars I and II made clear how control of global sea lanes determined the outcome of those conflicts.

"Free trade" in a time of confrontation and crisis, then, is axiomatically counterproductive to achieving national survival and in constraining an opponent.

The crisis of 2020 ensured that, for the time being, the age of free trade was now ended.

That is not an ideological or philosophical position — concepts of markets determining free trade can endure — but rather a position of ensuring national survival, and minimizing the advantage of a competitor. Apart from the major power which wishes to dominate its trading partners, only those who do not recognize that a war has begun will continue to insist on "free trade".

So if trade is to be emphasized between trusted partners, then that would assume that trade pacts would need to include security provisions to ensure the carriage of that trade. This re-emphasizes, of course, the security of sea lanes, straits and waterways, and air traffic routes. The assumption of a continuation of the old "rules-based world order" is no longer guaranteed.

The PRC, in announcing (in September 2018) its "new Thirty Years War" indicated that at the end of that war (in 2049) it would have in place a "new Treaty of Westphalia" — by some new name — to emplace a Beijing-dominated "rules-based world order". Saying it does not make it so, but the intention was clear: the PRC does not accept the pre-2020 order of theoretically-equal nation-states to be valid.

The new trading objectives of post-2020 governments, then, need to be defined, because it is clear that they have not been defined up until this point. These objectives would need to define national goals, needs, and methods of achieving the desired ends.

It means that trading patterns must overlay security patterns. In other words, if trade is critical, the means must be there to ensure that it can be achieved.

Trade, then, becomes not merely about commodities, but about the means and routes of delivering them, and the security to guarantee that pattern.

5. Repurposing Strategies

How CAN STRATEGIES designed for different times be applied in the post-2020 world?

Economic, geopolitical, and trade dependency factors changed with the crisis of 2020. Yes, much business would continue as usual, but the underlying strategic inflection changed, and the global debt position transformed economic capabilities.

More to the point, the People's Republic of China made it clear that it had already embarked on a war from which it could not resile. That war, for the PRC, as noted, was to be dominated by a strong interactive pattern of population, sociological, economic, technological, and information dominance factors, quite apart from military factors.

Indeed, the PRC hoped that the war would be won before any resort to formal military confrontation.

Does that mean that one response would be to force the PRC to fight its war on terms it considers disadvantageous? Because that would indeed be a military aspect of the "total war".

So, by 2020, the PRC was embarked on a defensive military strategy *vis-à-vis* the United States, while posturing with symbolic military actions in some areas, such as the South and East China Seas and around Taiwan. But Beijing is highly aggressive in its power projection by diplomatic and non-military means against other targets. And it only had economic levers to sustain that attempted use of "overwhelming force" on its trading and diplomatic partners.

And these were levers from a declining PRC economy. As noted, the PRC approach was to minimize resistance to its strategic offensive by minimizing the economic strength and independence of its targets.

Where have we seen a comparable model of strategic

projection in history? Nothing appears to be immediately comparable. This is very much a grand strategy of bluff, deception, and audacity. It was, for Beijing, effective until 2020, but the 2020 crisis then polarized much thinking against the PRC and CPC.

But did this also offer the PRC consideration of a military gamble to, for example, seize Taiwan and finish the civil war once and for all against the Republic of China? Until possibly 2021, the People's Liberation Army could have some possible ability to move against Taiwan while limiting US capabilities to help defend Taiwan. It would be a gamble, but Beijing might not get another chance at the roulette table.

6. Repurposing Defense

WHAT MILITARY STRUCTURES and doctrine would survive the 2020 inflection point?

Clearly, for the first time in many years, most governments needed to force their defense planners to harmonize defense strategic plans with national grand strategic goals and options. That was difficult, because defense structures are heavily dependent on legacy capital items, legacy doctrine, and inherited postures. And government leaders are notoriously resistant to stating long-term goals.

Governments were, by 2020, revisiting their situations, but to what extent could long-term capital defense programs be re-calibrated for the new strategic environment? Even more significantly, how could defense forces even sustain operational capabilities when declining national economic outlooks would likely constrain defense spending growth, if growth was even feasible in the coming few years?

To a significant degree, because the "new total war" was likely to be less kinetic and less formal than in the 20th Century, efficiencies would likely emerge from more interdisciplinary cooperation than had been historically achieved. This was the most difficult aspect. In "war" situations, the military assumes it must lead.

The Russian Government in 2019 gave warfighting leadership, even in non-kinetic frameworks, to the Russian General Staff on the basis that "non-military actions comprised 80 percent of contemporary conflict". But can careers of military discipline, logic, and chain of command adapt to the new, fluid, amorphous social face of "total war of the 21st Century"?

We are left with sufficient evidence to see not only that this amorphous new "total war" of the 21st Century is real, but that it was already upon us by 2020. It would continue throughout the lives of many of those who were born in the 20th Century and early 21st Century.

But it would be a grinding war of powers heavily weakened by their debts; their tools dulled by insufficient growth in resources. Many states would break apart and be rebuilt, perhaps in different forms and various pieces. The glittering process of delivering continually new capabilities would falter. Some societies would prosper, and to do so they would safeguard their borders. Do not expect, therefore, that the anticipated "fourth industrial revolution" will come like the miracle it was hoped to transform mankind in a way "unlike anything humankind has experienced before". It was supposed to be a linear extrapolation of the "third industrial revolution", building on the fusion of the 20th Century's use of information technology to automate production. Aspects of the new technological fusion *will* occur, but economic, energy, demographic, and strategic interruptions will make it a patchwork affair.

We will see that our patterns mirror the cycles of history. And for each vale of tears through which humanity must pass there is a vision of possibilities from the mountaintop.

We can think then of John Keating's words in his poem, "On First Looking into Chapman's Homer":

Much have I travell'd in the realms of gold,
  And many goodly states and kingdoms seen;
  Round many western islands have I been
Which bards in fealty to Apollo hold.
Oft of one wide expanse had I been told
  That deep-brow'd Homer ruled as his demesne;
  Yet did I never breathe its pure serene
Till I heard Chapman speak out loud and bold:
Then felt I like some watcher of the skies
  When a new planet swims into his ken;
Or like stout Cortez when with eagle eyes
  He stared at the Pacific — and all his men
Look'd at each other with a wild surmise —
  Silent, upon a peak in Darien.

Epilogue

Moving Through the Phony War Period

S O MID-2020 SAW THE WORLD AT WAR. It was actual strategic war as far as the Forbidden Palace in Beijing was concerned: a life and death issue for the communist governance of China.

This reality was gradually, almost disbelievingly acknowledged around the world.

It was a war which was viewed tentatively and with incredulity in much of the West because it was a war of a very new type. And it was a war in which the West — for the first time in a century or more — had not written the rules of engagement.

Indeed, because it had emerged from covert war to overt war, the People's Republic of China leadership was aware, certainly by early May 2020 (and probably even by January of that year), that it had to quickly use the cover of the global coronavirus preoccupation and lockdown to make and consolidate key strategic advances while it could do so unopposed.

Initial objectives for Beijing included:

➤ 1. Locking down control of the autonomous Hong

Kong region — a significant source of the PRC's access to foreign exchange generation — once and for all, and with minimal foreign reprisal;

➤ 2. Rebuilding a PRC position whereby it could resume global dominance of manufacturing, which it had been losing even before the 2020 crisis;

➤ 3. Consolidate military domination of the South and East China Seas regions, to include Taiwan;

➤ 4. Break up the revival of a coherent US alliance structure in the Indo-Pacific (including the Middle East) and ensure that there were no viable options to allow the Russian Federation to expand its *rapprochement* with the West. It needed to end the prospect that the "second Silk Road", dominated by Russia and supported by Japan (in particular), would not be strategically threatening to Beijing;

➤ 5. Shorten the timescale for a military-led option to remove Taiwan — the Republic of China (ROC) — from any chance of depending on strategic military cover from the United States and Japan.

There were no immediate, clearcut successes visible for Beijing by mid-2020, but the urgency was there, and so was the momentum.

The PRC had no option but to make gains quickly, and it was clear that it had done so, despite reviving fear, distrust, and counter-action by the US, UK, Australia, and others. Beijing's economic position and outlook, worsening for at least the previous decade, could not sustain the PRC's strategic competitiveness *vis-à-vis* the US and its allies much longer unless the crisis could be used to bring about the ruin of the relative economic and military positions of its opponents.

If Beijing could not succeed in recovering its economic (and therefore strategic) competitiveness, then all others needed to lose *their* ability to compete.

It was a war plan consciously written by the Communist Party of China (CPC), and particularly in the image of the CPC and PRC leader, Xi Jinping. It had its ideological origins in the globalism pioneered by the Communist Party of the Soviet Union (CPSU), but it took on maoist characteristics (consolidated by the updated maoism of Xi Jinping), including the clarity of the 1999 doctrinal watershed of the publication of the *Unrestricted Warfare* total war strategy.

So the new war doctrine — the 21st Century version of "total war" — was a long time in coming. Its development was also, most importantly, an evolution of the Allied victory of World War II, with its development of global supply chain thinking: logistics and industrialization.

The CPC, starting with Deng Xiaoping, learned to truly create "socialism with Chinese characteristics", but that meant something very much modernized over historical marxist-oriented interpretations. This led, progressively, to the understanding by Beijing that it needed to rebuild the traditional "global" supply chain pattern through which the Middle Kingdom had made itself the central power through much of ancient history. Its suppliant, or tributary vassals, had depended on the Silk Routes, overland through Eurasia and by sea through the Indo-Pacific (and beyond), and must be made to do so again.

This became Xi Jinping's "One Belt, One Road" (OBOR) initiative, which in May 2017 became the "Belt & Road Initiative" (BRI) when it was clear that Moscow, Tokyo, and Washington were attempting to create a "second Silk Road" across Russia, bypassing Beijing's attempted domination of the South China Sea (to control the Silk Road at Sea).[96]

But in the period up to mid-2020, the "new total war" was viewed — particularly in the West — as nebulous. This new total war format is, by definition, amorphous, and deliberately so. Direct, kinetic confrontation — the measure by which the uniformed

---

96 On June 8, 2017, this writer noted in *Defense & Foreign Affairs Special Analysis*: "Beijing is attempting to push Washington to 'peacefully decline' or retreat in certain areas, through a "Fourth Communiqué" between the US and the PRC. The new terms which Beijing seeks would see the US voluntarily surrender any ability to regard Taiwan as an ally, or to deal with it in any military or diplomatic terms. This would neutralize the ROC's ability to sustain a viable, independent military, and would therefore leave the PRC the ability to move strategic forces freely into the Central Pacific, a positioning which would, in fact, begin to challenge US and other nations' security of navigation and the US' ability to balance PRC strategic forces." The US recognition of the People's Republic of China in 1978 was followed by the passage, during the US Carter Administration, of The Taiwan Relations Act, in 1979, which allowed for the US defense of Taiwan, and which was further amended by three subsequent 'communiqués' with the PRC. The matter of a 'Fourth Communiqué' was raised by the PRC and rejected by the US White House before the April 6-7, 2017, meeting between PRC Pres. Xi Jinping and Pres. Donald Trump at Mar-a-Lago, Florida. It was raised again — although in what context is unclear — by former US Secretary of State (and now PRC advisor) Dr Henry Kissinger, then aged 93, at a meeting with Pres. Trump on May 10, 2017. Pres. Xi wanted the 'Fourth Communiqué' to crown his consolidation of power at the 19th National Congress of the Communist Party of China later in 2017. The architect of the planned "Fourth Communiqué" is former PRC Foreign Minister (2007-13) Yang Jiechi, still a senior diplomat and State Councilor, who orchestrated Beijing's approach to the Mar-a-Lago talks. He then met with US National Security Council Senior Director for Asian Affairs and former US Marine Matthew Pottinger on the sidelines of the 'Belt and Road Initiative' summit in Beijing in mid-May 2017 to unsuccessfully promote the idea."

military and much of society viewed "war" — was absent, although the threat of it had finally emerged by April-May 2020, and this galvanized thinking among Western policymakers. They were unprepared for it.

It even generated enough alarm to see the deep internal political schisms in the US and Australia heal to a small degree. In the US, the emerging threat saw Democratic Party and Republican Party politicians agreeing — largely unreported in the US media — to reject the PRC's threat to US and Western interests. It also caused the UK Government to finally be able to move, with broad public acceptance, to end the PRC's strategic leverage in Britain, including ending the question of reliance on the PRC's 5G communications technology from Huawei.

However, it was, to use the term at the start of World War II, a period of "phony war", just as it appeared from September 1939, until May 10, 1940. And it was akin to the thinking which, after World War I was enjoined in August 1914, saw soldiers happily reassuring their families that they would be "home by Christmas".

Both those episodes of wishful thinking characterized the start of the two total wars of the 20th Century.

But in both those conflicts, as with the new total war of the 21st Century, those who had long planned secretly for an offensive war knew that their canvases extended beyond formal military conflict. They planned for a victory which had global, and indeed globalist, ramifications: a total world system unified under the nexus of the visionary power.

But these titanic struggles are usually won or lost by factors determined well in advance of the opening shots of kinetic war, and during the "phony war" period before the targets of the initial aggressor are aware that they have been caught at a disadvantage. In the Napoleonic Wars, World Wars I and II, and the Cold War, the aggressors (France, Germany twice, and the Soviet Union coupled with the People's Republic of China) sensed that they were at a significant strategic disadvantage. This caused them to undertake strategic preparations and operations without and well before any formal declaration of war.

They needed to steal a march on their adversaries. Significantly, in all of those "total wars" — and the Cold War was even more total than the earlier great wars — the initial aggressor never overcame its fundamental lack of comprehensive strategic strength.

Was the new total war of the 21st Century likely to be different?

Was it likely to be as protracted as the four-decade Cold War? Certainly, given technologies and the extent to which some three decades of "peaceful" globalism had allowed Beijing to dominate supply chains so that its trading partners became dependent on it, it was to be a far more amorphous war than even the Cold War.

Pres. Xi had cause for optimism, but also — because of the PRC's fundamental and increasing economic weakness — needed to accelerate the timescale for initiating operations which he knew would bring a major strategic response, a pushback, from his adversaries.

The late 2019 outbreak of the COVID-19 crisis provided the trigger point for open offensive operations by the PRC, but they were operations which were still within the boundaries of amorphous warfare.

Beijing, going into the 2020 break-out, understood *completely* the limitations and strengths of its existing formal military capabilities.

In the words of the US Country and Western song, it "knows when to hold 'em, knows when to fold 'em, knows when to walk away, knows when to run". Beijing knew that it must essentially win the new total war before it became globally kinetic, and therefore it must preclude the formation (or the re-joining) of Western alliances and strategic economic gains against it, and prevent Russia, in particular, from being drawn into the Western camp.

Although the PRC had depended heavily (and resentfully) on Moscow during the Cold War, by the 21st Century it was Russia — still, in many ways, technologically more innovative than the PRC — which now depended on Beijing. Russia was, to draw an imperfect parallel from World War II, Italy to Beijing's Germany in the new total war.

Relative Foundational Strategic Capabilities

THEN-US SECRETARY OF Defense Donald Rumsfeld said: "You go to war with the army you have, not the army you might want or wish to have at a later time."

It is even more important to note that "you go to war with the government and economy you have, not the one which you might wish for or need".

On the military side, while that Rumsfeld comment was as true today as it was in the early post-Cold War period when he made his comment, it is also true that all aspirant powers attempt to gain as much force development — and technology — as possible before having to show their hand in a major war.

This was the particularly the case with the PRC since Pres. Xi Jinping came to supremacy in 2012.

It may not be reasonable to say the same about the Russian Federation in this timeframe. Russia was indeed, in the post-Cold War era, able to step out from the shadow of the Soviet-era to prepare its forces, doctrine, and technology to a state where the US regarded it as its "pacing threat": the *capability* which most challenged US capabilities. But it was the PRC which worked discreetly to pose the *actual* threat.

To a significant degree, the economics of Eurasia and the Russian dependency on cashflow from the PRC meant that Beijing largely had access to Russian technology during its critical build-up period for war against the US and its allies. But the PRC also had access (even in the pre-Xi era) to much Western strategic technology through intelligence-driven acquisition of Western intellectual property. This included the very technology of strategic precision targeting and guidance for ballistic weapons and hypersonic weapons which threatened US and allied capabilities in the offshore oceans of East, and South-East Asia, by 2020.

Beijing knew that, if it needed to force the US to "go

to war with the army it has", rather than the defense force it needed to have, it had best do so before the defense modernization plans driven by the US Donald Trump Administration could take effect.

Beijing had clear confirmation by early 2019 that the intended Trump upgrades to the US defense capabilities had not yet taken hold, and that some of the US capability improvements were unlikely due to long-term commitments to, for example, the Lockheed Martin F-35-series combat aircraft. On March 7, 2020, a RAND organization warfare analyst, in a speech to the (significantly, Democratic Party-controlled) Center for a New American Security, announced that RAND conflict simulation had seen the US fail to prevail in a comprehensive military engagement with either the PRC or Russia. RAND analyst David Ochmanek noted: "We lose a lot of people. We lose a lot of equipment. We usually [in these engagements] fail to achieve our objective of preventing aggression by the adversary."[97]

The conclusions were supported by a presentation by former US Deputy Defense Secretary Robert Work. "In every case I know of," said Work, "the F-35 rules the sky when it's in the sky, but it gets killed on the ground in large numbers." But subsequent failures of the F-35 to achieve anything like acceptable operational readiness rates do not even justify DepSec Work's qualified optimism.

---

97 See, Freedberg Jr., Sydney J.: "US 'Gets Its Ass Handed To It' in Wargames: Here's a $24-billion Fix", in *Breaking Defense* (website), March 7, 2019.

A gathering of the Aspen Security Forum in the US in July 2019 brought further reinforcement of the relative weakness of US forces in the Pacific. Much of this analysis was based on the 2015 RAND study, *The US-China Military Scorecard: Forces, Geography, and the Evolving Balance of Power, 1996-2017,* but with follow-on simulation strengthening the case.

The 2018 bipartisan official study for the US Defense Department, entitled *Providing for the Common Defense: The Assessment and Recommendations of the National Defense Strategy Commission,* noted: "If the United States had to fight Russia in a Baltic contingency or China in a war over Taiwan, Americans could face a decisive military defeat." The Commission highlights the PRC's and Russia's ongoing efforts to develop advanced anti-access/area-denial (A2/AD) weaponry, systems which could result in "enormous" losses for the US military in a conflict. It went on: "Put bluntly, the US military could lose the next state-*versus*-state war it fights".

The Trump Administration, however, was moving rapidly to attempt to rectify the challenge, moving belatedly to accelerate the introduction of maneuverable hypersonic weapons for offensive and defensive operations. Indeed, the speed with which the Trump White House was committed to recovering US defense capabilities clearly played a key rôle in spurring Beijing to action to achieve essential objectives in the "near-abroad" before the US could rectify its disadvantage.

Already, Xi had moved the PRC's defense emphasis

from ground force operations of the People's Liberation Army (PLA) toward the PLA Navy (PLAN) and the PLA Air Force (PLAAF) and — even more importantly — the Strategic Rocket Force and the Strategic Support Force. Essentially, the PRC was attempting to do something which it had not achieved since the first half of the 13th Century: to become a (if not *the*) globally dominant maritime power. But the first order of business was to dominate the First Island Chain (and particularly Taiwan) and subdue the US control of the Central Pacific (based on Guam) into defeat or at least a defensive impotence.

That a window of opportunity continued to exist into 2020 for the PRC to use its largely mobile ballistic missile (and hypersonic payload) capabilities to neutralize both US fleets at sea within around 1,000 n.miles from the PRC coastline and against US air (particularly B-52, B-2, and B-1 bomber) and missile assets on Guam and the Japanese islands was evident.

An open report in the UK newspaper, *The Times*, on May 16, 2020, indicated that continuing US simulation exercises showed that US forces would be overwhelmed, and that the situation was worsening with the introduction of new PLAN attack submarines, aircraft carriers, and destroyers through 2030. *The Times* article quoted Bonnie Glaser, director of the China Power Project at the Center for Strategic and International Studies in Washington, DC, and a consultant for the US Government on East Asia, as saying: "Every simulation that has been conducted looking at the threat from China by 2030 have all ended up with the defeat of the US. … Taiwan is the most volatile issue because that could escalate to a war with the US, even to a nuclear war. In the Pentagon and State Department and the White House, China is now seen as the biggest threat. We have been too passive in the past."

PRC military and intelligence analysis clearly recognized that short-term military success would not necessarily equate to long-term victory.

The Japanese decision to strike at US naval and air assets at Pearl Harbor, Hawaii, on December 7, 1941, actually *ensured* long-term Japanese defeat in World War II, and Beijing had no desire to create a similar outlook for itself.

But Beijing had no option but to initiate conflict with the US alliance at this time if it wished to avoid short-term implosion due to economic and internal resource shortcomings.

There is no doubt that Beijing has had a decade to consider this, and to formulate its broader strategic plan to help foment a more comprehensive collapse of US and Western strategic and economic resilience. Well, at least sufficient to enable the PRC to consolidate its geo-strategic space and sufficient economic strength to ensure domestic population control.

Initial PRC Targets

Xi Jinping needed, by May 2020, to show early strategic progress for substantive and prestige reasons. Both were critical to ensure domestic support and compliance, and to move regional and global competition into a defensive and possibly conciliatory posture.

Consolidation and demonstration of PLA capabilities in the South China Sea and against the ROC on Taiwan were ongoing, but did not yet reach the level of a definitive, iconic, and durable outcome for Beijing.

Beijing, through its National People's Congress on May 22, 2020, introduced a new national security law for Hong Kong to suppress "sedition, secession, and subversion" as well as foreign involvement, "terrorism", and autonomy. Despite Beijing's denial, this represented the effective end of the "one nation, two systems" policy guaranteed under the terms of the July 1, 1997, handover of Hong Kong to the PRC by the United Kingdom.

Politicians from 23 nations had, by May 24, 2020, signed a petition of complaint against Beijing for the action, but the real test of how much it would impact the economy of the PRC would be determined by whether the US ended its special economic relationship with Hong Kong. That would be a significant blow for Beijing, but the CPC had calculated that the pro-democracy movement in Hong Kong had already effectively destroyed significant contributions by Hong Kong to the PRC economy, and the coronavirus shutdowns had merely cemented that reality.

So bringing Hong Kong under direct Beijing control was worth the loss of whatever economic benefits the territory might still have had. And it would send a firm indication of Beijing's resolution to Taiwan. But real questions persisted as to how much the act would calm or inflame unrest against Beijing in Hong Kong, and whether it would caution or inflame anti-Beijing sentiments being aroused by economic and COVID-19 related issues around the rest of mainland China.

Again, clearly, Beijing could not accept the situation in Hong Kong, and had no option — if the CPC wished to retain control — but to suppress by force the "pro-democracy movement" which had refused to bend to any other entreaties. Similarly, internal security in the rest of the PRC would be undertaken forcefully. And Beijing was aware of the escalation of US and Turkish fomenting of the Uighur (Turkic) population of Xinjiang (with the "East Turkestan" independence movement). The now-naked US-PRC hostilities meant that Washington would be less discreet in its support for the Uighurs against their suppression by Beijing.

The question there was how much Beijing could pressure Moscow to on-pass pressure against Turkey to cease cooperation with the US on this issue. Ankara saw itself as the pan-Turkist patron of the East Turkestan movement.

Beijing had, by early May 2020, begun (once again) to probe a military flexing against India in the Pangong Tso Lake and Galwan Valley areas of Eastern Ladakh, part of Kashmir, along the "Line of Actual Control" in the unresolved border area. The Indian Army immediately matched the PLA buildup which had taken place in the two weeks to May 22, 2020. At least five rounds of talks at local levels there had, by May 22, 2020, failed to calm the tensions, and there had been violent confrontations between Indian Army and PLA forces on May 5, 2020, and a similar incident in North Sikkim on May 9, 2020.

From the PRC perspective, this manageable exercise was a form of *probasila* (Soviet term): reconnaissance to the point of contact, to gauge enemy strength, reaction, and resolve. It gave Beijing an option to escalate or distract, and possibly to divert India away from broader cooperation with the US and other South-East Asian nations on the question of PRC advances. But the PLA operations were also key to its resolve to support Pakistan's claims to its part of Kashmir which determines the PRC's critical overland access to the Indian Ocean, something threatened by India's 2019 invasion of Kashmir. And the mountains control water flows into the Indus Valley in Pakistan, and to China.

So the Ladakh escalation was a key indicator of Beijing's need to ensure a consolidation of its close geographic links in the Indo-Pacific region as well as its concerns over control of the water resources originating in the Central and South Asian mountains.

But of overriding importance to Beijing was its campaign to ensure that US Pres. Donald Trump was not re-elected to the Presidency in the November 3, 2020, election, and that the Republican Party would lose its majority in the House of Representatives and the Senate. In some respects, and using the contrived narrative of US initiation of, engagement in, and mismanagement of the COVID-19 crisis, the CPC was able to make common cause with such anti-Trump US influencers as *The New York Times* and the CNN cable network. Yet as tempting as this tactical alliance was in helping the Democratic Party to seek the ouster of Trump and the Republicans in November 2020, it was clear by mid-May 2020 that many in the Democratic Party leadership were also turning against Beijing over the COVID-19 issue and its hostility toward both the US and its allies, and Hong Kong.

Beijing might never have expected an overt alliance with anti-Trump elements in the US, but it aimed at achieving sufficient "nett effect" with them to sustain momentum against a Trump/Republican victory in November 2020. There was little doubt in Beijing that had Hillary Clinton defeated Trump in the 2016 election, the PRC would not have seen the sharp end to two decades of unopposed PRC strategic expansion in the Indo-Pacific and the Africa-Middle East regions.

In this light, it must be construed that Beijing supported in many ways the initiation of riots in US cities in the final days of May and early days of June 2020, as a sign of the PRC's retaliation against Western support for Hong Kong rioters.

Initial Strategic Operations

BEIJING'S INITIAL strategic operations in the new total war had been underway for some time before the 2020 watershed.

However, with the watershed of the COVID-19 crisis, the PRC's most urgent initial strategic operation was to ensure that it consolidated its hold on markets around the world. It had been losing market share gradually to other manufacturing states as labor costs mounted in the PRC.

The initial strategic operation of the CPC in early 2020 was to ensure that the PRC's factories returned to full production as quickly as possible so that an abundance of PRC-made goods could be dumped at concessionary prices onto the world market. This would, if done rapidly and at enticing prices, make it more difficult to stimulate the re-establishment of manufacturing in the major "pseudo-post-industrial" client states of North America, Europe, and Australasia.

This operation was a race against time for Beijing. It relied on the marketplace lure of cheap goods to overturn the instinct to resist Beijing and re-create — and incentivize and protect — revived local industry. The ability of client states to resist the dependence on the PRC would require legislation and government programs, and Beijing hoped that, over time, the urgency of those efforts would fade and the client states would fall back into the slumber of dependency on the PRC as the supplier of goods.

Beijing also hoped that by returning to robust economic production early in 2020 it could reinforce its claims that its form of governance had triumphed over the chaos of liberal democracy as evidenced by the COVID-19 malaise in Western and other "Western-style democracies".

These were reasonable strategic exercises, but there was no evidence by June 2020 of success, or that, on the other hand, the US and its allies would have the ability to re-grow their independent strategic capabilities in the near-term. And Beijing clearly hoped that, by dampening a return to vigorous Western dominance in the short-term, it could then deliver, with kinetic operations as well as ongoing splitting operations within target societies, a further process of reducing US-led abilities to withstand the relative growth and dominance of the PRC.

Initial Kinetic Operations

PRES. Xi WAS, IN May 2020, clearly hoping to postpone initial kinetic operations of the new war for as long as possible. It was in his interests to make as much progress as possible before his opponents began their own strategic revival.

That "strategic revival" by Beijing's opponents was the prospect that the US and other PRC client states would quickly reduce or substantively end their supply chain and general trade reliance on the PRC. In fact, public and governmental reaction against the PRC in Beijing's trading partners was swift and strong. Beijing's attempts to bully the Australian Government into withdrawing its demand for an independent inquiry into the origins of the coronavirus epidemic were successful in that the World Health Assembly (WHA) in Geneva on May 18-19, 2020, dampened down the Australian-led call for an independent inquiry in favor of a World Health Organization (WHO) commitment to a "lessons learned" inquiry "soon".

This actually only served to anger the US and its allies further, something compounded by a statement on May 19, 2020, from the PRC embassy in Canberra noting that the terms of the COVID-19 resolution were "totally different from Australia's proposal of an independent international review ... All those who know the consultation process that led to the resolution understand this. To claim the WHA's resolution [as] a vindication of Australia's call is nothing but a joke."

PRC Ambassador to Australia Cheng Jingye had, until a few months earlier, been able to get lead articles in Australian national media to berate Australians into thanking Beijing for Australia's economic success. By mid-May 2020, every appearance or statement by Amb. Cheng generated more Australian calls to rebuild Australian industry and reduce reliance on trade with the PRC.

Beijing had numbed, or paralyzed, North American, European, Australasian, South-East Asian, and other target audiences for a decade. It had made resistance to the "rise of China" unthinkable. But that period was now over. The war had been enjoined.

So where and how would kinetic operations begin?

Beijing was reluctant to initiate military action, but was ready to engage once it has begun. Both the PRC and US saw advantages and disadvantages in delaying decisive tactical or theater action. The path to escalation to nuclear engagement was also far less clear —

and deterrence far less sure — than during the NATO-Warsaw Pact "mutually-assured destruction" era. There seems a greater willingness by the PLA to engage in theater-nuclear capabilities (ie: against military targets).

Military action in the near-term could well consolidate the PRC position in its "near abroad". It could even achieve *de facto* or *de jure* control of Taiwan, a critical legitimizing goal for the CPC, if the US did not rush in tripwire assets and support to show a pre-emptive tripwire to deter PRC escalation. But what after that? Would it give Beijing the breathing space to "fight another day", given that — had it left matters as they were — it would not have had that chance, due to its growing economic difficulty (and the potential for collapse)?

Like Japan in 1941, the CPC had to buy time if it was to survive and consolidate control over markets and sources of supply. But, like Japan in 1941, would a precipitate action cause not just the US, but a variety of its allies, to rebuild in the longer-term?

The wager was now in the air.

A Strategic Glossary

Amorphous Warfare: Amorphous Warfare is this author's definition of the defining characteristic of total warfare in its 21st Century format: without clear form or absolute definition. Meant as a definition of strategic warfare format, rather than such definitions as "hybrid warfare", which tends to be far more clearly definable and identifiable as to the protaganists, and which tends to be more theater in nature. Like hybrid or other forms of non-linear warfare, it tends to employ all means available for weaponization and warfighting.

Hybrid warfare, including proxy warfare, tends to use disguised and unpredictable paths largely to compensate for strategic weakness; in other words, it attempts to make gains while blunting, deflecting, or deferring response capabilities from strategically more powerful adversaries; or to avoid adversaries coalescing into an effective opposing *bloc*. Consciously-conceived amorphous warfare, while retaining those shorter-term qualities, enables the protaganist to initiate and coordinate a range of over-arching and longer-term strategically offensive operations. These restrict — to a far greater degree than hybrid warfare — kinetic operations, and not only employ means "immediately available" for conflict prosecution, but mobilize larger-scale elements, including macro-economic, national-level population or cultural factors, and kinetic-preventing technological warfare strategies. [See also: Technology Warfare.]

"Black Swan events": A term, re-popularized in the early 21st Century, to describe catastrophic or transformative large-scale events which could not have been forecast. Lebanese-American author Nassim Nicholas Taleb popularized the modern use of the phrase in his 2007 book, *The Black Swan*, to describe events which, although of major importance to a society, could not be forecast.

It is Copley's contention that very few of these occurrences, in fact, defy forecasting. Rather, as Copley pointed out in his 2012 book, *UnCivilization: Urban Geopolitics in a Time of Chaos* [in the chapter entitled "Flying With Black Swans"], all such "black swan events" were merely the result of those who were taken by surprise failing to have had sufficient intelligence warning or contextual knowledge to have anticipated the event. Taleb uses the historical analogy that because white swans prevailed in Europe, residents there could never have anticipated seeing a black swan. But that analogy alone merely expressed the lack of information on the part of the European audience, not that such a sighting was unable to have been forecast. Rather, as this writer remarks, "black swan events" tend, in reality, to be failures of intelligence.

City-state, micro-state: A city-state or a micro-state — the terms are not necessarily synonymous — are, by definition, sovereign, at least to degrees greater than cities which are merely urban centers of larger geopolitical entities. The historical city-states, dating to antiquity, were often able to sustain independence because of the lack of threats, or the reality that the relative wealth of a well-defended urban trading state gave it sufficient military power to resist conquest. Some chose to be suzerain or imperial powers by virtue of less direct control over geopolitical dominions, such as Venice or Rome.

Micro-states retain an interest in current geopolitical life because they are offered nominal protection by the international system (the United Nations, in particular, which grants these states equal voting rights in the global forum, an asset which can be of use for a variety of major power purposes), or because they are of more use, physically, to larger powers as nominally sovereign entities. The use by the People's Republic of China (PRC) in the second decade of the 21st Century of several Pacific Island micro-states, for example, enables discreet power projection into the Central Pacific by the PRC, without attracting the same attention as the incorporation of these territories as colonies or possessions of the PRC.

But the emerging use of the term "city-state" is of rising importance because it implies that certain urban entities act as though they were sovereign, and regard the national hinterlands — with which they were ostensibly once equal partners within the nation-state — as, effectively either suzerain holdings (vassal entities left to their own devices in some respects), or as satrapies, or of no importance whatever. This current phenomenon has been mirrored frequently in historical patterns, with the most common outcome being that the cities lose their pre-eminence upon the arrival of a militarily greater power, or lose significance because trading patterns bypass the urban society.

The Free City of Danzig (*Freie Stadt Danzig*; note the German-language version of the name as a "Free State", not a Free City) was a micro-state created by the political outcome of World War I, and lasted from 1919 until 1939, when German military power subsumed it. The end of World War II saw it restored as the Polish city of Gdansk. The ruins of Nabatean Kingdom spice route cities, such as Petra (now in Jordan) and Mada'in Saleh (now in Saudi Arabia) showed how the Kingdom declined, and essentially disappeared, by the Second Century CE because of changing trade patterns which robbed Nabatea of its world-class power status; its remnants were subsumed into the Roman Empire. Its port city, Gaza, survived and remains, essentially, a city-state of the 21st Century as a *de facto* part of the Palestine National Authority (PNA), although distinct from control (even suzerain control) by the PNA.

The case of current major power attention on Djibouti as a micro-state has already alerted the inhabitants to the reality that the sovereign entity might be better protected if it resumed its historical rôle as an entrepôt but integral component of the Ethiopian Empire.

City-states and micro-states, then, often lack the comprehensive support and protection of a nation-state; support which would enable them to survive vicissitudes of military threats or changing trading and climatic patterns. The "new city-states" — the great modern urban centers (such as New York City, London, and Paris) which act as though they were sovereign — appear to have some protection because, in fact, they control the resources of the nation-states which surround them. However, the 21st Century urban globalist view that the sovereign borders and definitions of the nation-state no longer matter would, if left to pursue its ultimate rejection of the hinterlands, spell an end to the nation-state and "nationalism". This means that the resultant, isolated city-states would again become vulnerable as the patterns of history have demonstrated.

Despite the fact that urban globalist ideologues have not thought this process through — given that urban-centric élitism is also highly materialistic and transactional in a short-term sense — such bodies as the UN's extensive Habitat organization, ostensibly working toward better governance and conditions for urban societies, have actively been coopted and transformed into vehicles to oppose the concept of nation-states and nationalism.

Cratocide: A word created, in discussion with the author, by Dr Marios Evriviades in 2006 for *The Art of Victory* to define the process of the deliberate destruction or erasure of a nation-state.

Cratogenesis: A word created, in discussion with the author, by Dr Marios Evriviades in 2006 for *The Art of Victory* to describe the process of the birth of a nation-state.

Cratometamorphosis: A word created, in discussion with the author, by Dr Marios Evriviades following the 2006 edition of *The Art of Victory* to define the process of the comprehensive re-shaping and reorganization of a nation-state.

Civil Society: Civil society is the phrase usually meant to embrace groups outside the governmental structure of a nation-state, but not including the commercial sector. The phrase has come, in the late 20th and early 21st centuries, to be a deliberate formalization of a rôle for "non-profit" activist groups, including so-called "non-governmental organizations" (NGOs), which have assumed *de facto* power as "legitimate" voices of authority based solely on their activism and sometimes the power of their discreet funding. So the phrase, "civil society", has become psychologically loaded and no longer actually implies the civilian body of a population, which includes a wider range of individuals and organized bodies, whether they be religious institutions or corporations.

Cyber Warfare: To distinguish it from electronic warfare, to which it is related, cyber warfare specifically implies the use of computer technology and (usually) digital tranmission to disrupt the electrically- and electronically-based systems, infrastructure, and networks of an adversary power at either a tactical or strategic level, and in the civil and military spheres. It is not merely the use of technology to attack an adversary, but is specifically digital and computer-related. The Wikipedia definition of "cyberwarfare" is inaccurate and incomplete. Cyber warfare and cyber operations are subsets of the larger strategic information dominance (ID) spectrum of operations, which also includes psychological strategy, psychological warfare, information warfare, signals operations and security, electronic warfare and electronic countermeasures, communications and communications security, and deception operations of other varieties.

Democracy: The Greek-derived word (from *demos*, meaning the common people, and *kratos*, meaning to rule) obscures the fact that what we think of as democracy — the will of the population to determine its own governance — is not in itself a concept or a political theory, but an innate human tendency which enables cooperative social behavior through the assigning and acceptance of rôles and responsibilities in group activity. The Greeks, by giving the characteristic a name, co-opted the phenomenon and began its political, abstract life. The word has evolved different meanings in different societies throughout history, so it should be used carefully and related to the context of the time and location.

Financial Maoism: The Communist Party of China's "Belt and Road Initiative" (BRI; formerly called the "One Belt-One Road" scheme) was created not so much as a practical economic framework (although it was partially that, too, with the PRC at the hub of economic and political activity) but as an *ideological* weapon to overturn the power of sovereignty of states which needed to be bent to Beijing. It was a definitive expression of globalism. It was maoist marxism put into transactional, materialistic terms to bind adherents to Beijing.

The BRI has been called a form of "predatory capitalism", but, in fact, it is not based on market capitalism in any way, or on capitalist cost-benefit thinking. It is based on political cost-benefit thinking, using cash as a replacement for intellectual or philosophical appeal. The BRI, in essence, is *financial maoism*. The ideology of the European Union "visionaries" is similar; it is not based on economic or market reality.

Globalism versus Globalization: In essence, *globalism* is an ideology; *globalization* is the phenomenon of actual trade infrastructure and mechanics. It is recognized that the words are often used, incorrectly, interchangeably, and that their use is often imprecise.

Globalism is often used to imply the structure of free and unfettered global trade, equating it in some senses to a component of libertarian philosophy, but this also misrepresents the word. In modern use in the 21st Century, "globalism" represents not just (or sometimes not even) a *lassaiz-faire* marketplace unrestricted by national borders, but implies an anti-nationalism, anti-border philosophy, and, at the same time a favoring of global governance and an "international law" set of regulations. In that sense, it is the opposite of *lassaiz-faire*, and has come to imply a transactional, material framework.

Globalization, on the other hand, speaks of the phenomenon, mechanism, and infrastructure of global physical and services trading. While this framework can, of course, be used for unrestricted trading, and therefore accommodate the needs of globalism, it can also be used for politically- and strategically-determined structured trading patterns.

Certainly, "globalization" literally implies the ability to trade in goods and services anywhere in the world through physical and electronic infrastructure and vehicles. But merely because the ability to function globally exists does not imply an ideological commitment to using the entirety of that infrastructure, nor to allowing that infrastructure to be used unilaterally against the wishes of sovereignty.

Grand Strategy: Grand strategy is the concept and practice of consciously defining and achieving an over-arching perception and management of a society into the indefinite future. It implies particular regard to the external human and natural context surrounding that society, and recognizes and adapts to the constant fluidity of the evolving overall model.

It is called "grand" strategy not because it is grand in the theatrical sense, but because it embraces global elements; its scale and timeframe are of an overarching nature.

It is also constantly and dynamically interactive to a degree of complexity unknown in other forms of strategy.

Grand strategy, then, comprehends a society's identity and its fundamental and long-term aspirations. It then identifies and manages intrinsic and emerging threats and opportunities at the largest realistic scale. It creates and manages capabilities to achieve what goals have been defined. The grand strategist must achieve all of that within the fluid context of constant global change. And that context is, to the greatest degree, what is outside the control of the single sovereign entity.

All aspects of life and policy form interlocking parts of the grand strategy matrix. Nothing is remote from it, from politics and the social sciences, as well as science and technology, medicine and health care, religion and beliefs, agriculture and water supply, economics, military security, education, linguistics, and so on. See the author's book, *The Art of Victory*, for further elaboration.

Hybrid Warfare: *See also* Non-Linear Warfare.

Legal Warfare: Legal warfare or "lawfare" is a sub-set of psycho-political or political warfare, functioning usually in the "white" (acknowledged sponsor) spectrum. Despite operating ostensibly in the white spectrum, however, motivations and goals for lawfare are usually disguised or deliberately obfuscated, or, conversely, emphasized to weaponize intimidation aspects.

Dean Cheng, a Research Fellow in Chinese Political and Security Affairs in the Asian Studies Center at The Heritage Foundation, in Washington, DC, in May 2012 published a document entitled "Winning Without Fighting: Chinese Legal Warfare". He noted that while the US was focusing on the interplay between the law and counterinsurgency operations, the People's Republic of China was approaching lawfare from a different perspective: as an offensive weapon capable of hamstringing opponents and seizing the political initiative. Indeed, PRC planners were almost certainly preparing legalwar plans aimed at controlling the enemy through the law or using the law to constrain the enemy.

This is not a new aspect of strategy, but has been particularly employed by the major communist states — but not restricted to hem — to achieve a number of strategic goals. These include:

➤ (1) The use of legal international treaties to (a) underscore the legitimacy of the government of the weaker state in the eyes of its own domestic audience by demonstrating that the government must be legitimate because it has been recognized by a foreign government of accepted stature, and (b) to create a bargaining position and bedrock position in the international community by the weaker government.

➤ (2) The use of treaties to ensure advantage to the weaker or sponsoring state by hampering or constraining its adversaries. The PRC manipulation, for example, of the Paris Climate Accords to ensure that its rival states were economically and strategically constrained while the PRC — by virtue of an exemption clause (that it was not a developed state) — remained unconstrained.

➤ (3) The use of international membership organizations, such as the United Nations and its agencies to penalize non-members of the UN, or to build conensus *blocs* within international bodies to penalize specific targets. The PRC, for example, by displacing the ROC (Republic of China-Taiwan) as a UN member meant that Beijing could constantly ostracize Taiwan from international acceptance. This included, for example, the use of the UN's International Civil Aviation Authority (ICAO) to re-allocate air transport corridors around Taiwan so that the PRC could encroach on Taiwan's geopolitical space and zones. This was, in the early 21st Century, an example of such legal manipulation. So, too, was the PRC's use of its UN position to unduly influence the leadership of the World Health Organization (WHO) in 2019-20 to shape perceptions of responsibility for the COVID-19 epidemic outbreak away from Beijing.

The creation and manipulation of the UN's International Criminal Court (ICC) in The Hague through the 1990s and early 21st Century was a clear case of using the *appearance* of legality to gain strategic advantage. Significantly, in this case, it was the United States Government — which was not a signatory to the ICC — which leveraged the ICC to great effect to achieve political outcomes against Serbia, and some key African leaders. This was part of an effort to create, out of whole cloth, an attempt to use what it defined as "international law" to constrain and vitiate the concept of national sovereignty. This process was as much driven by urban globalist ideological agitation and pressure as by governments using "international law" and the ICC as proxy weapons.

Lawfare is a distinct subset of psycho-political warfare, even though Dean Cheng noted: "Chinese writings often refer to the 'three warfares' (*san zhan*): public opinion warfare, psychological warfare, and legal warfare. Chinese analyses almost always link the three together, as they are seen as interrelated and mutually reinforcing." Significantly, the PRC utilizes lawfare strategically, while the US has tended to look at legal warfare as a tactical tool to constrain non-governmental adversaries.

Where the US *does* use lawfare strategically, or semi-strategically, is usually in the area of sanctions against foreign individuals or organizations. These have the advantage (in the short-term) of enabling the sponsoring government (in this case, the US) to create domestic laws which sanction certain foreign individuals, organizations, or governments, and then use the ability provided by these laws to punish in the US any third party foreign entity which trades with or sustains the sanctioned target. Thus, the US often then has no need to use multinational instruments (such as the UN) to offer broad consensus for its legal actions against foreign targets.

Media Warfare: Media warfare is essentially propaganda carried out within the modern framework of news, information, entertainment, and social media networks. As with classical propaganda, it falls within the white, grey, and black spectra.

As well, the use of communications media as a weapon of warfare includes many of the aspects of intelligence warfare and propaganda, being in mind that all these aspects of statecraft fall within the information dominance (ID) context. "False-flagging", involving disguised sourcing or attribution for content, is critical in grey and black media operations. In the case of social media manipulation, disguised routing is critical to disguising or obfuscating sourcing or sponsorship.

The use of the phrase, "media warfare", rather than the classical terms "propaganda" or "psychological warfare", tends to move thinking on this capability away from the most important elements: profound knowledge of the target, and focus on message content. In essence, the delivery mechanisms — the media themselves — represent the straightforward component, whereas target comprehension and selection, and associated message crafting, requires deep and intimate research and understandings. These are different skills than the technological transmission skills.

Most media warfare operations are undertaken, as a result, brutishly and often (ultimately) in a self-destructive fashion because the technology of transmission has become increasingly accessible and rapid. Successful professional practitioners, then, often rely on finding sympathetic intermediaries to "translate" their messages into political tools closer to the targets, thus further disguising the sources of origin of the campaign.

Military Strategy: The concept is widely understood, so it is not critical to look at new concepts. The art evolves with technology. However, it is worth repeating the fundamental: Military strategy is the formulation and goals of a military leadership under the broader direction of national, or grand, strategy, which are then pursued and implemented by military organizations. Very specifically, then, it is the use of military forces — which by definition are state-controlled forces — and formal paramilitary forces, possibly working with proxy forces, to achieve goals through the use or presence of force. It is, therefore, clearly delineated from other forms of strategy, with which it must often be partnered, under grand strategic direction.

Non-Linear Warfare/Hybrid Warfare: Non-Linear warfare was a name given by Russia analyst Mark Galeotti in 2013 to describe what has also been called "hybrid warfare". However, Non-Linear Warfare can be an adequate description of warfare which covers and falls beyond the lines of conventional warfare and embraces a range of kinetic, non-kinetic, unofficial, psycho-political, economic, population, and other forms of conflict.

In other words, it goes beyond the standard view of "hybrid warfare" (or at least the Western interpretation of how hybrid warfare doctrine was used in Soviet warfare or post-Soviet Russian warfare). So although non-linear war and hybrid war may, arguably, also be used to describe amorphous warfare, that term — amorphous warfare — created by this author actually implies a strategic-level, or total war, whereas hybrid and non-linear warfare implies a theater or tactical level process of engagement or doctrine.

Moreover, although hybrid warfare tends to include proxy warfare and also tends to be formally undeclared, in the same way that amorphous warfare exhibits these attributes, hybrid warfare tends to function more in the "grey" spectrum. That is, it is formally deniable by its sponsor(s) but generally accepted to be at the behest of a known sponsor. Both amorphous and hybrid warfare are heavily within the range of psycho-political actions, although amorphous warfare tends to utilize more large-scale operations such as population warfare and economic warfare.

Sacro Egoismo: *Sacro egoismo* (Italian), literally translated as "sacred egoism", often interpreted as "sacred selfishness" or "sacred self-interest", has meanings in an individual social sense as well as in a national sense; and both are strategically important.

In the national sense, Italian Prime Minister Antonio Salandra (1914-16) used the term to determine on which side Italy would enter the Great War. In other words, his Government would determine the economic and strategic benefit of the perceived outcome of the war before determining on which side to enter the fray. Thus, on the basis of this material calculus, purely on the analysis of which side was likely to be the victor and therefore in Italy's benefit, Salandra took Italy into the Triple Entente (United Kingdom, France, and the Russian Empire) and on May 23, 1915, declared war on Austria-Hungary.

At an individual, or sociological level, *sacro egoismo* has been defined in two ways, both of which are related. Dr John Knox, of the University of Birmingham, in the UK, in 2009 defined it as "the ultimate authority regarding religious thought and interpretation rests with the individual". This, he indicated, evolved with the 19th century move toward liberalism defined by a number of theologians, such as the German philosopher Friedrich Daniel Ernst Schleiermacher (1768–1834). This may have coincided, or helped cause, the movement of the individual away from obedience to (in the Western sense) the Christian church.

In a 21st Century sense, it also has evolved — as this writer would aver — to embrace the post-Christian, essentially urban dogma in which the individual sees immediate gratification of material desires as the most important manifestation of entitlement. This has a direct impact, then, on voting patterns and mob behavior.

Technological Warfare: The phrase, "technology warfare" was devised by Dr Stefan T. Possony and Jerry E. Pournelle in their groundbreaking — and still highly relevant — 1970 book, *The Strategy of Technology: Winning the Decisive War*. They noted: "Victory in the Technological War is achieved when a participant has a technological lead so far advanced that his opponent cannot overcome it until after the leader has converted his technology into decisive weapons systems. The loser may know that he has lost, and know it for quite a long time, yet be unable to do anything about it." The weaker power has the option of being able to rapidly redress the technological imbalance; counter it through pre-emptive, surprise kinetic warfare (or other strategic means to redress the technology imbalance); or surrender.

Possony and Pournelle note: "Proper conduct of the Technological War requires that strategy drive technology most forcefully; that there be an overall strategy of the Technological War, allocating resources according to well-defined objectives, not merely strategic elements which make operational use of the products of technology. … We do not advocate that the Technological War be given over to the control of the scientists, or that scientists should somehow create a strategy of technological development. We mean that an understanding of the art of war is more important than familiarity with one or another of the specialists of technology."

Terroir: In its strictest sense, *terroir* is defined as the set of environmental factors which affect a crop's phenotype, including unique environmental contexts, farming practices, and a crop-specific growth habitat. Clearly, it has a cross-species application to all mammalian life. In a strategic and sociological sense, *terroir* can define the physical geographic/geophysical, and spatial, climatic, and atmospheric environment which governs the behavior of species in a given area.

In other words, under this writer's interpretation, *terroir*, or a sense of *terroir*, defines the logic of behavior of human and other species in relationship to their geographic surroundings. The terrain defines the logic of survival. In rural settings, that could imply the relationship of a farmer to his soil, water, and seasons of growing and harvesting. In an urban setting, the "concrete jungle" defines how an individual must behave in order to survive.

Terrorism is, as its designation implies, a tool or doctrine within the framework of psychological warfare in which the process is intended to create a state of terror in a target audience in order to achieve a desired political or strategic outcome. It falls, as an operational doctrine, within what the Soviets, during the period of the Union of Soviet Socialist Republics (USSR: 1917-1990), called "agitprop": agitation propaganda. It uses physical actions to create visual or audio-visual imagery to achieve psychological, political, and ultimately hard outcomes. It should not be confused with guerilla warfare and subversion, which, like all forms of human behavior, also induce a psychological result, but which have physical warfighting goals as the primary objective.

Terrorism is designed specifically to have psychological impact, in turn inducing a socio-political response. Specifically, by using actions which induce fear or terror in the target audience, the target audience becomes either paralyzed, or moves politically in a direction which suits the perpetrator's objectives. However, direct practitioners of terrorism may also have as an objective merely the perpetuation of the importance of their own societies which the terrorist fears may be overwhelmed and destroyed forever by an overwhelming hostile force (the target of the terrorism). So terrorism is a weapon of asymmetric response to a formal adversary which cannot be challenged in any other way by the weaker society. Terrorism, then, is seen by its practitioners as a doctrine or weapon of last response. As a result, those willing to sacrifice themselves in terrorist actions are often susceptible to patronage by a hidden, sponsoring power which sees advantage in using the sacrifice of the terrorist against a common foe. Sustained terrorism, therefore, is usually only possible when it is supported deniably (in black, or at least grey operations) by a state power. It is, then, a tool of proxy warfare.

Tyranny and Autocracy: *Encyclopædia Britannica* in 2020 noted: "Tyranny, in the Greco-Roman world, an autocratic form of rule in which one individual exercised power without any legal restraint. In antiquity the word tyrant was not necessarily pejorative and signified the holder of absolute political power. In its modern usage the word tyranny is usually pejorative and connotes the illegitimate possession or use of such power. For the ancient Greeks, a tyrant was not necessarily a bad ruler; in its original form (*tyrannos*) the word was used to describe a person who held absolute and personal power within a state, as distinct from a monarch, whose rule was bound by constitution and law. Some tyrants were usurpers who came to power by their own efforts; others were elected to rule; and still others were imposed by intervention from outside." Use of the term "tyranny" in the 21st Century had come to embrace autocracy, in which absolute control lies in the hands of a single person or with the grasp of a tightly-held group. The reality is that the ability of any society to apply autocratic governance across entire societies is, in practicable terms, difficult for any protracted period, given the reality that the almost infinite variables in societies — expanding as they become larger and more diverse — precludes management of ubiquitous governance.

Westphalia, Peace of: The Peace of Westphalia describes the agreements reached in Westphalia in 1648, marking the end of Europe's Thirty Years War. It was far-reaching in its import, because it essentially, for the first time, codified a common understanding of the modern "nation-state" as a geopolitical entity, rather than just the "nation", which implied a human phenomenon rather than human populations tied to a specific geographic region, whether rural or urban. So the "Westphalian state" came to represent a recognized geographical area and the people it contained as the unit of sovereignty which commanded the recognition of other such entities.

White, Grey, and Black (operations): In psychological warfare or intelligence operations, the fundamental categories are "white", being totally open and attributable to the originating body; "grey", being assumed to be linked to the originating body, but with plausible ambiguity; and "black", being totally covert and deniable (by the originating body), with the prospect of the actions being false-flagged to be attributed to a third party.

Selected Bibliography

These are some of the works accessed by the author for this volume, but the list does not include many of the standard historical works. Neither does it list the author's use of the Global Information System (GIS) current intelligence database covering 287 countries and territories worldwide (compiled and managed by the International Strategic Studies Association for its government members), and the ISSA/*Defense & Foreign Affairs* archives, and the archives of the *Defense & Foreign Affairs Handbook Online* which have been assembled under the author's direction since 1972.

Alinsky, Saul: *Rules for Radicals: A Practical Primer for Realistic Radicals.* New York, 1971: Random House.

Babkin, B. P., Dr: *Pavlov: A Biography.* Chicago, 1949: University of Chicago Press.

Beaufre, André, Général d'Armée (France): *Introduction to Strategy.* New York, 1965: Praeger. [*Introduction à la stratégie.* Paris, 1963.]

Beaufre, André, Général d'Armée (France): *Deterrence and Strategy.* London, 1965: Faber. [*Dissuasion et stratégie.* Paris, 1964: Armand Colin.]

Beaufre, André, Général d'Armée (France): *La guerre révolutionnaire...* Paris, 1972: Fayard.

Bernhardi, Friedrich von: *On War of To-Day.* Translated by Karl von Donat. London, 1912: Hugh Rees Ltd.

Bodansky, Yossef: "Beijing's 'New Thirty Years War'", in *Defense & Foreign Affairs Strategic Policy,* 10/2018.

Bodansky, Yossef: "The PRC's Strategic Support Force: Key Focus of US Concern", in *Defense & Foreign Affairs Strategic Policy,* 2/2020.

Bricker Darrell and Ibbitson, John: *Empty Planet: The Shock of Global Population Decline.* New York, 2019: Crown Publishing.

Brinton, Crane: *The Anatomy of Revolution.* New York, 1938: Vintage Press.

Broadberry, Stephen, and Howlett, Peter: In a chapter entitled "Blood, Sweat and Tears: British Mobilisation For World War II" in Chickering, R. and Förster, S. (eds.), *A World at Total War: Global Conflict and the Politics of Destruction, 1939-1945,* Cambridge: Cambridge University Press.

Brooks, Rosa: *How Everything Became War and the Military Became Everything: Tales from the Pentagon.* New York, 2016: Simon & Schuster.

Canetti, Elias: *Crowds & Power.* New York, 1981: Continuum. Originally published by Claassen Verlag, Hamburg, in 1960 as *Masse und Macht*.

Carroll, Lewis (Charles Lutwidge Dodgson): also known as *Alice's Adventures in Wonderland*. London, 1865: Macmillan and Co.

Clausewitz, Gen. Carl von: *Vom Kriege* (*On War*), 1832.

Copley, Gregory R.: *The Art of Victory*. New York, 2006: Simon & Schuster's Threshold Editions.

Copley, Gregory R.: U*nCivilization: Urban Geopolitics in a Time of Chaos*; Alexandria, Virginia, 2012: the International Strategic Studies Association (ISSA).

Copley, Gregory R.: *Sovereignty in the 21st Century and the Crisis for Identity, Cultures, Nation-States, and Civilizations*; Alexandria, Virginia, 2018: The Zahedi Center for the Study of Monarchy, Traditional Governance, and Sovereignty, at ISSA.

Copley, Gregory R: *Defense & Foreign Affairs **Strategic Policy** journal*; various editions, 1972-2020, and *Defense & Foreign Affairs Special Analysis* (and related newsletters), various editions, 1972-2020.

Copley, Gregory R.: *Defense & Foreign Affairs Handbook*, online and print editions, 1972-2020.

Fioramonti, Lorenzo: *The World After GDP*. Cambridge, UK, and Malden, MA, USA, 2017: Polity Press.

Foch, Ferdinand, Gen.: *The Principles of War*. Translated by J. de Morini. New York, 1918: H.K. Fly Company.

Fukuyama, Francis: *The End of History and the Last Man*. New York, 1992: Free Press.

Fuller, Maj.-Gen. J. F. C. : *Generalship: Its Diseases and Their Cure*. Harrisburg, Pennsylvania, 1936: Military Service Publishing Co.

Glubb, Sir John: *The Fate of Empires and the Search for Survival*, published in Edinburgh, Scotland, 1976-77.

Hoffer, Eric: *The True Believer: Thoughts on the Nature of Mass Movements*. New York, 1951: Perennial Library, Harper & Row.

LeBon, Gustave: *The Crowd: A Study of the Popular Mind*. Viking, 1960. Our edition: New York, 1896: The Macmillan Co.

Machiavelli, Niccolò: *The Prince*. First English edition, 1640. Current English translations include the 1961 edition by George Bull (Penguin).

Machiavelli, Niccolò: *The Discourses*. Various English-language translations by, for example, Penguin Classics.

Newton, Maxwell: *The Fed: Inside the Federal Reserve, the secret power center that controls the American economy*. New York, 1983: Times Books.

Possony, Stefan T.: *To-morrow's War: Its Planning, Management, and Cost*. London, 1938: William Hodge & Comany Ltd. It was particularly important with its original German title, *Die Wehrwirtschaft des totalen Krieges* (*The Economy of Total War*).

Possony, Stefan T.: *Strategic Air Power: The Pattern of Dynamic Security.* Washington, DC, 1949: Infantry Press.

Possony, Stefan T., and Pournell, J. E.: *The Strategy of Technology: Winning the Decisive War.* Cambridge, Mass., USA, 1970: University Press of Cambridge Dunellen.

Possony, Stefan T.: *Waking Up The Giant: The Strategy for American Victory and World Freedom.* New Rochelle, 1974: Arlington House.

Possony, Stefan T.: "The Invisible Hand of Strategy" in *Defense & Foreign Affairs Digest,* 8/1975.

Possony, Stefan T.: "Ethnomorphosis: Invisible Catastrophic Crime", in *Plural Societies,* Autumn 1976, Vol. 7, No. 3. Published by the Foundation for the Study of Plural Societies.

Qiao Liang and Wang Xiangsui, Senior Colonels, People's Liberation Army, PRC: *Unrestricted Warfare* (the Mandarin title literally translates as "Warfare Beyond Bounds"). Beijing, February 1999: PLA Literature and Arts Publishing House. Subsequently translated and published by the US Foreign Broadcast Information Service (FBIS) in 1999 (FBIS is now Open Source Enterprise, part of the US Central Intelligence Agency's Directorate of Digital Innovation).

Rousseau, Jean-Jacques (1712-1778): *The Social Contract or Principles of Political Right;* Paris, 1762.

Spengler, Oswald: *The Decline of the West* (originally: *Der Untergang des Abendlandes*). Vol. I first appeared in 1918; Vol. II in 1922; first published in the US in 1926 by Alfred A. Knopf, Inc. (with the second volume in 1928). A single-volume edition published in the US in English in 1932.

Sun-tzu: *The Art of War.* Particularly the 1910 edition translated, and with notes, by Lionel Giles. Many publishers have produced this work; our copy printed anonymously in Taipei, undated. Also: New York, 2004, Barnes & Noble (Classic Series).

Yoshihara, Toshi, and Holmes, James R.: *Red Star Over the Pacific: China's Rise and the Challenge to US Maritime Strategy.* 2nd Ed. Annapolis, Maryland, 2018: US Naval Institute Press.

Acknowledgments

A BOOK SUCH AS THIS ENTAILS more than direct research and the immediate scribbling. It is the product of a lifetime.

There are those of my "gang", as well as Members of the International Strategic Studies Association College of Fellows to thank. Many of us discuss events daily. They remind me of our obligation to the concepts of nobility, freedom and individual sovereignty, and respect.

Names? My parents, Brian and Marjorie Copley, for the bedrock of values, curiosity, literacy; my brother, Howard, for making me justify my views. Maxwell Newton for sheer inspiration and a conceptual understanding of political economics: his teachings were formative, instructive; a lesson in courage, individualism, and wit. Dr Stefan T. Possony for illuminating the world to show the interplay of sociology, sciences, military arts, economics, psychology, and grand strategy: he gave me a quarter-century of daily lessons, humor, and appreciation. A further quarter-century after his death and I still learn from him.

Every friend gave something. My wonderfully philosophical friend, the late Dr Assad Homayoun, who left us during work on this book, was a constant encouragement and teacher. His Imperial Highness Prince Ermias Sahle-Selassie Haile-Selassie inspired decades of deep appreciation and learning about Ethiopia, and all of Africa, and traditional governance, as did Lt.-Gen. Aliyu Mohammed Gusau and his dedicated officers in Nigeria. HE Amb. Ardeshir Zahedi, the former Iranian Foreign Minister, embroiled me in the history of Iran, and opened my discussions with the Shah. Former UK Defence Minister the Rt. Hon. Sir Geoffrey Pattie strengthened my appreciation of statecraft; Vice Adm. Ko Tun-hwa — Tony — my love of Asia and appreciation of a true humility I could never emulate. There have been so many great influences: Field Marshal Mohammed Abd al-Halim Abou-Ghazala, Egyptian Defense Minister (1981-89); Elkana Galli, Israeli Prime Minister Ben Gurion's political advisor; Dr Joan Vernikos, the most senior woman ever at NASA and an innovative thinker; Sir Charles Court, Australia's great statesman; and my friend from 1973 until his death, former US Secretary of State Gen. Alexander M. Haig, Jr.

My inspiring friends Andrew Pickford, Yossef Bodansky, Stephen Ryan, Australian astronaut and mathematician Dr Paul Scully-Power, Hon. Shane Stone, Dr Harold Clough, Prof. David Flint, Kerry Collison, George Bougias, George Chapman, and Craig Lawrence. The Gnomes of Perth. They are pillars of abiding value, and they caused my interests and circles to widen. No less than did friends and inspirations US broadcaster and thinker John Batchelor, and his producer, Lee Mason.

There are many, alive and passed, who unknowingly guided my pen. May it have written faithfully. But without the loving partnership I have with my wife, Pamela, and her inspiration, nothing, and *particularly this volume and this life*, would have been possible.

About the Author

Western Australian Gregory Copley has served for almost five decades as an adviser on strategic issues to a number of national, military, and intelligence leaders around the world.

He is Editor-in-Chief of *Defense & Foreign Affairs* publications, and Director of Intelligence at the Global Information System (GIS), a global strategic intelligence service solely for governments. He is President of the International Strategic Studies Association (ISSA), based near Washington, DC.

Mr Copley founded, within ISSA, The Zahedi Center for the Study of Monarchy, Traditional Governance, and Sovereignty, and earlier established specialist ISSA centers to study issues in the Balkans and Eastern Mediterranean, Africa, the Middle East, Central Asia, the Indian Ocean, Battlefield Survival, and so on.

He has authored or co-authored 36 books (including this volume), and several thousand articles, papers, and lectures on strategic issues, history, energy, aviation, and so on. Recent books include *Sovereignty in the 21st Century and the Crisis for Identity, Cultures, Nation-States, and Civilizations* (2018), *UnCivilization: Urban Geopolitics in a Time of Chaos* (2012), and *The Art of Victory* (2006), and others listed elsewhere in this volume.

Gregory Copley has received a number of orders and decorations, including, in 2007, being made a Member of the Order of Australia for his contributions to the international community in the field of strategic analysis. He received the Asian Council Award in Japan in 1990, and the Erebus Medal from the Royal Canadian Geographic Society in 2015. He was made a Fellow of the Royal Society of New South Wales in 2017.

He was, in 2020, created hereditary Marquess of Tana for decades of service to the Ethiopian Crown.

Copley has been a keen yachtsman, aviation enthusiast, and industrialist, owning several shipyards, heavy engineering firms, a ship design bureau, chemical and water companies, media organizations, and other ventures. He serves also as President of the Water Initiative for Africa, and is on the Board of Advisors of the Canadian Forces College Foundation.

He has been married since 1986 to an American, Pamela von Gruber Copley.

Index

Praise for some of Gregory Copley's earlier work

Sovereignty in the 21st Century

"Sovereignty may be the most powerful asset possessed by human societies, and yet we were in danger of forgetting it, or misunderstanding it, until Gregory Copley's vital new book."

— His Imperial Highness Prince Ermias Sahle-Selassie Haile-Selassie
President of the Crown Council of Ethiopia

"In this *tour de force*, Gregory Copley identifies the vital factors which make societies work, and explores the challenges facing us in the 21st Century."

— Prof. David Flint, AM
Convenor of Australians for Constitutional Monarchy

UnCivilization: Urban Geopolitics in a Time of Chaos

"This is a life changing book. Very brave in this politically correct world." … "Uniquely intelligent in its presentation and thought provoking in its idea development. ... prescient and clear".

The Art of Victory

"Gregory Copley has defined in this unique and important book the scope of what victory really is, and how it can be sustained and nurtured."

— Gen. Alexander M. Haig, Jr., former US Secretary of State

"*The Art of Victory* is an eye-opening study of the strategic realities of man's eternal challenges. It bypasses our day-to-day battles to focus on who we are, where we need to go — as individuals and societies — and what we must do to get there. *The Art of Victory* is not abstract pontificating: Gregory Copley, our only conscious grand strategist and exponent of psychological strategy, provides vital new insights into the key challenges facing us today: terrorism and globalism. If Sun-tzu's *Art of War* is the marshal's baton in the knapsack of every soldier, then the beautifully written *Art of Victory* should be the secret strength of all who wish to lead society."

— Yossef Bodansky, renowned geo-strategist and best-selling
author of *Bin Laden: the Man Who Declared War on America*

"A masterful, thought-provoking look at conflict and the critical grand strategy of winning."
— Best-selling military writer W. E. B. Griffin

"I know what it takes to get on top and stay there, and Copley shows how it's done at every level of society, and why it's the critical skill we must all understand. *The Art of Victory* is a *tour de force* on leadership and success which every business leader should read."
— Fred Turner, former CEO, McDonalds Corporation

"Copley's *The Art of Victory* is an outstanding work ... a most thorough, ordered and lucid exposition, on a subject he defines as "the ability of peoples to survive down the generations". The breadth of his book is immense, covering not just the rôle of war, but also the importance, for example, of technology, belief in God, psychology and leadership. He has also managed to distill his ideas, using 28 maxims to simply and clearly convey the often-complex nature of victory, and how it must be pursued and secured. *The Art of Victory* is both highly philosophical and of practical value, being very much a book for our volatile and uncertain times. I found it inspiring, stimulating and enjoyable to read."
— Then Australian Head-of-State Gen. Michael Jeffery, AC, CVO, MC

A "Sun Tzu sequel" ... "a genuinely helpful book".
— National Review

"A great book; a truly great book".
— The Bauer and Rose Show, Radio Station WMET-AM, Washington, DC

To order these, and other books and journals by Gregory Copley and The International Strategic Studies Association, please go to:
www.StrategicStudies.org
or email:
Sales@StrategicStudies.org

Copley

Praise for **The New Total War**

Hon. Newt Gingrich
Former Speaker of the US House of Representatives

At this time of extraordinary change in every aspect of our lives — from a pandemic to a government-inspired worldwide depression to the rise of a more militant and aggressive China — this is the kind of new thinking and candid dialogue we need to prepare for a better future.

Hon. Bob Walker
Former US Congressman; CEO, MoonWalker Associates; Former Chairman of House Science Committee; NASA Distinguished Service Medal Recipient

Those who are leaders or who aspire to leadership must read Gregory Copley's new book, *The New Total War in the 21st Century*.

Trends like information dominance, depopulation, globalist vs. nationalist competition and weaponized fear create a platform for decision-making that looks nothing like the experiences of the past.

Two decades into this century everything consequential has changed and Copley captures that reality in a most inspiring way.

Edwin J. Feulner, PhD
Founder and former President of The Heritage Foundation

Gregory Copley, one of America's foremost strategists, invites us to re-think the current pandemic in its larger context, geographically and historically.

He challenges us to examine the reaction of "experts", and our own commitment to freedom.

The New Total War of the 21st Century is a provocative volume that ex-
pands our understanding of these challenges in their broadest context.
Read it to understand the challenge we are really facing.

Robert S. Wood, PhD
*Emeritus Dean and Nimitz Chair, Center for Naval Warfare
Studies, US Naval War College*

Gregory Copley has drawn together the disparate political, socio-economic, technological, and military forces of our century to show a
global transformation startling in its significance for our survival as a
people.

It signals a social and transnational struggle that can aptly be called total war aimed at preserving or changing our way of life and fundamental institutions. Military power and defense strategies remain critical but
their importance must be subsumed in a much broader grand strategy
touching unfolding struggles both within and without.

This study is a must-read for those who are entrusted with national defense as it will change the way we think about defense budgets, strategies, decisionmaking, and operations.

Rt. Hon. Sir Geoffrey Pattie
Former UK Minister of Defence

This excellent analysis increases awareness of the total war in which
democracies are involved.

John Batchelor
US National Broadcaster

Total War is a primer on the undiscovered country of the 21st Century's
yet-unloved tragedies, failures, vanities and mysteries. Not a crystal
ball. More a template for how we blunder when we think that war is
about firearms.

Total War is how we live now: everybody against everybody in competition for resources, narratives, markets, useful lies. Gregory Copley reminds that George Clemenceau dryly summated the lessons learned
of the Great War by disdaining the generals: "War! War is too serious a
matter to entrust to military men."

Copley reminds that war is too serious to be left to the victors and van-
quished.

Imagine Copley writing after the Third Punic War that Rome would re-
consider its lordly savagery when what was done to Carthage came to
Rome, six hundred years from now.

Total War is rethinking the Big Picture for this century and the next
locked in a pitiless existential conflict: Chinese and Russian
revanchism, American exceptionalism, European defeatism, English-
speaking élitism, homegrown nationalism, plutocratic globalism, scientific authoritarianism, parasitic nihilism.